Hands-On MS-DOS® 5

Learn By Doing

Dr. J.D. Watson

QUE

Hands-On MS-DOS 5

Library of Congress Catalog No.: 91-66193

ISBN: 0-88022-683-8

95 94 93 92 4 3 2 1

Interpretation of the printing code: the rightmost double-digit number is the year of the book's printing; the rightmost single-digit number, the number of the book's printing. For example, a printing code of 92-1 shows that the first printing of the book occurred in 1992.

Hands-On MS-DOS 5 is based on MS-DOS 5.0.

Publisher: Lloyd J. Short

Product Development Manager: Thomas Bennett

Acquisitions Manager: Rick Ranucci

Managing Editor: Paul Boger

Book Designers: Scott Cook and Michele Laseau

Production Team: Jeff Baker, Michelle Cleary, Keith Davenport, Brook Farling, Dennis Clay Hager, Audra Hershman, Carrie Keesling, Bob LaRoche, Cindy L. Phipps, Linda Seifert, Kevin Spear, Johnna VanHoose, Lisa Wilson, Allan Wimmer, Phil Worthington, Christine Young

Acquisitions Editor
Tim Ryan

Product Director
Charles O. Stewart III

Production Editor
Fran Blauw

Editors
Sara Allaei
Jo Anna Arnott
Tracy L. Barr
Susan M. Shaw

Technical Editor
Lynda Fox

Composed in *Cheltenham* and *Macmillan* by Que Corporation

To Mark Phillippo, who first told me about what a PC could really do. Who would have thought?

ABOUT THE AUTHOR

Dr. J.D. Watson

Dr. J.D. "Doc" Watson is an independent consultant, database developer, and college instructor. He teaches DOS, dBASE, and Windows at Colorado Mountain College and Colorado Northwestern Community College, both located in the Colorado Rockies. His first book, *MS-DOS PC Tutor*, was the first book in Que's PC Tutor series, and he also provided technical support to two other titles in the series. Doc is the technical editor of *Christian Computing Magazine*, for which he writes a monthly technical column and a Windows column.

TRADEMARK ACKNOWLEDGMENTS

ACKNOWLEDGMENTS

I want to thank Chuck Stewart for his direction on this project; Chuck, we finally made it! Thanks also to Fran Blauw for her input, Greg Bowers for his review, and all the professionals at Que who gave me a chance to do what I've always wanted to do—write.

Most of all, thanks to my wife, Debbie, and son, Paul, for their patience when dad was down in the dungeon working.

CONTENTS AT A GLANCE

TABLE OF CONTENTS

IV Going Beyond the Basics

Introduction

> **Attention Please**
>
> We all occasionally have the tendency to skip Introductions and go right to sections of interest. But it is highly recommended that you read this one. It presents foundational concepts and conventions that are essential to your understanding of the individual lessons in this book. No actual computer use is required, so you simply can sit down and read this Introduction at your leisure. You'll be glad you did.

As the user of an IBM Personal Computer (PC), an IBM PC XT (XT), an IBM Personal Computer AT (AT), an IBM Personal System/2 (PS/2), or an IBM-compatible machine, you have one of the most powerful tools ever invented. Like most new PC users, you probably purchased your computer to run applications programs like word processing, spreadsheets, or accounting. But also like most new users, you are not aware that the system itself has many powerful capabilities that you can use independently of your applications programs.

The purpose of this book and disk set is to teach you how to use your operating system, MS-DOS. It provides both background information about MS-DOS and, most importantly, hands-on experience in using DOS commands. The book and disk were written specifically for MS-DOS Version 5 and contain instructions for PC, XT, AT, and PS/2 users. You can use this book and disk independently or with *Using MS-DOS 5*

(Que Corporation) if you want more information. Additionally, you can use *Hands-On MS-DOS 5* as individualized instruction or in a classroom as part of large-group instruction.

What Is DOS?

DOS (short for *disk operation system*) is a collection of software programs built into the computer. The most important function of the operating system is to help manage the computer hardware (the system board, disk drives, printers, keyboard, display, and so on) and to direct the fundamental operations of the computer. The operating system does this so that applications programs (such as word processors, spreadsheets, and so on) don't have to.

Like all operating systems, MS-DOS gives you control of your computer. Without an operating system (and other software), a computer is a useless piece of hardware.

A simple way to compare hardware and software is:

> *Hardware makes it possible, while software makes it happen.*

But DOS also does more than just operate the hardware. As you will learn, DOS also enables you to manage files and many other things that would usually require additional software (computer programs).

Why Should You Know How To Use DOS?

As a computer user, you will find that the more you know about your disk operating system, the more useful your computer will be. Certain DOS functions are absolutely essential to all computer users; for example, you cannot use your computer without knowing how to *boot* (start) the computer and how to *format* disks (how to prepare them to receive information).

Other DOS functions, like copying files and diskettes, calling up directories, and renaming files, make your life as a computer user much easier. If you don't know how to make *backup* (extra) copies of important disks, you risk losing important information through data loss or damage. Learning the simple copying process and taking the time to back up disks may save you hours of work and frustration in the long run.

Knowing some of the more advanced functions of DOS—especially the functions that are unique features of Version 5—will develop your knowledge of the system, as well as save you time and work.

> Some beginning DOS users think that a DOS Shell can do all the work for them. While this is true to some extent, experienced DOS users know that being able to use their computers at the DOS level is sometimes much faster and more efficient than using a DOS Shell. Although *Hands-On MS-DOS 5* focuses on the DOS Shell, it will also teach you how to use your computer at the DOS command line level, thereby making you more productive. Once you learn how to use DOS, you will discover when it is advantageous over the DOS Shell.

Who Should Use This Book?

This book was written with the following users in mind:

- *Beginning DOS users: Hands-On MS-DOS 5* is particularly valuable to the new PC user. Part I introduces you to your computer and to the disk tutor. Part II presents the fundamentals of using the DOS Shell. Part III then teaches you the essential functions of DOS, while Part IV introduces you to a few simple ways to customize DOS and the DOS Shell.
- *Individual users and instructors of group sessions:* This book and disk set is designed to be used as individualized instruction guides for those interested in learning more about DOS on their own, as well as a training manual for group seminars or workshops.
- *Users of DOS-compatible applications programs:* This book will be especially helpful for those who use programs such as 1-2-3, WordPerfect, and many others that rely upon a basic knowledge of DOS.
- *Business and industrial training personnel and other instructors who need training for teaching DOS: Hands-On MS-DOS 5* is a great way to "teach teachers how to teach."

What This Book Includes

As an introduction to DOS, this book and disk set is a unique approach to learning. Together they provide both practical background information and hands-on practice in using DOS functions. This book and disk set features the following:

- An ATI (American Training International) disk tutorial (hereafter called disk tutor) that enables you to actually get hands-on experience with DOS without any of the dangers that are possible in a DOS environment.
- Introductory descriptions of each function, including definitions and explanations of applications.
- Detailed and easy-to-follow steps for performing each DOS function.
- Figures showing actual screen shots of DOS, the DOS Shell, and the disk tutor.
- References for further reading in *Using MS-DOS 5* and other Que books.
- A summary of terms and key concepts near the end of each lesson.
- An "Exercises" section at the end of each chapter that gives you more hands-on experience.
- Five appendixes (three of which are also included in disk files) containing additional information and reference material.

The 17 lessons in this book are divided into four major sections:

Part I, "Getting Started," introduces you to the components of your computer and teaches you how to start DOS. This section also explains how to install and use the disk tutor.

Part II, "Introducing the DOS Shell," presents the basics of working with the Shell. It teaches you how to use the Shell's menus, dialog boxes, and scroll bars. It also presents the fundamental procedures for changing the Shell's display, working with files and directories, and getting on-line help.

> Some users will choose not to use the DOS Shell program that is supplied with MS-DOS 5, but will choose rather to work with another shell program or from the DOS command line itself. Whether or not you choose to use the DOS Shell, it is still highly recommended that you read Lessons 4 and 5. These lessons not only introduce the Shell, but also introduce some very foundational principles of the MS-DOS operating system.

Part III, "Working with DOS," contains nine lessons for the beginner. The sequence of these lessons duplicates as closely as possible the process by which a beginner learns DOS. This section contains lessons on formatting disks; copying, renaming, and erasing files; copying and comparing disks; and more—all the basic DOS functions every user should know.

If you are a beginning computer user or a newcomer to the MS-DOS operating system, you will want to work systematically through these nine lessons in order. If you are already familiar with some of the DOS functions presented in these lessons, you may choose to work through only the lessons or parts of lessons with which you are not familiar.

Part IV, "Going Beyond the Basics," teaches you how to work with programs in the Shell and how to customize the Shell. One lesson even teaches you some basic principles for customizing your computer.

How To Use This Book

The best way to use this book is to complete all of the disk tutor, and then the book lessons, occasionally looping back to the disk tutor if desired. You then can use the book for a desk reference.

One of the first things you will notice at the beginning of each lesson in this book is the **Estimated Time of Completion** line. These times are an average of the time it took test subjects to complete the lesson. The test subjects ranged from beginning DOS users to advanced DOS users. This estimate will help you determine if you currently have enough time to complete that lesson and to allow you to gauge your progress. You should never feel pressured by these times, however; they are merely a guide. You should always work at your own pace. ***Note:*** The estimate does *not* include the time involved in the "Exercises" section at the end of each lesson.

In working through the individual lessons in this book, you first should read the overview presented at the beginning of the lesson, and then follow the step-by-step instructions throughout the lesson. At the end of each lesson, you may use the "Key Terms" and "Lesson Summary" sections to review the major concepts presented in the lesson. For additional practice and review, an "Exercises" section is provided at the end of most lessons.

Special Note to Instructors and Corporate Trainers

One of the strongest points for using *Hands-On MS-DOS 5* is that it enables students to actually use DOS in a totally safe environment. As every experienced DOS user knows, DOS has some dangers, so it is difficult to teach DOS in a "hands-on" course. With the disk tutor, however, a student can't do anything wrong. An excellent way to use *Hands-On MS-DOS 5* in the classroom is to allow students to do each disk tutor lesson privately (at home, for example), and then to do the book lessons in class. This approach will cut down greatly on the "intimidation factor" for which DOS is notorious.

Conventions Used in This Book

A number of conventions are used in *Hands-On MS-DOS 5*:

- References to keys are as they appear on the keyboard of the IBM PC AT.
- Direct quotations of MS-DOS screen prompts and messages appear in a `digital typeface`.
- Information that you are to type appears in **BOLD, UPPERCASE** letters (although capitalization usually does not matter).
- File names and DOS commands appear in UPPERCASE letters.
- Key combinations that must be pressed together are separated by a hyphen. For example, Ctrl-Break means that you press and hold down the Ctrl key as you press the Break key.
- The following icons are used throughout this book:

A Tip icon designates a user tip from the author's experience that makes the present subject easier or more efficient.

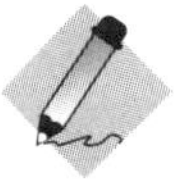

A Note icon draws attention to a particular aspect of a subject.

A Warning icon indicates a definite danger or destructive action.

A Caution icon points out a potential problem.

How To Use the Disk Tutor

If you plan to use the DOS tutorial program included with this book, you need to install the disk tutor files onto your hard disk. To install the disk tutor, follow the easy instructions in Lesson 3. You don't need to do this now, because you won't need the disk tutor until Lesson 3.

> Remember that the disk tutor is a separate program from DOS itself. When you work with the disk tutor, you are *not* actually working with DOS; it is only a highly realistic *simulation* of DOS.

Equipment You Need for the Lessons in This Book

To make full use of this book and disk set, you need the following hardware and peripherals:

- IBM PC, PC XT, AT, PS/2, or an IBM-compatible machine that uses the MS-DOS operating system
- At least 384K of RAM (for running the disk tutor)
- One floppy disk drive and one hard disk drive
- Blank disks suitable for use with your system and labels
- A monochrome or color monitor
- A printer hooked up to your computer and computer paper (optional but recommended)

> You need to install MS-DOS Version 5 on your computer in order to do the book lessons. The disk tutor, however, will run under DOS 3.x and later versions.

Continuing in This Book

You now are ready to begin your DOS training. To continue, choose one of the following:

If you are	Then go to
A novice to computer hardware *and* DOS, or want to review hardware fundamentals	Lesson 1
Very knowledgeable of computer hardware but not DOS	Lesson 2
Very knowledgeable of computer hardware and know how to start your computer	Lesson 3
Very knowledgeable of computer hardware, know how to start your computer, and are not planning to use the disk tutor included with this book	Lesson 4

Good luck to you as you learn MS-DOS Version 5.

Part I

Getting Started

The first three lessons in this book introduce new computer users or new DOS users to three very important subjects:

- Computer hardware and software (Lesson 1)
- Procedures for loading and starting DOS (Lesson 2)
- Procedures for installing and using the ATI disk tutor included with *Hands-On MS-DOS 5* (Lesson 3)

CPSIA information can be obtained
at www.ICGtesting.com
Printed in the USA
BVHW032319271018
531260BV00001B/1/P

9 781925 830958

Lesson 1

Getting To Know Your Computer

Before learning about *DOS*—your computer's operating system—you should familiarize yourself with computer hardware and software. Knowing about hardware and software will help you use your operating system and other computer software more effectively. If you are already familiar with hardware and software, you may want to move on to the next lesson, or you may choose to continue just for the sake of review.

In this lesson, you are introduced to the following:

- System unit
- Disk drives and disks
- Keyboard
- Display
- Printer
- Mouse
- Modem
- Software

Estimated time to complete this lesson: 20-25 minutes

Unlike the other lessons in this book, you do not need a computer for this lesson; you can just sit back and read at your leisure.

What is Computer Hardware?

As you may have already deduced, computer *hardware* refers to the mechanical devices that actually make up the computer system. These parts include the system unit, disk drives, keyboard, display, mouse, and printer.

The System Unit

Every personal computer system has a *system unit*, which houses all the electronics that make the computer work. A typical system unit is shown in figure 1.1.

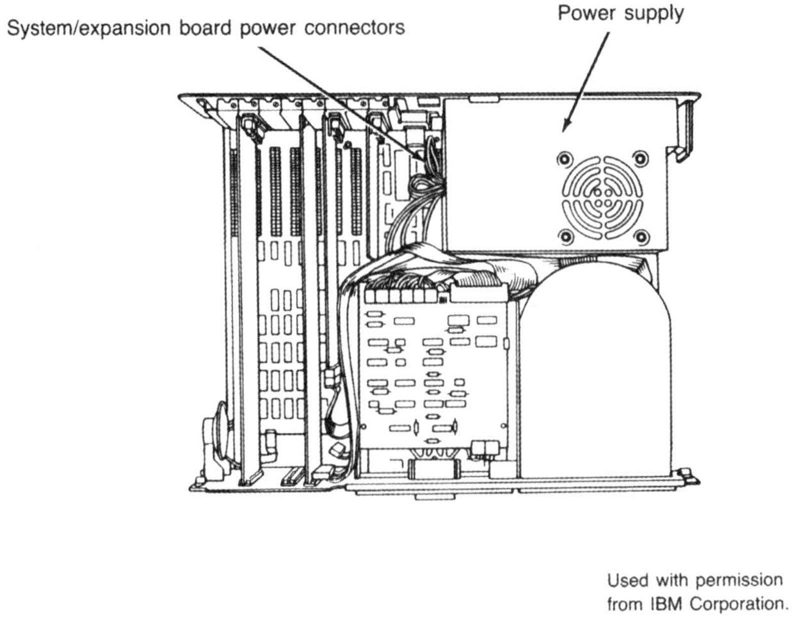

Fig. 1.1. A typical system unit.

The “brain” of the computer, the *microprocessor*, or *CPU* (central processing unit), is the main part of a computer that performs calculations and processes information. Examples of CPUs are the 8088, 80286, 80386SX, 80386, and 80486 microprocessors. Each one of these processes information faster than its predecessor. The microprocessor is truly a marvel of science. It is a single, 1- to 1 1/2-inch square silicon chip, in which thousands of transistors are imbedded.

The computer has two types of memory. The first type is called *ROM*, which means read-only memory. This type of memory contains non-erasable computer instructions that are embedded in hardware chips. The other type of memory is *RAM*, which means random-access memory. This is the electronic memory DOS uses for programs and data. RAM changes constantly as you use programs and is lost when the machine is turned off.

Another part of the system unit is the *power supply*. This plugs into a standard 120-volt AC electrical outlet, but has a transformer inside that converts this voltage to the lower-voltage DC current used by the computer. The power supply also has a fan that pulls air through the system unit to keep the components in it cool. *Expansion slots* are used to add *printed circuit boards* (also called *add-in cards*) to your computer. One example of a circuit board is the video card that controls the video display. PCs also have a small, built-in *speaker*, which many programs use to give you audible messages, such as “beeps” and other sounds.

Depending on the computer, there are a number of lights and buttons on the front of the system unit. Usually a light comes on to indicate when the hard disk is being accessed, and another light indicates that the power is on. Most computers can operate at two speeds, so they have a *turbo button*, which you use to select the speed at which the CPU operates. The best computers also have *reset buttons*, which you can use to restart the computer without physically turning it off and then on with the power switch.

The Keyboard

Your main means of communicating with your computer is through the keyboard. The original PC and XT came with the standard keyboard in figure 1.2. The early ATs came with the redesigned standard keyboard in figure 1.3. The IBM PS/2 computer and most newer XT and AT machines use the new 101-key enhanced keyboard, shown in figure 1.4.

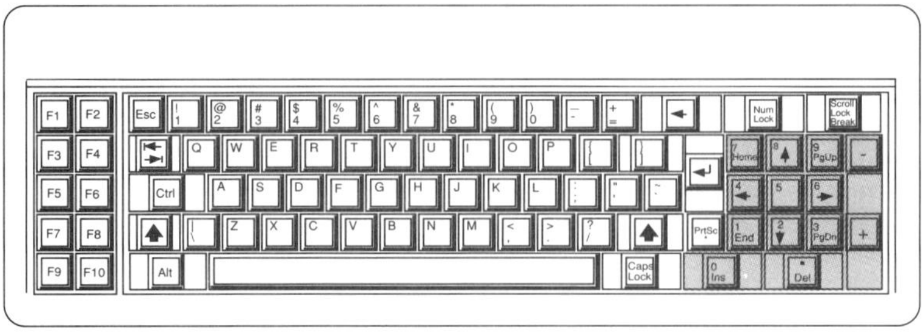

Fig. 1.2. The original IBM PC keyboard.

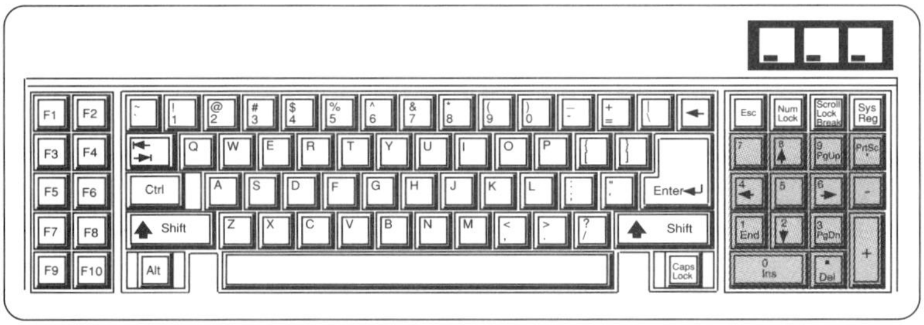

Fig. 1.3. The original IBM PC-AT keyboard.

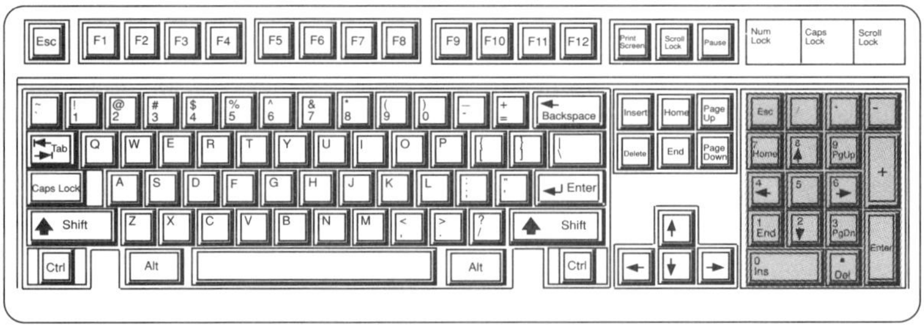

Fig. 1.4. The 101-key enhanced keyboard.

All three of these keyboards share similar groups of keys. The *QWERTY keys* (QWERTY comes from the letters on the left side of the top row of the keyboard) contain all the letters of the alphabet. You'll use this section of the keyboard to type the commands you want the computer to carry out. If you are unfamiliar with a typewriter keyboard, you may want to spend a few minutes studying how the alphabetic keys are arranged.

The meaning of the *function keys* changes depending on the program you are running—any program can redefine these keys. The word processing program WordPerfect, for example, makes extensive use of the function keys. When combined with the Shift, Ctrl, and Alt keys, the function keys can produce 40 (or 48) different functions. You will use the function keys for certain actions in DOS.

The *numeric/cursor-control keys* have two functions: they enable you to move around on the video screen, and they enable you to input numbers as you would on an adding machine. You can press the Num Lock key to toggle between these functions. Additionally, the enhanced keyboard provides a separate set of cursor-control keys, which makes both of these functions available at once.

Special keyboards also are available. Some users, for example, use an enhanced keyboard with the function keys on the left instead of across the top. The reason for this arrangement is that some "old-timers" learned on the original style keyboard and can't (or won't) give up the left side function keys. Other nonstandard keyboards are found on laptop computers. The keys are in a nonstandard layout to conserve space.

The lessons in this book use keys from all these sections. Before you work through the lessons, familiarize yourself with the locations of these keys. To help you learn your keyboard, refer to table 1.1, which lists some special keys and their descriptions.

Table 1.1. Special Keys on the Computer Keyboard

Key	Function
↵Enter	Signals the computer to respond to the commands you type. Also functions as a carriage return in programs that simulate the operation of a typewriter.
↑ ↓ ← → Home PgUp PgDn End	Changes your location on-screen. Included are the arrow, PgUp, PgDn, Home, and End keys.
←Backspace	Moves the cursor backward one space at a time, deleting any character in that space.
Del	Deletes, or erases, any character at the location of the cursor.
Ins	Inserts any character at the location of the cursor.
⇧Shift	Enables you to capitalize letters when you hold down Shift while you type the letter. When pressed with another key, Shift can change the standard function of that key.

continues

Table 1.1. continued

Key	Function
Caps Lock	When pressed to the lock position, all characters typed are uppercase, or capitalized. Caps Lock doesn't shift the numbered keys, however. To release, press the key again.
Ctrl	When pressed with another key, changes the standard function of that key.
Alt	When pressed with another key, changes the standard function of that key.
Esc	In some situations, enables you to escape from a current operation to a previous one. Sometimes Esc has no effect on the current operation.
Num Lock	Changes the numeric pad from cursor-movement to numeric-function mode.
Print Screen	Key found on AT Keyboards. Used with the Shift key to send the characters on the display to the printer.
Print Screen	Key found on enhanced keyboards. Same as PrtSc.
Scroll Lock	Locks the scrolling function to the cursor-movement keys. Instead of the cursor moving, the screen scrolls.
Pause	Suspends display activity until you press another key. (Not provided with standard keyboards.)
Break	Stops a program in progress from running.
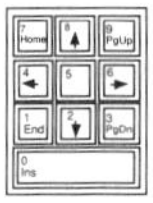	A cluster of keys to the right of the standard keyboard. The keypad includes numbered keys from 0 to 9 as well as cursor-movement keys and other special keys.

The Display

You communicate with your computer through the keyboard, but your computer communicates with you through the video display. Other names for the display are *monitor* and *CRT* (cathode-ray tube). The quality of a monitor's display is measured in *pixels*, that is, dots; the greater number of dots, the finer the *resolution* (detail). A monitor's quality also is judged by the number of colors that it can display. Table 1.2 summarizes the common video displays.

Table 1.2. Common Video Displays

Adapter Type	Name	Graphics Mode	Pixel Resolution	Number of Colors Available
MDA	Monochrome display adapter	Green or amber text only	N/A	N/A
CGA	Color graphics adapter	Medium resolution	320 x 200	4
CGA	Color graphics adapter	High resolution	640 x 200	2
EGA	Enhanced graphics adapter	All CGA modes	All CGA resolutions	All CGA colors
EGA	Enhanced graphics adapter	CGA high resolution	640 x 200	16
EGA	Enhanced graphics adapter	EGA high resolution	640 x 350	16
MGA	Monochrome graphics adapter	Monochrome graphics	720 x 348	2
VGA	Video graphics array	All CGA and EGA modes	All CGA and EGA resolutions	All CGA and EGA colors
VGA	Video graphics array	Monochrome	640 x 480	2
VGA	Video graphics array	VGA high resolution	640 x 480	16
VGA	Video graphics array	VGA medium resolution	320 x 200	256

EGA or VGA is the most desirable for running DOS 5, especially if you are using the DOS Shell, because the higher resolution yields much better eye relief and gives you much more control over the screen display.

Most monitors have contrast and brightness controls, as well as an on/off switch. It's a good idea to turn the brightness control down all the way if you are going to leave the monitor for a long period of time. Images can be "burned-into" the screen, especially with the high resolution screens of today. You also may install a screen-blanking program, which blanks the screen automatically after a certain length of time. Numerous screen-blanking programs are available today. One excellent program is ScreenSaver, from Signature Software (1-804-287-5053), a shareware product that is designed to work with almost every hardware and software configuration possible (except Microsoft Windows).

The Printer

A computer is great, but a printer provides *hard copy*, a permanent record on paper of your work. The most inexpensive printers are dot-matrix printers, which are *tractor-fed*, which means that paper is pulled through the printer. A 9-pin dot-matrix printer doesn't produce very high quality print, but a 24-pin printer does a much better job.

The highest quality printing, however, comes from the laser printer. The laser printer is similar to a photocopying machine, except that it gets its images from a computer instead of through lights and lenses. But, as you may guess, with higher quality print comes a higher price tag.

The Surge Protector

The surge protector is an *absolutely essential* piece of computer hardware; you shouldn't use your computer without one. A typical surge protector is shown in figure 1.5.

Your computer uses 120-volt AC current with a frequency of 60Hz (cycles per second). Sometimes, however, there are fluctuations in the current that come from the power supplier or nearby appliances. These can cause errors in data. You can prevent this by plugging your computer, monitor, and printer into the surge protector. You also can use the switch on the surge protector to turn on all the components at once. This will increase the life of your power supply switch.

Actual hardware damage can be caused by another enemy—the *voltage spike* (a sudden, unexpected, and dramatic increase in line current). Small spikes can be protected against by the surge protector, but contrary to popular belief, the average surge protector will *not* protect against a direct lightning strike. If there is a danger of this in your area, you should consider buying a lightning arrestor, or at least unplugging your computer when the weather threatens.

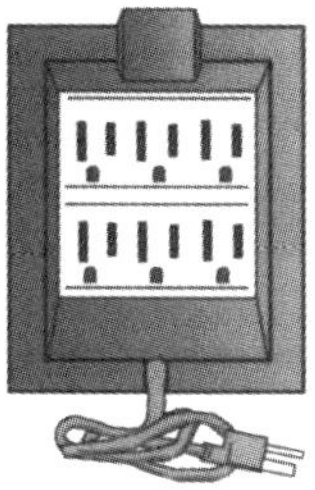

Fig. 1.5. A typical surge protector.

The Mouse

This small box with one, two, or three buttons on it usually is attached to the computer with a cable (although some are made wireless). Figure 1.6 shows a typical two-button mouse.

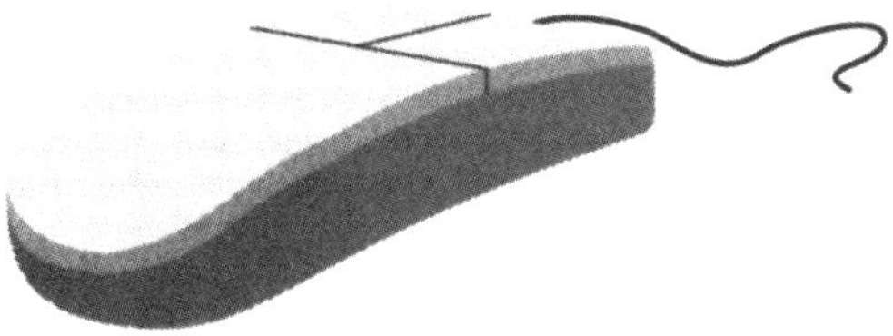

Fig. 1.6. A typical mouse.

A mouse fits comfortably in your hand, enabling you to move it around easily and press each button as required. As you move the mouse around on the desk, this motion is registered on the computer display, usually by a *mouse pointer*—an arrow or small box—that moves around the screen. Pressing a mouse button does the same thing as pressing a key on the keyboard.

A mouse can be used only with programs that were designed for it, although many mice today include add-on mouse menus for popular programs that do not have their own mouse support. The DOS Shell supplied with Version 5 makes extensive use of the mouse, as you will soon discover.

The Modem

The *modem* (short for modulator-demodulator) is a device that enables data to be transferred over telephone lines. While not a necessary piece of hardware, modems are becoming more and more popular all the time. A typical modem is shown in figure 1.7.

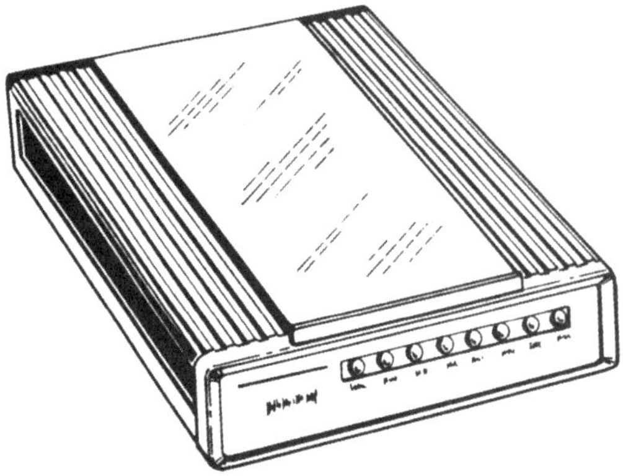

Fig. 1.7. A typical modem.

Modems are popular with users who want to communicate with electronic bulletin board systems (BBSs); these are used to communicate with other users and to upload (send) and download (receive) public domain and shareware software. With the emergence of *computer viruses*, however, the BBS has suffered. A virus (Trojan horse, logic bomb, and so on) is a destructive program that is designed to attack a specific part of the computer. One common virus action is to destroy hard disk data. For this reason, if you use a BBS, use virus-protection software (such as FluShot+) on any programs you download before using them on your computer.

Another popular use for the modem is to call on-line information services, such as CompuServe. With CompuServe, you can get the latest news, weather, and sports; play on-line games; go shopping on-line; send and receive electronic mail; make airline and hotel reservations; read *Consumer Reports*; access Grolier's *Academic American Encyclopedia*; and upload and download software.

Modems are rated according to their *baud* rate, which is the rate at which information is transmitted through a communications line. Baud rates are expressed in bits per second. As a rule of thumb, a baud rate divided by 10 equals characters per second. A baud rate of 300, for example, is equal to 30 characters per second. Typical rates are 1200 (120 characters per second) and 2400 (240 characters per second) baud, but 9600-baud modems are becoming more popular. Most of these modems also have facsimile (fax) capabilities.

Bits, Bytes, and Other Terms

The information used in computer memory or stored on disks is measured in *bytes*, a collection of eight binary digits, or bits.

A *bit* (short for binary digit) is the smallest unit of storage on a computer. A bit can have a value of 0 or 1. You can think of a bit like a light switch; it is either on or off.

A *byte* is a collection of bits, usually 8. Depending on the value of each bit (or whether each switch is on or off), a byte can have a value of 0 through 255. A byte is basically equivalent to one character or letter. The English alphabet is 26 bytes; therefore, a double-spaced, typewritten page is about 1,500 bytes.

Because bits and bytes are very small, the computer manipulates them in units. The most common unit is called a *kilobyte* (K), which is 1,024 bytes; a common practice is to round off a K to 1,000 bytes. A double-spaced typewritten page is about 1.5K. A *megabyte* (M) is 1000K or about one million bytes. This would equal about 666 double-spaced, typewritten pages. Large hard disks are very common these days. A 40M hard disk, for example, will hold about 26,640 double-spaced, typewritten pages. Even larger hard disks, such as 200M, are getting more common all the time.

Some businesses need even larger storage capacity. Another unit of measuring bytes is the *gigabyte* (G), which is 1,000M or about 1 billion bytes. This is a staggering amount of space, roughly equalling 666,666 double-spaced, typewritten pages. Even more staggering is the *terabyte* (T), which is 1,000G, or about 1 trillion bytes. Think about it! That's roughly 666,666,666 double-spaced, typewritten pages.

Memory (as well as disk space) is measured in bytes. When the original IBM PC was introduced in 1981, it could only address a whopping 64K of memory, because no one ever thought that a user could possibly need more than that! Well, things change. Today, the bare minimum for RAM is 640K, and many manufacturers put one megabyte in their machines as a standard. But it is quite common to see 4, 8, 16, and even 32 megabytes of memory in PCs today. This memory demand is due to large applications programs, such as Lotus 1-2-3, and *multitasking* (multiple programs running at once) environments, such as Microsoft Windows.

Floppy Drives and Disks

Technically, any device other than the system unit is a *peripheral device*. A peripheral enables you to do things such as store data on a disk, type letters with the keyboard, or print what you type on the keyboard. The following sections present various peripheral devices.

One or two floppy disk drives also are contained within the system unit. In general, disk drives provide a way to store data and programs permanently and to transport information from one computer system to another. Depending on the computer you are using, disk drives are a 5 1/4-inch minifloppy or a 3 1/2-inch microfloppy drive. Many computers have both types of floppy drives; this way they are more flexible in storing and transferring data. Figure 1.8 shows a typical 5 1/4-inch floppy disk drive.

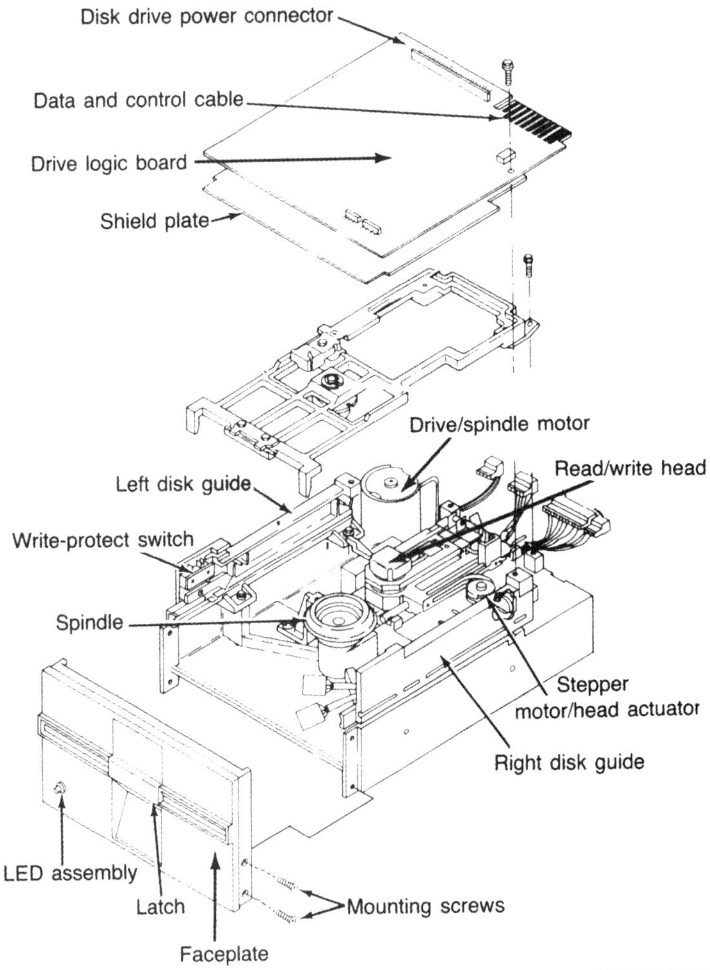

Used with permission from IBM Corporation.

Fig. 1.8. A 5 1/4-inch floppy disk drive.

Floppy disks are circular pieces of mylar or other plastic-like material coated with a magnetic oxide film and enclosed in plastic cases. You can store data on the disk, retrieve the data, use it, change it, or erase it.

IBM-compatible computers use two types of removable disks: 5 1/4-inch disks (sometimes called minifloppy disks) are housed in jackets made of flexible plastic (see fig. 1.9). Smaller 3 1/2-inch disks (sometimes called microfloppy disks) are housed in square, hard plastic cases, which are thicker and sturdier than minifloppies (see fig. 1.10).

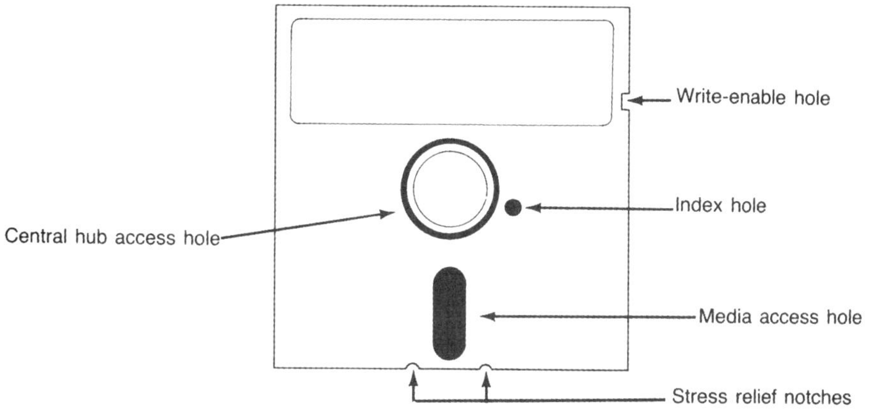

Fig. 1.9. A 5 1/4-inch floppy disk.

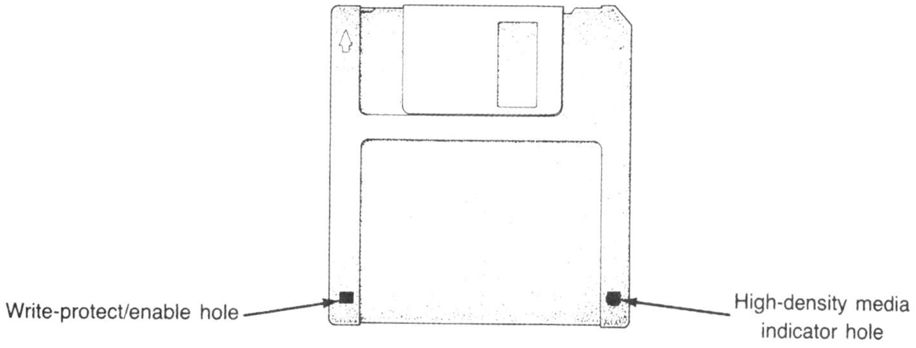

Fig. 1.10. A 3 1/2-inch floppy disk.

When you insert a floppy disk into a disk drive, a spindle comes up through the spindle hole, grabs the disk, and spins it. A moving read/ write head mounted inside the disk drive reads and writes information on the magnetic surface of the disk through the read/write slot. The index hole aligns the disk; as the disk spins, a light beam is projected through the index hole of the disk and the hole in the jacket, enabling the computer to determine the exact position of the disk. The stress-relief notches help to prevent the jacket from warping. Finally, if covered, the write-protect notch prevents information from being written to the disk. Small tabs for this purpose, which resemble pieces of tape, are included with disks when you buy them.

The anatomy of the 3 1/2-inch disk is very similar to the 5 1/4-inch disk. One important difference is that the sliding cover protects the disk surface when the disk is not in the disk drive; it slides open when the disk is inserted. Another difference is that the write-protect tab is built-in. To write-protect the disk, you simply slide the tab so that you can see through the hole. The high capacity hole is open if the disk is a high density disk, which you will learn about in a moment.

On any disk, the read/write head writes on concentric circles called *tracks*. These tracks are divided into pie-shaped wedges called *sectors*, which serve as a disk's smallest storage unit. Figure 1.11 shows this disk organization. The number of tracks and sectors on a disk determines the *density* (storage capacity) of a disk, as you'll see in a moment.

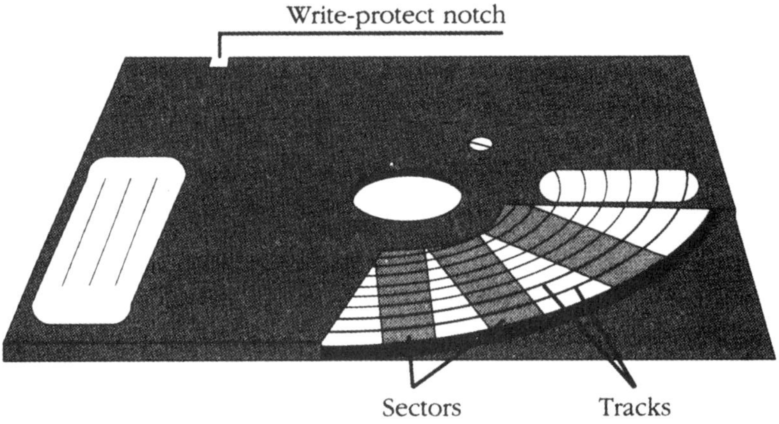

Fig. 1.11. Tracks and sectors on a disk.

The disks used in PCs today are termed *double-sided* (DS) because they are used on both sides. At one time, IBM produced a few PCs that used *single-sided* (SS) disks, but these early PCs are now ancient history. Disks now record information in *double-density* (DD) or *high-density* (HD) form. High-density disks also are called *quad-density* (QD) because they hold four times the number of those early standard disks.

Table 1.3 summarizes the most common floppy disk formats used today. You will learn more about these disk formats in Lesson 6.

Table 1.3. Common Floppy Disk Formats

Format	Tracks	Sectors per Track	Usable Capacity
DSDD-9	40	9	360K
QD-9	80	9	720K
QD-15	80	15	1.2M
QD-18	80	18	1.44M
QD-36	80	36	2.88M

As you can see, the total capacity of a disk is actually quite simple to calculate; total capacity equals the number of tracks times the number of sectors.

Inserting a Floppy Disk into a Disk Drive

Whether you are using a 5 1/4-inch disk or a 3 1/2-inch disk, the procedure for inserting it into the disk drive is easy. If you are using a 5 1/4-inch drive, follow these steps:

1. Open the door of the disk drive, if it is closed; it's closed if the latch blocks the drive slot.
2. Grasp the disk at the top, label side up, with the write-protect notch on your left.

> If the disk drive has a vertical opening, the labeled side should be facing left with the write notch on the bottom.

3. Gently insert the disk into the drive.

   Do not force the disk into the drive. If the disk does not go in easily, take it out and try again. Forcing the disk may cause it to bend or to be scratched.
4. Close the drive door.
5. To remove the disk, open the drive door, take the disk out of the drive, and return it to the disk envelope (or sleeve).

If you are using a 3 1/2-inch disk drive, follow these steps:

1. Grasp the disk at the top, label side up, with the insertion arrow on your left and pointing forward.
2. Gently slide the disk into the drive until you hear a click; this means the disk has seated into place.
3. To remove the disk, push the button located just below the drive slot (or to the right of the slot, if the slot is vertical).

Guidelines for Protecting Your Disks and Disk Drives

- Insert disks carefully into the disk drive.
- Store minifloppy disks in their protective envelopes when the disks are not being used.
- Label every disk, using only a felt-tip marker on 5 1/4-inch disks (never use a pencil or ball-point pen, because it may damage the disk). Or, just fill out the label *before* you place it on the disk.
- Make backup (extra) copies of important disks. Lessons 9 and 14 provide more information on making backup copies of disks.
- Store infrequently used disks and backup copies of disks away from your computer.
- Store disks in a perfectly flat or vertical position.
- Keep your disks at a comfortable temperature; avoid extremes of hot and cold.
- Buy good quality, certified disks; avoid "bargain basement" disks.
- Remove the disks from the drives before you turn off your computer or move it.
- Don't touch the disk's magnetic surface. Always hold it by the outside edges.
- Don't put your disks near magnetic fields, such as a photocopier, typewriter, telephone, or even the magnetic strips on credit cards.
- Don't "clean" your diskettes—that is, wipe them with a cloth, or anything else.
- Don't keep your disks near potential contaminants, such as food, liquids, smoke, and open windows.

- Don't fold or bend a disk.
- Close the drive door carefully after inserting a floppy disk.
- Don't clean the recording heads too often; once a year is usually enough (see your owner's manual).
- Be careful not to shock the disk drive by bumping or jarring it.
- Put the cardboard protector or an old floppy disk in the disk drive and close the doors when moving or shipping your drives for long distances. This locks down the read/write head and prevents it from being jarred loose.

Hard Disk Drive

Most computers today have a *hard disk* (also called *fixed disk*). A hard disk is similar to a floppy disk in reading and writing information. The main difference is that the hard disk uses a rigid metal platter, or multiple platters for large capacity drives, thus making the disk "hard." The platters are coated with metal oxide. Because the hard disk drive and sealed read/write heads are combined into one nonremovable unit, it is also called *fixed*. Figure 1.12 shows a cut-away view of a typical hard disk drive.

The hard disk spins much faster than the floppy disk—usually at 3,600 rpm compared to the 300 rpm of a floppy disk. This faster spin provides much faster transfer of information than is available with floppy disks. Other advantages of hard disks are that they store much more information than floppy disks and provide much faster access to information.

What is Computer Software?

To reiterate what was mentioned in the Introduction of this book, without software, a computer is a useless piece of hardware. Remember:

> *Hardware makes it possible, while software makes it happen.*

Simply put, a *software program* is a list of instructions that tells a computer what to do and how to do it. The term *applications program* takes in just about every software program there is. Examples of applications programs include word processors (which manipulate text), spreadsheets (which manipulate numeric information), and databases (which store and retrieve almost any kind of information). Additionally, other software is available on the market for practically any need you may have.

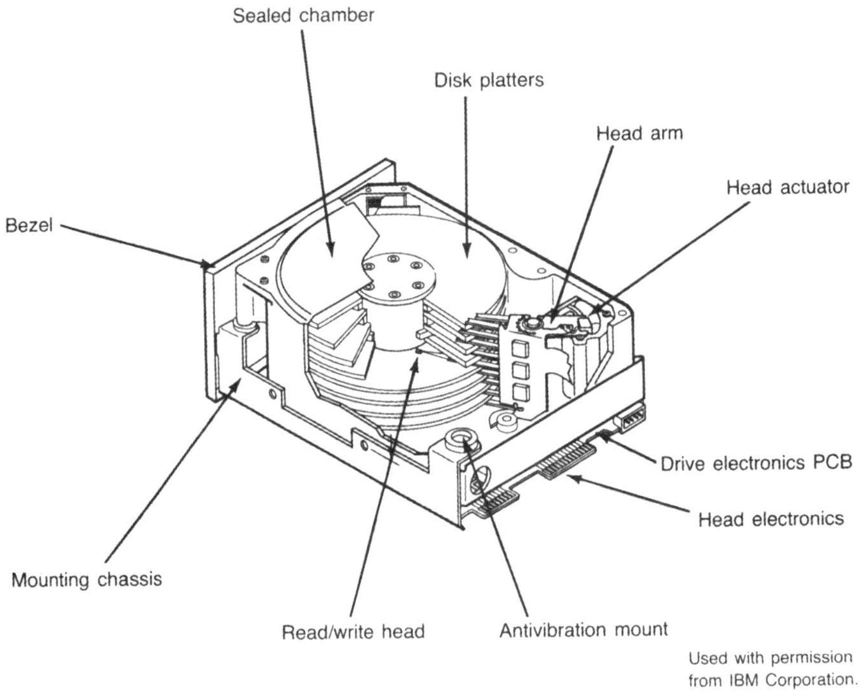

Fig. 1.12. A typical hard disk drive.

In contrast, a *system program* controls the computer system itself. DOS is such a program, or set of programs. It manages the computer hardware (the system unit, disk drives, keyboard, display, printer, and mouse) and directs the fundamental operations of the computer. The system program does all this so that applications programs don't have to.

Lesson Summary

- ☐ Computer hardware is the equipment that makes up your computer system—the IBM PC, XT, AT, PS/2, or IBM-compatible system.

- The essential parts of your computer system are the system unit, disk drives, keyboard, display, and surge protector. A printer is not essential, but is highly recommended.
- For some programs, you can use a mouse instead of the keyboard to select from a list of items shown on-screen. As you move the mouse around on a desk, the motion is reflected by the motion of the cursor on-screen.
- A modem is a valuable asset for calling on-line information services, public bulletin boards, and other computers.
- 5 1/4-inch (minifloppy) and 3 1/2-inch (microfloppy) disks are removable. Hard disks are fixed and nonremovable.
- Disk capacity depends on the type of disk drives that are installed in a system unit and the density of the disks used in the drive.
- Software programs come in two types: applications programs accomplish useful tasks such as word-processing, while system programs control the computer hardware.

Key Terms

Bit	Binary digit—has a value of 0 or 1
Byte	A collection of bits—usually 8
Disk	A plastic disk or metal platter coated with a magnetic material used to store information
Disk density	The storage capacity of a disk
Disk drive	A device that records and plays back information on disks
Hard copy	A printout on paper of computer data
Hardware	The mechanical devices that make up the computer system
Kilobyte (K)	1,024 bytes
Megabyte (M)	1,000K or about one million bytes
Microprocessor	The main part of a computer that performs calculations and processes information
RAM	Random-access memory—electronic memory used for programs and data
ROM	Read-only memory—nonerasable computer instructions embedded in hardware chips

Sector	Pie-shaped section of a track that serves as a disk's smallest storage unit
Software program	A list of instructions that tells a computer what to do and how to do it
Surge Protector	An electronic device which protects computer equipment from electrical current fluctuations and spikes
Track	An invisible, electronically produced circle on a disk where data is stored

In addition to the terms used in this lesson, here are a few other terms that you will explore in more detail as you progress through this book.

Back up	To make copies of files for storage in case the originals get damaged or lost (Lesson 14)
Command	An instruction you give to the computer that executes a DOS function or a program (Lesson 6)
Copy files	To make duplicate copies of individual files (Lesson 10)
Ctrl-Alt-Del	Pressing this key combination will reboot (restart) the computer (Lesson 2)
Ctrl-C (or Ctrl-Break)	Key combination that will interrupt and cancel a DOS command (Lesson 9)
Directory	An area of the DOS file system that holds information about files and directories. The root directory is the highest directory of the tree structure, and every disk has a root (Lesson 5).
Erase files	To remove files from a disk (Lesson 11)
Extension	An optional suffix of one to three characters that helps to identify a file more precisely (Lesson 8)
File	A named collection of information stored on disk. Usually contains data or a computer program (Lesson 8).
File name	A one- to eight-character string which identifies a file. A file must have a file name (Lesson 8).
Formatting	To prepare a disk for use by DOS (Lesson 6)
Hierarchical Directory	An organized, multilevel structure of directories (Lesson 12)
Launch	To start a program (Lesson 15)

Path	The list of directory names, separated by a backslash (\), that defines the location of a specific directory or file (Lesson 7)
Shift-Print Screen	Prints what is presently on-screen (Lesson 13)
Wild-card character	Character DOS uses to represent one character (?) or multiple characters (*) in a file name or extension (Lesson 8)

Exercises

Identify the following parts of your computer system:

1. System unit (what microprocessor is it)
2. Floppy disk drive (what format is it)
3. Floppy disk
4. Printer (is it a dot-matrix or laser)
5. Display (what type is it)
6. Keyboard (what type is it)
7. Function keys
8. Numeric/cursor-control keys
9. Surge protector
10. Mouse (if you have one)
11. Modem (if you have one)

For More Information

If you would like further information about computer hardware and software, consult Chapter 1 of *Using MS-DOS 5* (Que Corporation).

Lesson 2

Loading and Starting DOS

In this lesson, you learn how to do the following:

- Load and start (*boot*) DOS
- Set the date and time
- Correct mistakes you make while booting

Estimated time to complete this lesson: 10-15 minutes

What Is Booting?

Like every other aspect of computers, there is even a term for starting the computer—it is called *booting up*. This term is taken from the old expression "pulling yourself up by the bootstraps." This expression describes how a computer can almost start itself.

When you turn on (or *power up*) your computer, it does a *power-on reset* (POR), which means that the microprocessor, RAM, and other electronics zero out and start from scratch. The system then begins its *power-on self-test* (POST), which simply means that it tests system components (such as the RAM and disk drives) to ensure that they are working properly. Then the *bootstrap loader* (or *bootstrap program*—a tiny program built into the computer), loads DOS into the computer's memory.

This book assumes that you have a hard disk and, therefore, boot from the hard disk. You also can boot the computer from a floppy disk, however, if it has DOS on it. You will learn in Lesson 6 how to create a floppy disk that will boot the computer, but for now you will just turn on the computer and boot from the hard disk.

As part of the booting operation, MS-DOS gives you the opportunity to enter the current date and time, if your computer does not automatically keep track of these for you. Although entering the date and time is optional, it's a good idea for record-keeping purposes to get into the habit of entering the information every time you boot DOS or reset your computer. This information can come in handy later if you need to know the date you worked on a project or you want to check the time of day the project was finished. (You see how this identification procedure works in Lesson 8.) Date and time information becomes increasingly important as you use your system and create more files.

There are two types of booting: the *cold boot* and the *warm boot*. This lesson explores both of these methods.

Performing a Cold Boot

A *cold boot* simply means that you start the computer from a power-off condition. You do this simply by turning on the switch. Most computers sold nowadays automatically keep track of the date and time, even when the computer is not on; therefore, you may not need to do much when you go through the following procedure. You may need only to turn on the computer and allow it to "do its thing" before it turns control over to you.

To perform a cold boot, follow these steps:

1. If your computer is on, make sure that you are at a DOS prompt (C:\> or similar prompt), and press the Reset button on your computer (if you have one). If not, turn the power off and wait for about 30 seconds.

2. Turn the computer on (unless you pressed the Reset button).

   Notice the self-test information that comes on-screen, which is similar to the following:

   ```
   Memory check
   640K  OK
   ```

   The moving numbers represent blocks of memory that the computer is testing. After the memory check, notice that the light on your floppy drive(s) comes on showing that the computer is testing it. The computer now loads the bootstrap program into memory.

3. If a message similar to the following is displayed on your screen,

```
Current date is Thu 11-22-1991
Enter new date (mm-dd-yy):
```

   then you need to enter today's date if it is not the current date. To accept the suggested date, just press Enter. To enter a date, enter the month as a number between 1 and 12 in place of `mm` and the day as a number between 1 and 31 in place of `dd`. DOS assumes the 20th century, so just enter the two-digit year in place of `yy` (such as 92 for 1992). Separate each part of the date with a hyphen (-) or a slash (/). When you're done, press Enter.

   Don't worry if you make a mistake. DOS will just prompt you again with the following message:

```
Invalid date
Enter new date (mm-dd-yy):
```

   Some common mistakes are explored a little later in the lesson.

4. If a message similar to the following appears on your screen,

```
Current time is 1:21:42:54a
Enter new time:
```

   you need to enter the time if it is not the current time. To accept the suggested time, just press Enter. If, for example, you want to enter 2:21 P.M. as the new time, you can enter it in one of two ways:

   2:21p (12-hour format)

   or

   14:21 (24-hour format)

> If you are using a version of DOS prior to Version 4.0, you *must* use the 24-hour format.

   Be sure to separate the parts of the time statement with a colon (:) or a period (.). When you are done entering the time, press Enter.

   Again, if you make a mistake, no problem; DOS just prompts you to try again with this message:

```
Invalid time
Enter new time:
```

Depending on how your computer is configured, when the booting process is complete you see a DOS prompt similar to the following:

C:\>

Or, you see the DOS Shell (see figs. 2.1 and 2.2).

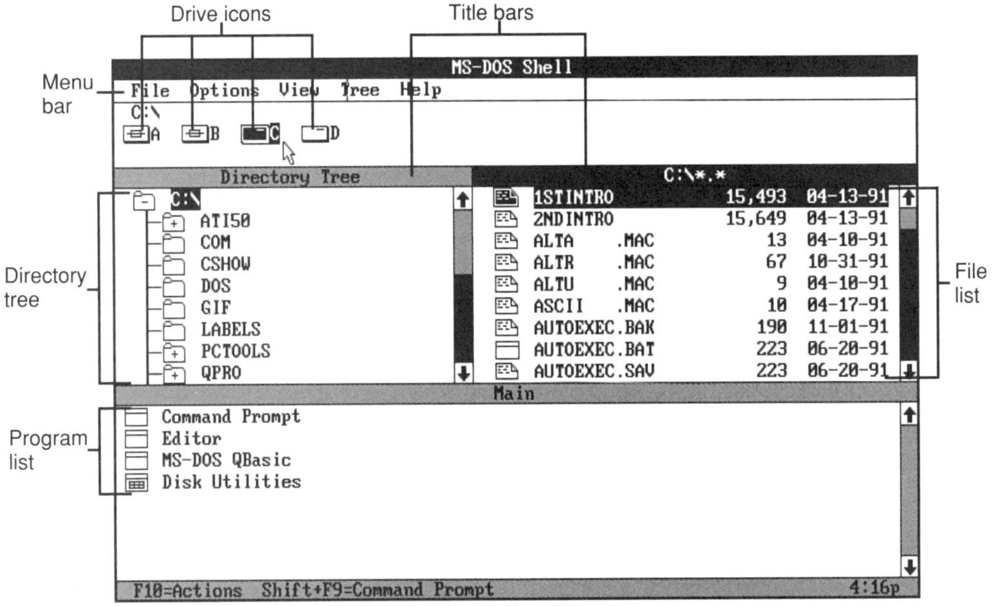

Fig. 2.1. The DOS Shell in graphics mode after bootup.

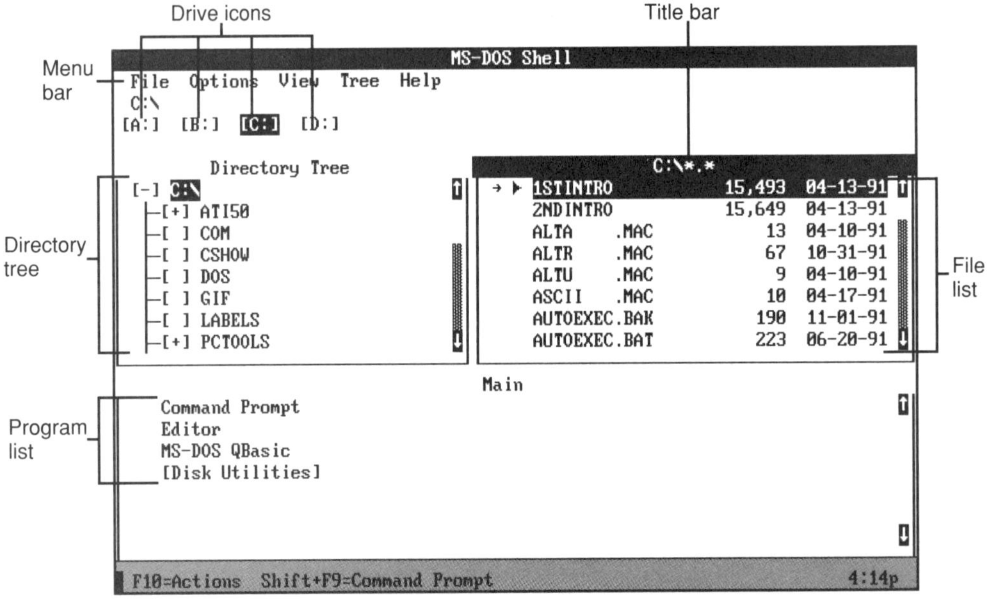

Fig. 2.2. The DOS Shell in text mode after bootup.

> If you have an AUTOEXEC.BAT file (which is explored in Lesson 17), DOS does not prompt you for the date or time unless the DATE and TIME commands are in the AUTOEXEC.BAT file.

Most computers nowadays provide a reset button on the front panel of the system unit that enables you to do a cold boot without actually turning off the computer. You will see the advantages of this in a moment.

Performing a Warm Boot

A *warm boot* is the process of restarting a PC while the power is on. You perform a warm boot by pressing Ctrl-Alt-Del, which you will do in a moment. The physical difference between a cold boot and a warm boot is that a warm boot does not go through the memory-checking process and is, therefore, faster. It is far better for you to perform a warm boot rather than a power up cold boot because powering up your computer puts more strain on the electronics.

One great advantage of having a reset button on your computer is that a cold boot with the reset button does not put the stress on the electronics that a power up cold boot does. Another advantage is that a reset button provides an easy way to reboot when the computer and keyboard lock up, making a warm boot with Ctrl-Alt-Del impossible.

To perform a warm boot, follow these steps:

1. Make sure you are at a DOS prompt, such as C:\>.

   If the DOS Shell is on-screen, press the F3 key to get to a DOS prompt.

2. Press Ctrl-Alt-Del (press and hold down the Ctrl key, press and hold down the Alt key, press the Del key, and then release all three).

3. Perform steps 3 and 4 in the "Performing a Cold Boot" section, as needed.

Making Mistakes Entering the Date and Time

Everyone makes mistakes—even the most experienced computer users (who often are called *power users*). When you're a newcomer to computing, however, or when you're using an unfamiliar computer or operating system for the first time, mistakes can be especially frustrating unless you know what causes them and how to correct them.

Not all mistakes in computers can be corrected, and recovery from some errors is simply impossible. These errors—and how to avoid making them—are discussed in later lessons. But fortunately, errors in date and time are easy to fix. Some of the most common mistakes you can make at the booting stage follow:

- Making a simple typing error
- Typing a nonsense date or time
- Using incorrect punctuation or format
- Trying to use the numeric keypad on the right side of the keyboard instead of the numbers along the top of the keyboard when the keypad is in cursor mode

DOS can identify only mistakes caused by an impossibility in logic, such as entering 13 for the month or 75 for the seconds, and mistakes caused by invalid format. If you make such errors, DOS simply prompts you again for a valid entry. Be aware: DOS does not recognize an incorrect date or time if the entry is plausible and the format is valid.

Using the DATE and TIME Commands

Even if your computer keeps track of the date and time for you, you should know how to enter the date and time manually. DOS has two commands you can use to set the date and time. You can run these commands—DATE and TIME—whenever the computer displays a system prompt (C:\>, for example).

Use these two commands to correct the date and time or change the date and time as recorded by your computer. A good example of when you will need to change the time is if your area changes to daylight savings time in the spring and back to normal time in the fall.

You do not have to reset the system to change the date and time. Starting with DOS 3.3, in fact, the DATE and TIME commands reset the built-in, battery-backed clock of AT-class machines ('286, '386, and '486 computers).

You can use the DATE or TIME command anytime by typing it at the DOS prompt and proceeding as outlined earlier. You can use a shortcut, however. Instead of typing **TIME** and then entering the time at the prompt, just include the time you want to enter with the command. If you want to change the time to 8:00 A.M., for example, type **TIME 8:00A**.

In the "Exercises" section, you'll intentionally make a few mistakes, find out what happens, and correct them.

Shutting Off Your Computer

You should never reboot or turn off (*power down*) your computer unless there is a system prompt on-screen. To do so at other times, such as when a program is running, may cause you to lose information you want to save. Additionally, never reboot or turn the computer off when a disk drive light is on; doing so may cause data damage or even disk damage.

A misunderstood area of computers concerns how often a user should turn the computer on and off. Some users mistakenly think that the computer should be turned off when not in use, but this is not true. Believe it or not, it does not harm your computer if you leave it on 24 hours a day, 7 days a week, 52 weeks a year. In fact, this is actually the best thing to do for the computer.

The start-up current draw for the computer and the motors in your disk drives is much higher than the normal operating current draw. Starting the computer puts a tremendous demand on the power supply, because all the circuitry and components get their power from that supply. This demand often overloads a weak circuit and causes a power supply failure. Many people have replaced power supplies because of this. Additionally, allowing the computer to remain on keeps the temperature of the system constant. Frequent power downs and start-ups cause the system to cool down and then heat up, again putting great strain on circuits and components.

If you are not able to leave the computer on all the time, there is an alternative—*power on the system only once a day*. If you power up in the morning to do an hour's worth of word processing, for example, but don't think you'll need the computer again until the afternoon, don't power down. If several people use the computer during the day, make sure that everyone knows to leave it on when they are done. Don't power down until the working day is over.

The fewer start-ups your computer has to go through means the fewer component failures *you* will have to go through.

Although it is best to leave your computer on as much as possible, there is one thing to be wary of—leaving an image on the monitor screen for an extended period of time. This can cause *screen burn-in*, which means that the phosphor used to coat the inside of the monitor screen can have an image permanently burned into it, thereby ruining the monitor. To prevent screen burn-in, you should turn down the brightness and contrast controls on the monitor if you will be away from the computer for an extended period (over 30 minutes). An alternative is to install a screen-blanking program, which will blank the screen after a certain time of keyboard inactivity.

Lesson Summary

- ☐ *Booting* means loading and starting DOS. Booting DOS is the first step when you use your computer for any reason.
- ☐ A system reset causes the computer to start again or reboot. You can perform a system reset by pressing Ctrl-Alt-Del (performing a warm boot).
- ☐ You should make sure that your computer has the date and time set correctly, because both are attached to any files you create or change. This information is useful for identifying files and keeping records.
- ☐ If you enter a date or time in an incorrect format, you see the error message `Invalid Date` or `Invalid Time`. You then can enter a valid date or time.
- ☐ You can use the DATE and TIME commands independently to verify or change dates and times.
- ☐ The DOS prompt (or system prompt) is the computer's signal that a new command is needed.

Key Terms

Boot up	To load and start DOS.
Cold boot	To start the computer from a power-off condition.
Ctrl-Alt-Del	Reboots (restarts) the computer (warm boot).

DATE command	Changes the system date.
DOS prompt	Characters DOS displays to inform you that you can enter a command. For example, `C:\>` is a DOS prompt.
Power down	To physically turn off the computer.
Power up	To physically turn on the computer.
Reboot	To restart DOS.
Reset button	A button, usually mounted on the front panel of the system unit, which enables you to perform a cold boot without shutting off the computer.
TIME command	Changes the system time.
Warm boot	Restarting a PC while the power is on.

Exercises

In this section, you will intentionally make a few mistakes with DATE and TIME to find out what happens and how to correct them. To practice using the DATE command, follow these steps:

1. From the DOS prompt (if you are in the Shell, press F3 to exit it), type **DATE** and press Enter.
2. Enter the nonsense date **15/45/99**, or a similar entry of your own making, and press Enter.

   If you want, you can consolidate the command into the following statement:

   DATE 15/45/99

   Then press Enter. The following message appears on-screen:

   ```
   Invalid date
   Enter new date (mm-dd-yy):
   ```
3. Now try entering some other invalid date combinations, such as those in the following table:

Entry	Error
June 5, 1988	You can enter the date only in numerical format; you cannot use words.
2/29/93	Too many days for that month
070288	No punctuation between *mm-dd-yy*
12 13 88	You cannot use spaces to separate *mm-dd-yy*. You must use only hyphens (-) or slashes (/).
3/5/79	The year predates this version of DOS, which was created in 1980. DOS 3.3, 4.0, and 5.0 accept any year from 1980 to 2099.

Each time you enter an invalid date, you get the same message and another opportunity to enter the date correctly. In fact, DOS gives you an unlimited number of opportunities to enter a valid date.

If you do not want to enter a new date, simply press Enter when you see the prompt to keep the suggested date.

> On some computers, if you press Enter instead of typing the date, the files you create may not be identified by the current date in your directory.

4. To set things right, enter the current date.

> A handy use for DATE is to check the day of the week for upcoming dates. If you want to know on what day of the week December 25, 1992 falls, for example, type **DATE 12-25-92** and press Enter for the new date. Then type **DATE** again. DATE comes back with the day of the week! But don't forget to change the date back.

To practice using the TIME command, suppose that this is Monday morning after daylight savings time went into effect over the weekend. Your computer thinks it's 7:00 a.m. but you know it's 8:00 a.m. (partly because you lost an hour of sleep Saturday night). Just follow these steps:

1. At the DOS prompt, type **TIME** and press Enter. The current time appears on-screen.
2. Enter the new time, in this case **8:00A**, and press Enter.

Again, you can consolidate the command into the following statement:

TIME 8:00A

3. Now try entering some invalid time combinations, such as those in the following table:

Entry	Error
12/04/55/00	Incorrect punctuation. You can use only a colon or a period between the various parts of the time stamp.
1:30 pm	DOS Versions 3.3 and under operate on a 24-hour clock. For hours after noon, add 12 to the hour; 1:30 pm is 13:30. With DOS 4.0 and 5.0, you may type **1:30P** to use the 12-hour clock feature.

4. To set things right, enter the current time.

Now that you know how to start your computer, Lesson 3 guides you through the next step—installing and using the disk tutor.

Lesson 3

Installing and Using the ATI Disk Tutor

If you've completed the introduction to computer hardware and software in Lesson 1 and have used Lesson 2 to get DOS up and running on your system, you're ready to install the *Hands-On MS-DOS 5* disk tutor. Or, if you already know something about computer systems, have DOS running, and are eager to jump in and begin the computer-based training, you're ready to start this lesson.

As you learned in the Introduction, *Hands-On MS-DOS 5* has three parts:

- The computer-based training (disk tutor)
- The book lessons
- The book lesson files

The disk tutor gets you comfortable with DOS 5, and the book lessons reinforce and take you beyond what the disk tutor teaches you. By completing the disk tutor sessions and then working through the book lessons, you gain an immediate working knowledge of DOS 5. The book lesson files let you practice various commands with DOS 5 as you work through the lessons.

The disk tutor from American Training International (ATI) is an excellent, interactive training course that enables the beginner and intermediate DOS user to learn DOS in an easy, hands-on manner.

> Keep in mind that the disk tutor is a separate program from DOS itself. *When you work with the disk tutor, you are* not *actually working with DOS; it is only a realistic* simulation *of DOS.* After you complete the disk tutor sessions, you can return to the book and actually begin working with DOS. Remember: You need to install MS-DOS Version 5 on your computer in order to do the book lessons. The disk tutor, however, will run under DOS 3.x and later versions.

The next two lessons, Lessons 4 and 5, introduce you to the DOS Shell and cover some foundational principles for using DOS 5.

In this short lesson you learn the following:

- How to install the disk tutor and book lesson files
- How to use the disk tutor
- How to run the disk tutor from a floppy disk

Installing the Disk Tutor and Book Lesson Files

Hands-On MS-DOS 5 includes a 5 1/4-inch, 1.2M disk that contains the ATI disk tutor and the lesson files that go with the book lessons. An installation program on the disk automatically installs the software to the hard disk of your choice.

> If you need another disk format for your computer—that is, if the enclosed disk does not work in your system—see the offer at the back of this book. You can exchange the disk that came with this book for two 5 1/4-inch, 360K disks or one 3 1/2-inch, 720K disk.

If you prefer, you can run the disk tutor and access the book lesson files from a floppy disk. Although this is *not* the best way to use the disk tutor, it can be done (see "Running the Disk Tutor from a Floppy Disk," later in this lesson).

Install does a number of things during the installation process, including the following:

- Detects what version of DOS is on your computer and displays a message.
- Detects whether there is enough memory on your computer to run the disk tutor. If there is, Install displays no message.
- Detects what hard disk drives exist on your computer and enables you to choose which drive to install to.
- Determines whether your chosen drive contains enough space to hold all the disk tutor and book lesson files.
- Displays the default directory on the chosen drive that will receive the disk tutor and book lesson files. It would be a good idea to accept the default directory, because you will need to access this directory and the subdirectories under it in the book lessons.
- Creates all the directories and copies all of the files you will need in order to work with the disk tutor and book lessons.

To install the disk tutor and lesson files to your hard disk, follow these steps:

1. Place the *Hands-On MS-DOS 5* disk into drive A and close the drive door.
2. At the DOS prompt (probably C:\>), change to drive A by typing **A:** and pressing Enter.
3. At the A> (or A:\>) prompt, type **INSTALL** and press Enter.

From here on, just follow the simple instructions on-screen. You can exit the installation at any time by pressing Ctrl-X.

Using the Disk Tutor

Now that you have installed the disk tutor and book lesson files, you are ready to start learning DOS. You should complete all the lessons in the on-screen disk tutor *first* before turning to the lessons in the *book*.

Running the disk tutor is as a easy as installing it. Follow these steps:

1. You first must type the letter of the drive to which the tutor was installed, followed by a colon (**C:** for example), and press Enter. You then must type **CD\ATI50**, press Enter, type **ATI**, and press Enter once again.
2. From here on, the disk tutor is totally menu-driven. Just follow the simple on-screen instructions.

For a handy reference, table 3.1 lists the keys used in the disk tutor, when each is used, and what each does.

Table 3.1. Disk Tutor Keys

Key	When To Use It	What It Does
Home	Any time during the tutorial	Displays the most recent menu.
PgUp	Any time during the tutorial	Goes back to review a screen; goes back up to three screens.
PgDn	Any time during the tutorial	Goes on to next screen, bypassing any keystrokes you may otherwise have to type to get to the next screen.
End	Any time during the tutorial	Displays help screen with these four useful keys: Home, PgUp, PgDn, and End; also helps exit the disk tutor.
Esc	When prompted	Exits disk tutor.
Space bar	When prompted	Continues to the next screen, after you have read the information on the current screen.
Enter	When prompted	Tells the computer you have completed a command (for example, when you enter your name at the beginning of the disk tutor).

Running the Disk Tutor from a Floppy Disk

The disk tutor and book lesson files are specifically designed to work on a hard disk, and it is highly recommended that you install them there, for at least three reasons:

- The disk tutor runs much faster from a hard disk.
- The book lesson files are easier to access on a hard disk.
- Accessing the disk tutor and the lesson files on a hard disk teaches you to navigate directories.

If, however, you need to use the disk tutor and lesson files from a floppy disk, you can do so, but *only* if the floppy disk is a 1.2M or higher capacity disk.

To be able to run the disk tutor and access the book lesson files from a floppy disk, follow these steps:

1. Place the *Hands-On MS-DOS 5* disk into drive A and close the drive door; this is called the *source* disk.
2. At any C> prompt, type **DISKCOPY A: A:** and press Enter.
3. Follow the on-screen instructions, exchanging the source disk with a blank disk (called the *target* disk) each time you are told to do so.
4. When the copying process is finished, press N when you are asked if you want to copy another disk.

   See Lesson 9 for much more detailed instructions on using the DISKCOPY command.
5. To start the disk tutor, place the copy of the disk you just made into drive A, type **A:** and press Enter, and then type **ATI** and press Enter.

> Whenever a book lesson calls for a lesson file, you must access drive A instead of the drive and directory given in the lesson text.

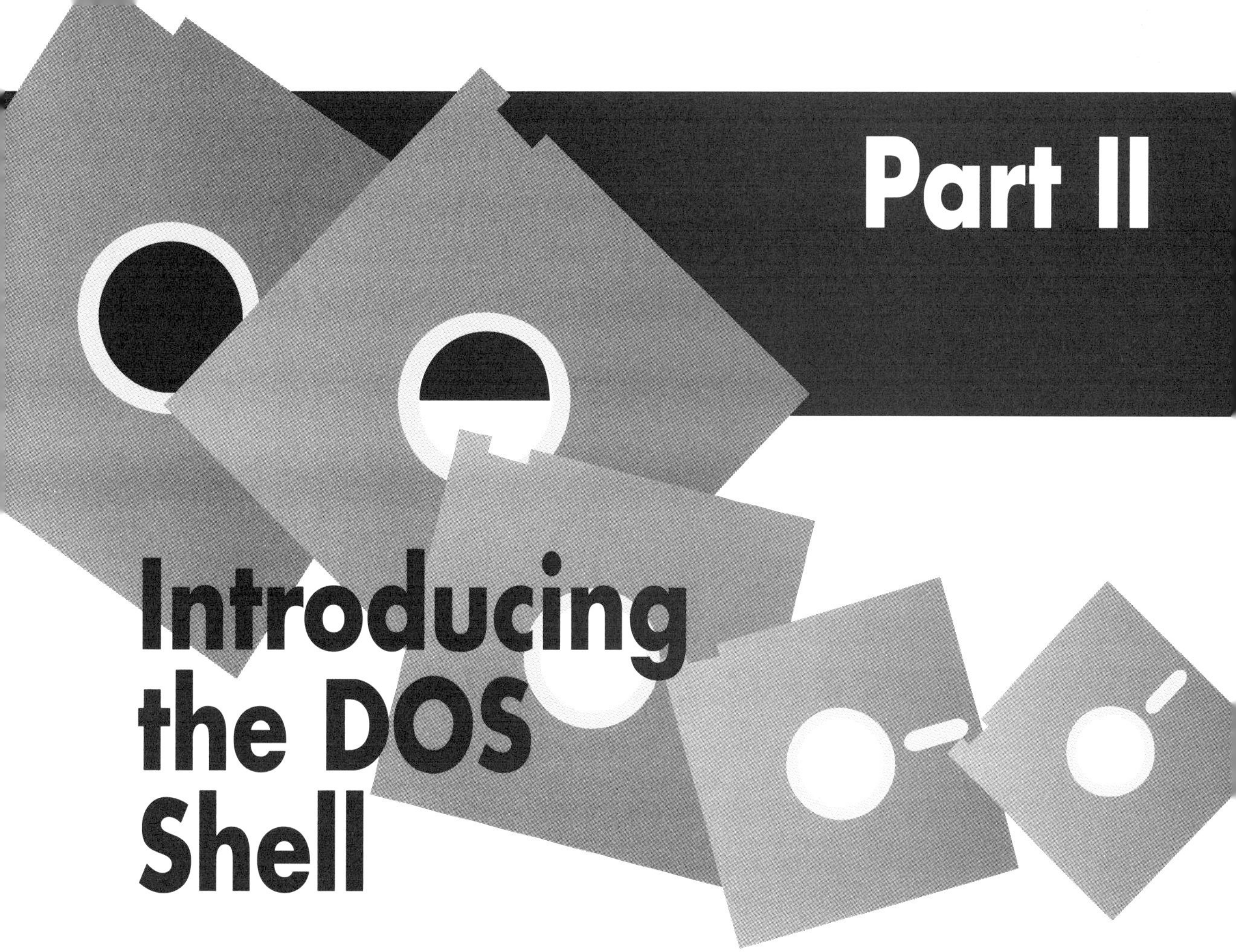

Part II

Introducing the DOS Shell

The DOS Shell is the foundation of DOS 5. The two lessons in this section introduce you to two important subjects:

- Basic procedures for using the DOS Shell (Lesson 4)
- How to work with the DOS Shell on a daily basis (Lesson 5)

Lesson 4

DOS Shell Basics

A DOS shell is a sophisticated computer program that "insulates" the user from DOS, making DOS much easier to use. Just as a hot pad enables you to touch a hot dish, a DOS shell enables you to use DOS without handling it directly (see fig. 4.1). With a DOS shell, you can choose commands, files, and directories without typing them manually.

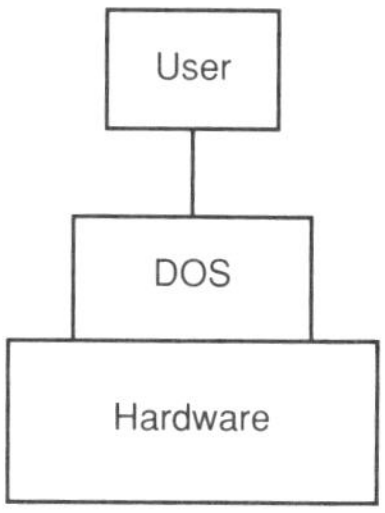

Fig. 4.1. The layers of DOS.

The hardware is the foundation of the computer system, and DOS controls the hardware. You interact with the hardware through DOS.

DOS Version 5, however, adds an additional layer of software between you and the fundamental parts of the computer. Figure 4.2 shows you how the DOS Shell makes using DOS easier.

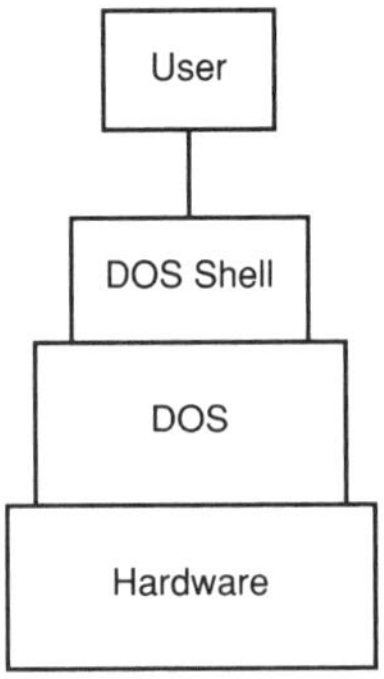

Fig. 4.2. The layers of DOS Version 5.

The DOS Shell that comes with DOS 5 is not technically a part of DOS; that is, DOS will still operate without the Shell. In fact, prior to DOS Version 4, there was no Shell at all. The user had to enter commands manually from the DOS command line. The new Shell is a computer program that forms a friendly interface between you and DOS.

Most shells graphically display an organized list of DOS commands, directories, and files. They also enable you to work with files, directories, and disks with ease. Most shells even have easy program-launching (starting) capabilities with the touch of a key or the click of a mouse.

The DOS Shell included with DOS 5 is also a contender with many commercial shells; although not as powerful as some, it is still an excellent DOS shell. Many users find it to be all the shell they ever need.

The DOS Shell makes DOS easier to work with and control than ever before. Through the use of color and graphics, the Shell makes working with DOS more of a visual experience rather than a drab text-based experience. To use the Shell effectively, you need to learn only a few basic skills. In this lesson you learn how to do the following:

- Start the DOS Shell
- Use the Shell's menus
- Use dialog boxes
- Use scroll bars
- Change the Shell's display
- Exit the Shell

Estimated time to complete this lesson: 25-30 minutes

Starting the DOS Shell

If you chose during installation to have the Shell activated each time you turn on your computer, you simply need to turn on your computer; the shell is displayed automatically.

As the Shell starts, you see the message

```
Reading Disk Information
```

in the center of your screen. This message indicates that the Shell is making note of what is on the disk and is storing it in memory. After starting the Shell, your screen should look similar to figure 4.3 or 4.4.

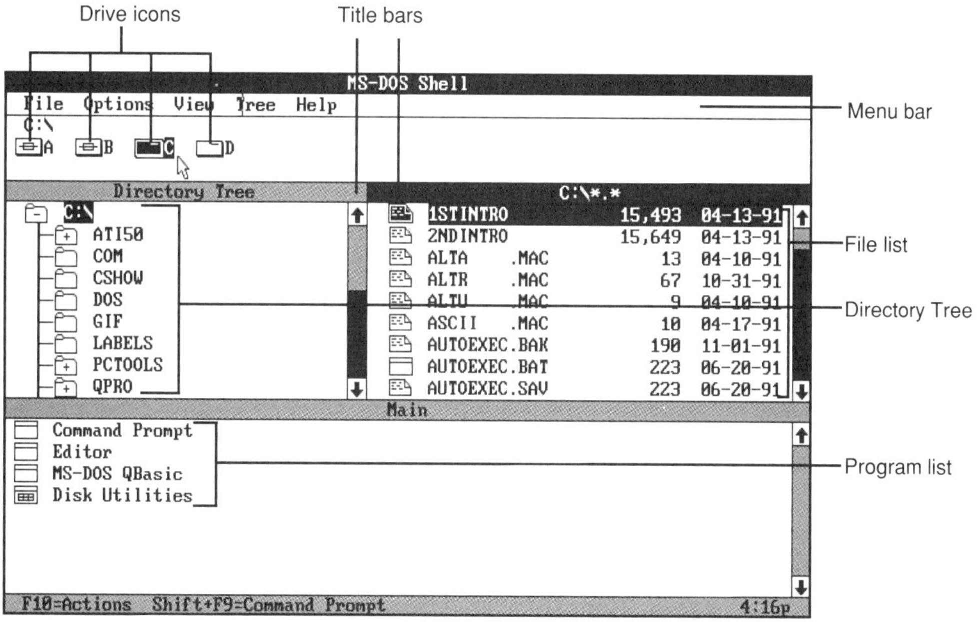

Fig. 4.3. The DOS Shell in 25-line, low resolution graphics mode.

The difference between figures 4.3 and 4.4 is that figure 4.3 appears in graphics mode, whereas figure 4.4 shows the DOS Shell in text mode. If you have a monochrome monitor that cannot display graphics, the DOS Shell is displayed in text mode. If you have a graphics monitor, you can choose from a number of color schemes and display modes. You learn about these display options in Lesson 16.

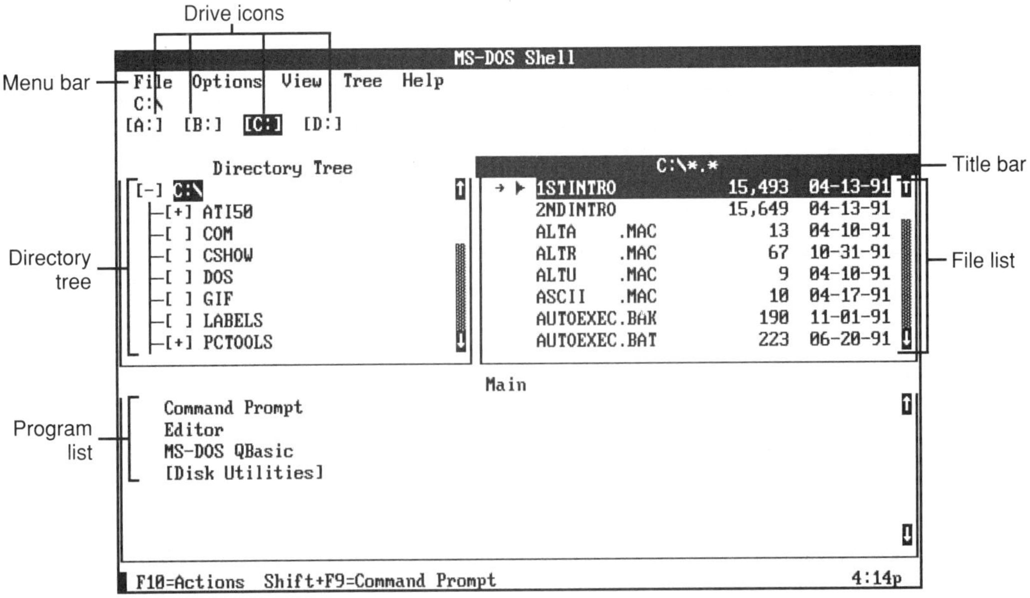

Fig. 4.4. The DOS Shell in 25-line, low resolution text mode.

The Shell's display mode in no way affects its capabilities; regardless of which mode you are in, all the Shell's features are available to you.

If the Shell does not appear automatically when you turn on your computer, follow these steps to activate the Shell:

1. At the DOS prompt (C:\> or a similar prompt) type **DOSSHELL** and press Enter.

   As the Shell starts, you see the message

   ```
   Reading Disk Information
   ```

   in the center of your screen. This message indicates that the Shell is making note of what is on the disk and is storing it in memory. After starting the Shell, your screen should look similar to figure 4.3 or 4.4.

   If the Shell appears on your screen, skip the remaining steps. If you receive the error message

```
Bad command or file name
```

continue with the next step.

2. Type **C:** and press Enter to make sure you are logged on to drive C.
3. Type **CD\DOS** and press Enter.
4. Type **DOSSHELL** and press Enter.

   The Shell now appears on-screen as in figure 4.3 or 4.4. If you still receive the error message

   ```
   Bad command or file name
   ```

   reinstall MS-DOS 5 according to the directions that came with DOS 5.

Taking a Quick Tour of the Shell

This section is a brief tour of what you see on-screen when you first activate the Shell. The Shell screen, also called the Shell *window*, is divided into four areas by default (the disk tutor calls these *areas*). Figures 4.3 and 4.4 illustrate these areas:

- *Drive icons:* Represent the available disk drives on your computer. Pictured here are drives A through D (in the upper left portion of the screen). Note that the mouse pointer is pointing to drive C in figure 4.3.
- *Directory Tree area:* Shows the directory structure of the current disk drive. The Directory Tree display changes according to the selected drive icon, and is located just below the drive icons.
- *File List area:* Shows a list of files in the current directory, which is displayed in the title bar above the list. In figures 4.3 and 4.4, the directory listed is C:*.*—that is, all the files (*.*) in the root (\) directory of drive C. This list changes when you select a different drive or directory, and is located to the right of the directory tree.
- *Program List area:* Lists the programs in the group (depending on what program group you are working with) in the area just below the directory tree. A *program group* is simply a collection of programs that are listed together, usually because they are in some way related. By default, the main program group is displayed, as in figures 4.3 and 4.4.

The Main program group includes two programs that you can start directly from the Shell. Editor starts the DOS text editor, which enables you to create text files, much like a word processing program. You can use MS-DOS QBasic to write programs in the BASIC programming language.

The Main program group also provides the Command Prompt choice, which takes you to the DOS command line. Finally, Disk Utilities displays the Disk Utilities program group in place of the Main program group. This group includes several DOS programs for maintaining your disks.

For some quick hands-on experience, activate the various areas and then display the Utilities group. If you have a mouse, follow these steps (if you are using the keyboard, skip to the next set of instructions):

1. Move the mouse pointer to the title bar of the Program List (Main) and click the left mouse button (press it once).

   Notice that the title bar changes its color or shade to indicate that the area is activated.

> If you are using a two-color monitor, the title bar will not change. You must watch for the small selection arrow (→) that moves to an item within an area when you click on it.

2. For practice, repeat step 1 for the other areas.
3. Move the mouse pointer to the Disk Utilities option in the Program List area.
4. Double-click the left mouse button (press it twice quickly) on Disk Utilities.

   Notice that double-clicking the mouse activates the area. The Disk Utilities program group now should be listed, as shown in figure 4.5. You learn how to use these simple programs for maintaining your disks in the following lessons:

   Lesson 6 (Format)
   Lesson 6 (Quick Format)
   Lesson 9 (Disk Copy)
   Lesson 11 (Undelete)
   Lesson 14 (Backup Fixed Disk)
   Lesson 14 (Restore Fixed Disk)

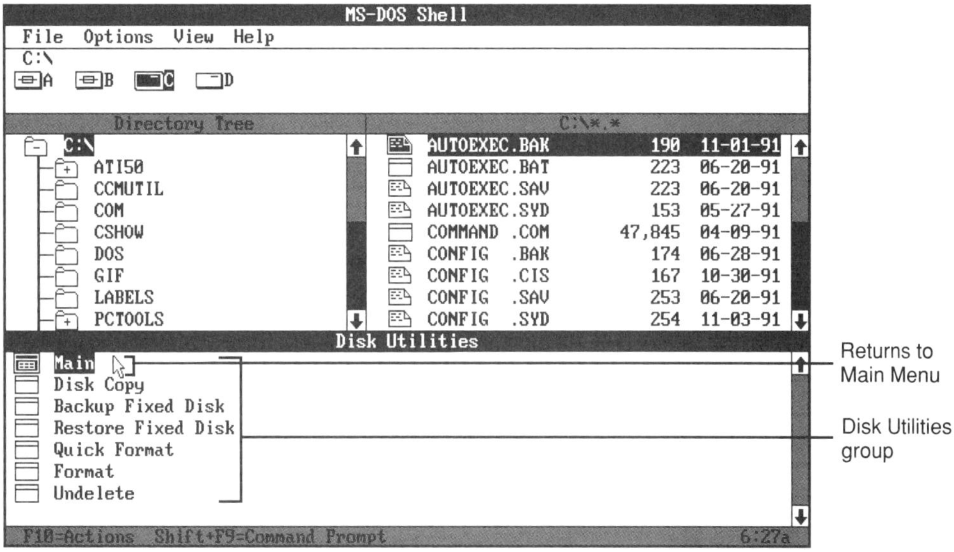

Fig. 4.5. The Disk Utilities program group.

5. To return to the Main group, double-click the Main option.

If you are using the keyboard, follow these steps to become familiar with the DOS Shell screen:

1. Press Tab to move from one area of the window to another.

   As you press Tab, notice that the title bar in each area changes its color or shade to indicate that the area is activated.

   If you are using a two-color monitor, the title bar does not change. You must watch for the small selection arrow (→) that moves to an item within an area as you press Tab.

2. Continue pressing Tab until the title bar of the Program List (Main) changes its color or shade. (You also can press Shift-Tab to move in the opposite direction.)

3. Press the up- and down-arrow keys to move to the Disk Utilities option.

4. Press Enter.

Notice that the Disk Utilities program group now is listed, as shown in figure 4.5. You learn how to use these simple programs for maintaining your disks in the following lessons:

Lesson 6 (Format)
Lesson 6 (Quick Format)
Lesson 9 (Disk Copy)
Lesson 11 (Undelete)
Lesson 14 (Backup Fixed Disk)
Lesson 14 (Restore Fixed Disk)

5. To return to the Main program group, use the arrow keys to move back to Main; then press Enter.

Using the Shell's Menus

Like many programs today, the MS-DOS Shell has pull-down menus. A *menu* is a list of commands grouped together for easy viewing. A *pull-down* menu is a list of commands in a box that drops down from the top of your screen. You simply choose the menu item that you want in much the same way that you would choose an item from a restaurant menu.

The figures given earlier in this chapter illustrate that the menu bar appears in the upper left corner of the Shell window. If the Directory Tree area or File List is active, you can choose from five menus: File, Options, View, Tree, and Help. These menus are discussed in detail in other lessons, but this section shows you how to select menus and choose commands within them.

Selecting and Canceling a Menu

Choosing a menu is simple. To choose the File menu with your mouse, follow these steps:

1. Move the mouse pointer to File in the menu bar and click the left mouse button.

   This action pulls down the File menu, as shown in figures 4.6, 4.7, and 4.8. Note that the File menu presents different choices, depending on which area is active.

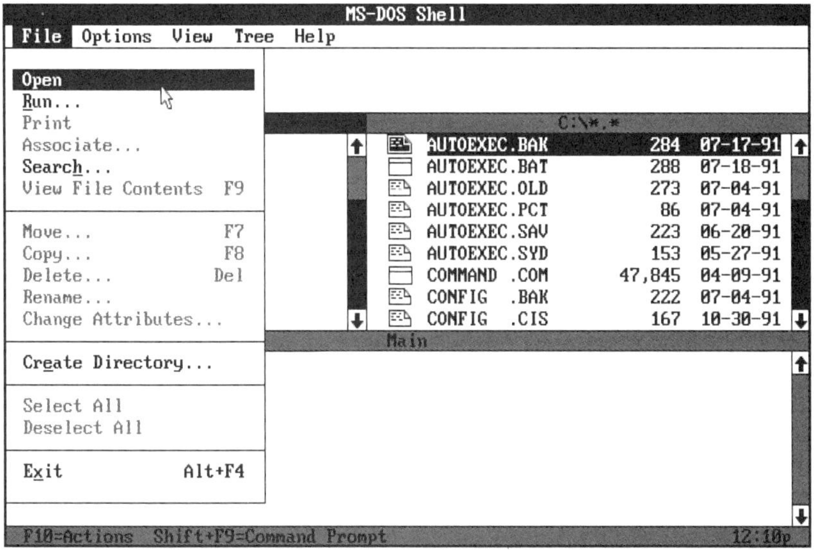

Fig. 4.6. The DOS Shell pull-down File menu for the Directory Tree area.

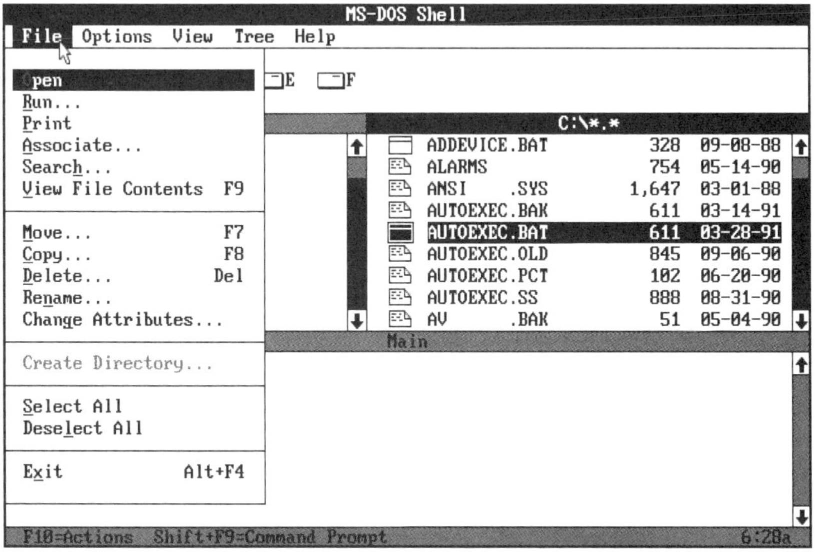

Fig. 4.7. The pull-down File menu for the File List area.

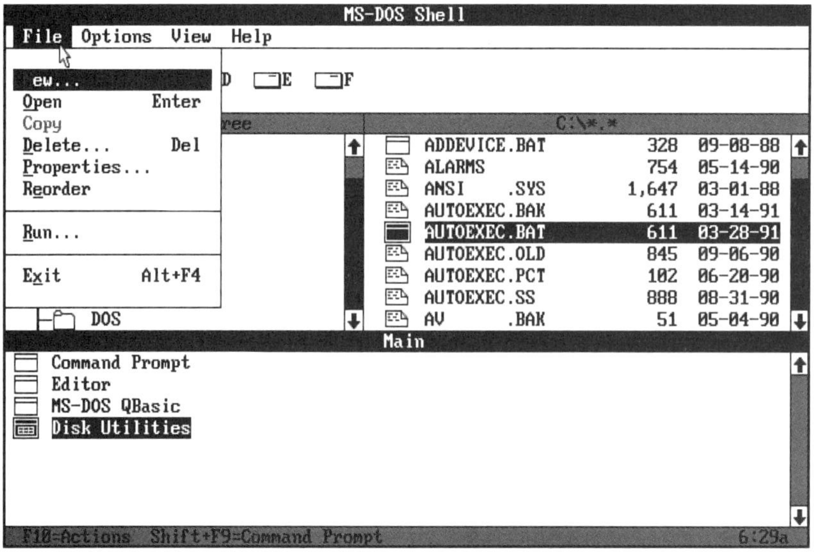

Fig. 4.8. The pull-down File menu for the Program List area.

2. To close the menu, just click the menu name again, click anywhere outside the menu, or click the right mouse button.

After selecting one menu, you easily can select another simply by clicking the menu name in the menu bar.

To choose a menu using the keyboard, follow these steps:

1. Press Alt or F10 to activate the menu bar.

   Notice that the color or shade of the menu bar changes and the first letter of each menu choice is highlighted.

2. Press the highlighted letter of your choice—in this case, F for File.

   This action pulls down the File menu.

> An alternate method for choosing a menu is to press the left- or right-arrow key to highlight your choice—in this case, the File menu—and press Enter.

   After selecting one menu, you easily can go to another simply by pressing the right- or left-arrow key.

3. To close the menu, press Esc.

Choosing Commands

Choosing a command from a menu is as simple as choosing the menu itself. Figure 4.9 illustrates other conventions used in Shell menus.

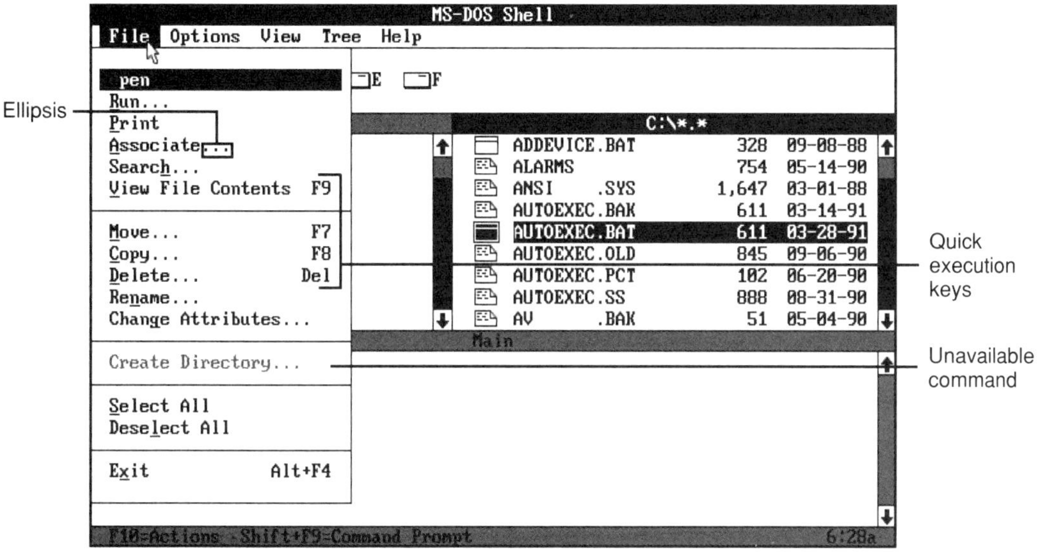

Fig. 4.9. Conventions used in DOS Shell menus.

Some menu choices are dimmer than others (or aren't visible at all, if you have a monochrome monitor), indicating that this option is not available for one of two reasons:

- You need to perform some other action before this command becomes available.
- The option is not applicable to the task you are currently performing.

Some commands are followed by an ellipsis (...), indicating that when you choose that command, a dialog box will appear. Dialog boxes are discussed in the next section.

Some commands also have a quick execution key at the far right. You can use this key combination to execute that command without choosing it from the menu. As you become more proficient with the Shell, these shortcuts will become second nature to you.

A few commands have a diamond (◆) to the left of their names. This diamond indicates that the command can be active or inactive, just as a light switch can be on or off. You will learn more about this feature as you continue to work with the Shell.

You choose a command from a selected menu in the same way you choose a menu. If you are using a mouse, simply click the command you want to select. If you are using the keyboard, press the highlighted letter in the command name (or highlight your choice with the arrow keys and press Enter).

Using Dialog Boxes

Sometimes DOS needs more information in order to carry out your command. When you choose a command followed by an ellipsis (...), the Shell responds with a *dialog box*. This box provides or asks you for additional information.

The File Search command is one command that makes use of a dialog box. In order to become familiar with the way dialog boxes operate, take the following steps to search for a file on drive C:

1. Click the Directory Tree or File List area to activate it, or cycle through the areas by pressing Tab (or Shift-Tab).
2. Click File or press Alt-F.
3. Click Search or press H. Your screen should look similar to figure 4.10.
4. To search for the file COMMAND.COM, press Backspace once to erase the *.* symbol and type **COMMAND.COM**. (You can use upper- or lowercase letters when typing commands; DOS is not case-sensitive.)

   For this example, you do not need to move within the dialog box. When you need to do so, just click the area you want to move to, or press Tab (or Shift-Tab) to move to the desired area.

   Notice the *check box*; many dialog boxes have similar options. The X in this box indicates that DOS will look for the listed file on the entire disk. If you click the X (or move to the box with the Tab key and press the space bar), DOS searches for the files only in the current directory.

   Dialog boxes also have *command buttons* at the bottom of the box. The OK button executes the command, and the Cancel button cancels the command. Some dialog boxes also have an Advanced button, which opens another dialog box of advanced features. To select these buttons, click them with the mouse or move to them using the Tab key and press Enter.

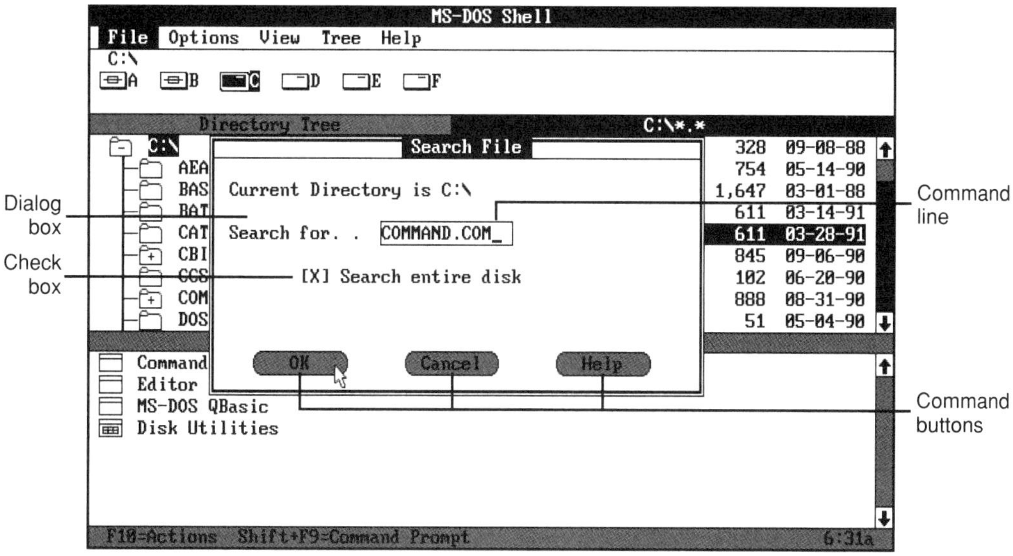

Fig. 4.10. The Search File dialog box.

Notice also the Help button in figure 4.10. Selecting this button will display help for the current procedure. In Lesson 5 you learn about the Shell's on-line help system.

5. Press Enter or click OK. Your screen should now look similar to figure 4.11 (you may have different files listed).

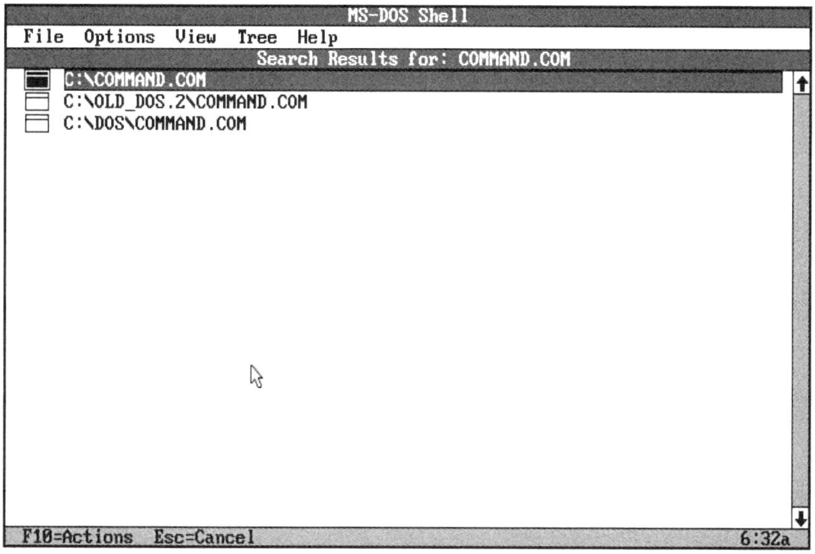

Fig. 4.11. The result of a file search.

> Even if you have a mouse, pressing Enter is often handier and faster, especially when you don't have to change any options or when you have to type something in a dialog box.

6. To return to the main Shell window, press Esc.

You will see many other examples of using dialog boxes in other lessons in this book.

> The File Search feature of the Shell is illustrated in this section as an example of dialog boxes, but the feature itself is important. You can use this procedure whenever you need to search for a file on your disk.

Using Scroll Bars

Most areas of the Shell and some dialog boxes contain *scroll bars* located vertically along the right side of the area (see fig. 4.12). Sometimes there is more information than can be displayed in one window, so the scroll bar enables you to display more information.

Each scroll bar contains a *scroll box*. The size of the scroll box tells you at a glance how much of the available information you can presently see.

The large scroll box in the Directory Tree area indicates that most of the available information is visible. The small scroll box in the File List area indicates that you are looking at only a small portion of what is available. Notice that the Program List area has no scroll box because all the available information is visible.

You can scroll through the information in a list or box by using the mouse or arrow keys. If you are using a mouse, follow these steps:

1. Click the File List title bar or, as a shortcut, click one of the arrows (↓, ↑) in the scroll bar to the right of the File List area to activate that area.
2. Place the mouse pointer on one of the arrows; then press and hold down the left mouse button to scroll through the list. If it doesn't scroll, you are at the beginning or end of the list.

An alternate method is to "drag" the scroll box by moving the pointer to the scroll box, holding down the left mouse button, and then moving the mouse up or down.

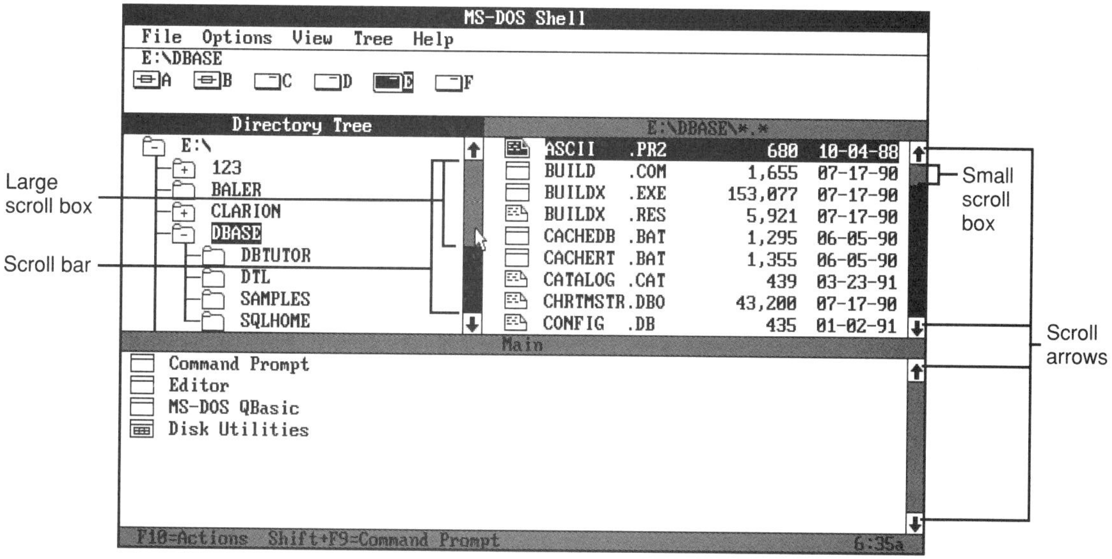

Fig. 4.12. Scroll bars, scroll boxes, and scroll arrows.

> Another way to scroll is to click any part of the scroll bar above or below the scroll box. This action scrolls up or down one page (as does pressing the PgUp or PgDn key).

To scroll using the keyboard, follow these steps:

1. Press Tab to move to the File List area.
2. Press the up- and down-arrow keys to scroll through the list. Hold down the arrow keys to scroll more quickly through the list.

You also can use the following keys to scroll:

Key	Action
PgDn	Scrolls down one window
PgUp	Scrolls up one window
End	Scrolls to end of list
Home	Scrolls to beginning of list

Even if you use a mouse, you may find that the greatest speed in using the Shell comes by integrating the mouse and the keyboard. If you are near the end of a directory or file listing and need to go to the top of the listing, for example, pressing Home is much faster than scrolling through the listing with the mouse.

Changing the Shell's Display

As you have learned, when the Shell first starts, it displays certain areas by default. But the Shell is quite flexible; it enables you to view your directories, files, and programs in several ways.

You can view the Shell in several ways by following these steps:

1. Choose View from the File List menu by clicking it or pressing Alt-V. The View pull-down menu appears (see fig. 4.13).

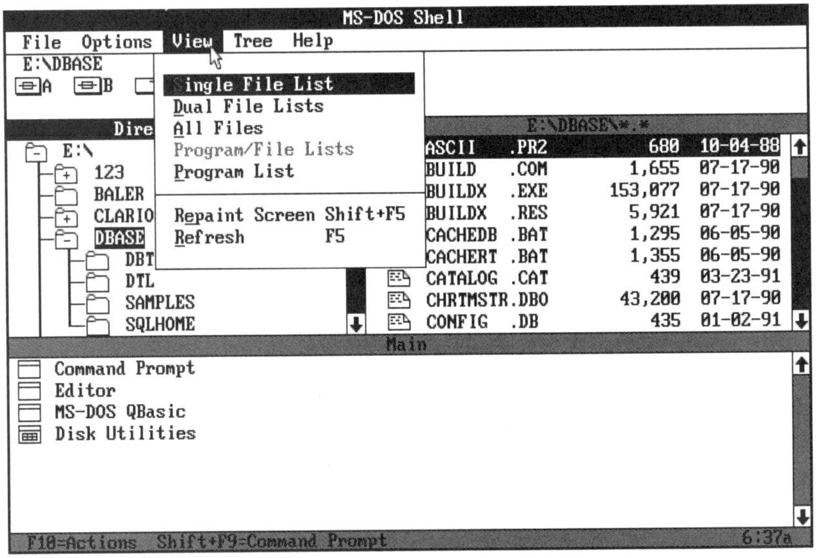

Fig. 4.13. The View menu.

2. Click the Single File List option or press S.

   The directory tree of the current disk drive appears at the left of the screen and a file listing of the current directory appears on the right. You learn much more about directories and files in Lesson 5.

3. Select View again and click Dual File Lists or press D.

   The window splits horizontally into two areas containing the same information. This view enables you to view two different file lists simultaneously. To see how this works, insert the disk that came with this book into drive A and press Ctrl-A. Notice how the display changes; then press Ctrl-C to return to drive C.

4. Choose View again and click All Files or press A.

   A list of all file names on the drive as well as information about the selected file appears.

5. Select View again and click Program List or press P.

   This view displays program groups and items. You can change to a different group by double-clicking the group name or by pressing the arrow keys to move to the group name you want to view and then pressing Enter.

6. Choose View again and click Program/File Lists or press F.

You return to the original (default) display.

Exiting the Shell

You can exit the DOS Shell temporarily or permanently and move to the DOS command prompt (C:\>, for example).

To exit the Shell temporarily, follow these steps:

1. Press Shift-F9 or choose Command Prompt from the Program List area.
2. To return to the Shell, type **EXIT** and press Enter.

To exit the Shell permanently (that is, to end the Shell program entirely), follow these steps:

1. Choose File from the menu bar
2. Click Exit or press X.

You also can exit by pressing F3 or Alt-F4.

To get back into the Shell, restart the program by typing **DOSSHELL** at the C:\> prompt and pressing Enter.

Lesson Summary

- ☐ You can have the Shell start automatically each time you turn on the computer. Otherwise, you can start the Shell by typing **DOSSHELL** at the DOS command prompt (C:\>, for example) and pressing Enter.
- ☐ The Shell *window* is divided into four areas by default: the drive icons, the Directory Tree area, the File List area, and the Program List area.
- ☐ You select a pull-down menu by clicking it with the left mouse button or by pressing Alt, followed by the first letter of the menu choice.
- ☐ You select a menu option by clicking it or by pressing the highlighted letter in the command name.
- ☐ A dialog box appears when DOS needs more information in order to carry out your command. Commands that use dialog boxes are indicated by an ellipsis (...).
- ☐ You use scroll bars, boxes, and arrows to view and scroll through boxes when all the available information cannot be viewed at the same time.
- ☐ The Shell enables you to view your directories, files, and programs in several ways. The options are presented on the View pull-down menu.
- ☐ You can exit the Shell temporarily by pressing Shift-F9 or choosing Command Prompt from the Program List area. Typing **EXIT** returns you to the Shell.
- ☐ You exit the Shell permanently by pressing F3 or Alt-F4.

Key Terms

Dialog box	An on-screen message box that provides or asks for additional information.
Directory Tree area	Located just below the drive icons, this area shows the structure of the directories on the current disk drive.
DOS shell	A sophisticated computer program that insulates the user from DOS, making DOS much easier to use. Most shells graphically display an organized list of DOS commands, directories, and files.

Drive icon	Located in the upper left portion of the Shell window, each icon represents an available disk drive on your computer.
File List area	Immediately to the right of the Directory Tree area, this area lists the files that reside in the current directory.
Menu	A list of commands grouped together for easy viewing.
Program List area	Located just below the Directory Tree area, this area lists the programs contained in the displayed program group.
Pull-down menu	A list of commands in a box that drops down from the top of the screen.
Scroll bar/box	A vertical bar or small box along the side of areas of the Shell window and some dialog boxes; it enables you to move the display in that area up and down.
Shell window	The main screen of the MS-DOS Shell.

Exercises

To become more proficient with the basic procedures for using the DOS Shell, explore the Shell on your own by doing the following:

1. Use the mouse and/or keyboard to choose the Disk Utilities group and then the Main group (see "Taking a Quick Tour of the Shell").
2. Practice selecting all the pull-down menus (see "Selecting and Canceling a Menu").
3. Use the File Search feature to locate the file named BACKUP.EXE on drive C (see "Using Dialog Boxes").
4. Practice scrolling with the scroll bars, boxes, and arrows (see "Using Scroll Bars").
5. Practice exiting the Shell temporarily and permanently (see "Exiting the Shell").

For More Information

For additional beginner-level information, as well as some intermediate information concerning what was presented in this lesson, refer to *MS-DOS 5 QuickStart* (Que Corporation). For a more in-depth handling of these subjects, refer to *Using MS-DOS 5* (Que Corporation).

Lesson 5 builds on the foundation in this lesson by teaching you additional Shell functions.

Lesson 5

Working with the Shell

Now that you have learned the basic procedures for using the MS-DOS Shell, you are ready to start working with it. This lesson continues to present basic procedures, but it also teaches you many skills that you need in order to work with DOS on a daily basis. In this lesson, you learn how to do the following:

- Select a disk drive and directory
- Change directories
- Collapse and expand directories
- Change how files are displayed
- *Tag*, or select, files
- Update and repaint the screen
- Get on-line help

Estimated time to complete this lesson: 25-30 minutes

Working with Disks, Directories, and Files

In order to use your PC effectively, you need to understand how disks, directories, and files function. A simple way of understanding disks, directories, and files is to think of them as an electronic filing system (see fig. 5.1).

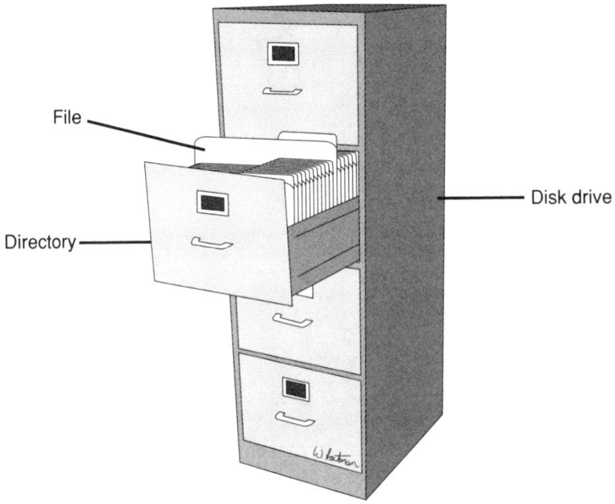

Fig. 5.1. Electronic files can be compared to a traditional file cabinet. The cabinet is like a floppy disk or hard disk. Drawers are like directories, and file folders are like files.

You can think of each of your *disks* as a file cabinet, each *directory* on the disk as a file drawer, and each *file* as a separate file folder in the drawer. Note the definitions of disk, directory, and file in the list of key terms at the end of this lesson.

Although DOS enables you to organize and work with disks, directories, and files, the DOS Shell makes these tasks even easier, as the following sections explain. You will learn much more about these components in other lessons.

Selecting Disk Drives and Directories

If you haven't started the DOS Shell, do so now by typing **DOSSHELL** at the C:\> prompt and pressing Enter.

When the Shell first starts, it displays a list of the directories (the file drawers) and files (the file folders) on the current drive (the file cabinet). Just as you may need to open another drawer in a file cabinet or even go to another cabinet altogether when you need a different file, you must likewise be able to change drives and directories on your computer in order to find the information you need. The Shell makes changing drives and directories easy and fast.

To select a disk drive, follow these steps:

1. Insert the disk that came with this book into drive A (or drive B, depending on your computer).
2. Click the drive A icon or press Ctrl-A. (If you put the disk in drive B in Step 1, click the drive B icon or press Ctrl-B.)

   Your screen should look similar to figure 5.2.

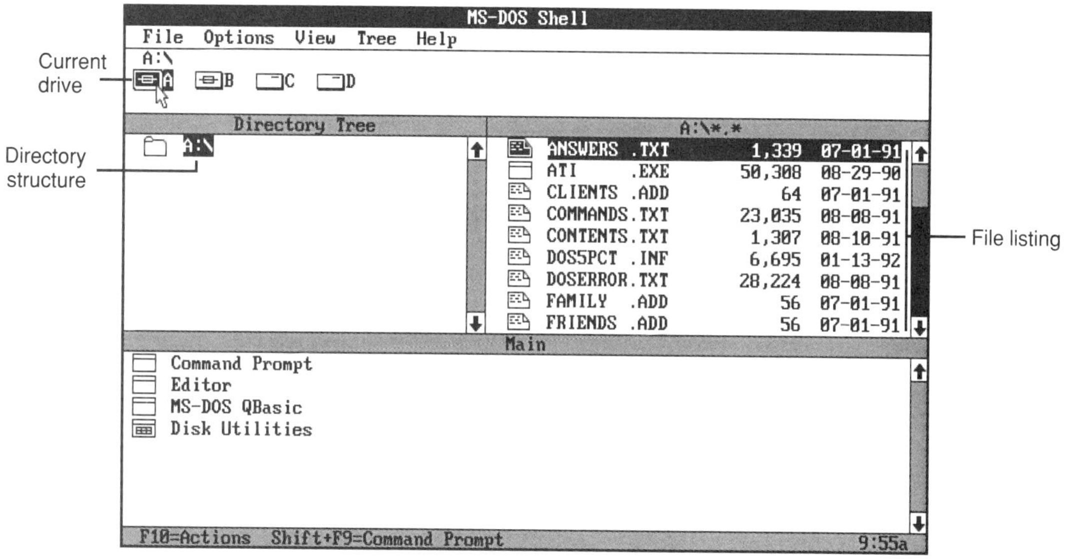

Fig. 5.2. Selecting drive A.

   An alternate method is to press the Tab key until one of the icons is selected; then use the arrow keys to choose the drive you want and press Enter.

3. Return to drive C by clicking the C icon or pressing Ctrl-C.

Changing Directories

As you know, the current directory is highlighted in the Directory Tree area. Changing to a different directory is as easy as changing to another drive. Follow these steps:

1. Make sure you are logged on to drive C, as explained in the preceding section.
2. Click the DOS subdirectory or press Tab to change to the Directory Tree area, use the arrow keys to highlight the DOS subdirectory, and press Enter.

   Your screen displays all the files in the DOS subdirectory.

> You also can use the scroll bars with your mouse or the other scroll keys on the keyboard to change directories and move around in the shell, as described in Lesson 4.

3. Change back to the root directory by clicking C or by highlighting it and pressing Enter.

Collapsing and Expanding Directories

The DOS Shell makes understanding the concept of a directory easy. A simple way to introduce the directory structure commonly used on hard disks is to compare it with an upside-down tree (see fig. 5.3).

When the Shell first starts, only *first-level* directories (the directories immediately down from the root) are displayed. To see the subdirectories below these directories, follow these steps:

1. Make sure you are logged on to drive C. Notice that only first level directories are listed.
2. Notice that the small box to the left of the root directory symbol has a minus (-) sign in it. Click this box or press the minus key.

   The directory structure collapses to display only the root directory.
3. Restore the directory structure by clicking the box again or by pressing the plus (+) key.
4. Move to the ATI50 subdirectory, which should appear in the Directory Tree area (see fig. 5.4).

> This directory may reside on a drive other than C, depending on what drive you have installed the disk tutor to. If the directory is not on drive C, change the drive and scroll to the correct directory.

DOS's directory structure is sometimes referred to as a tree-structured hierarchy. In simple form, the directory resembles an inverted tree. The root directory is the topmost directory. The numbered boxes represent directories on branches of the tree. For example, directories 1, 2, and 3 are on the same branch of the tree.

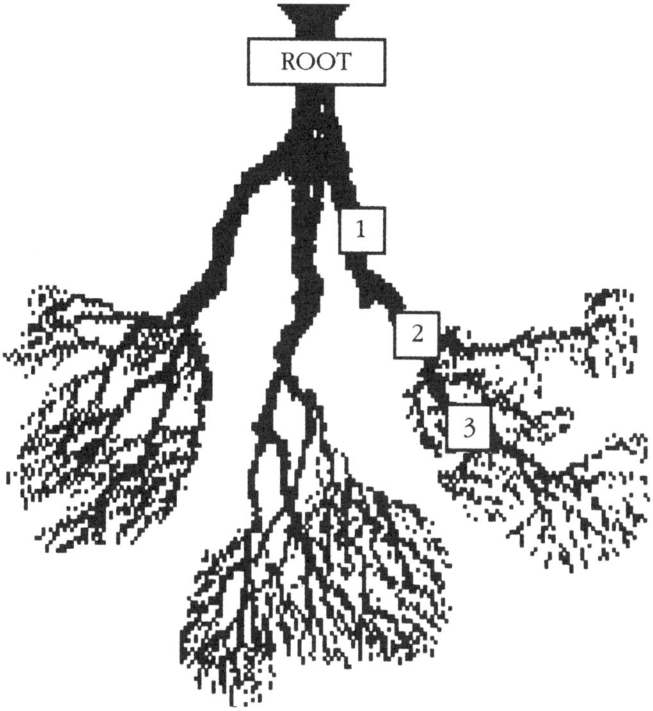

Similarly, the hierarchical directory structure has a root and multiple levels. Level 1 is the first branch off the root, level 2 is a branch off the first branch, and so on. Unlike a real tree, however, the directory structure can have as many subdirectories as needed.

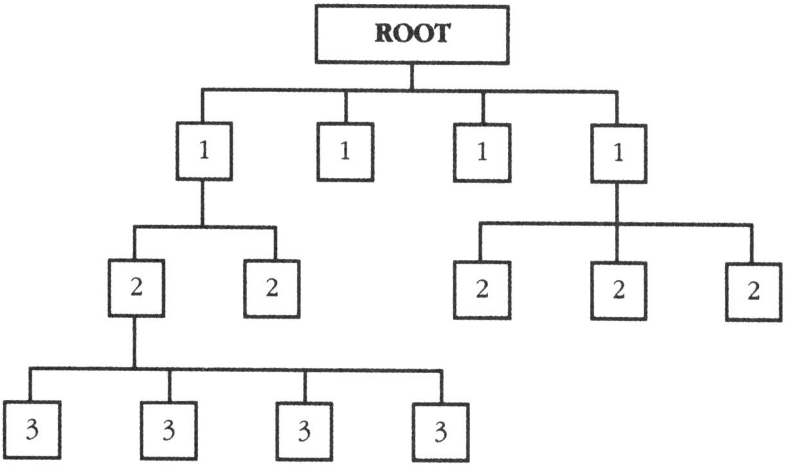

Fig. 5.3. A directory tree.

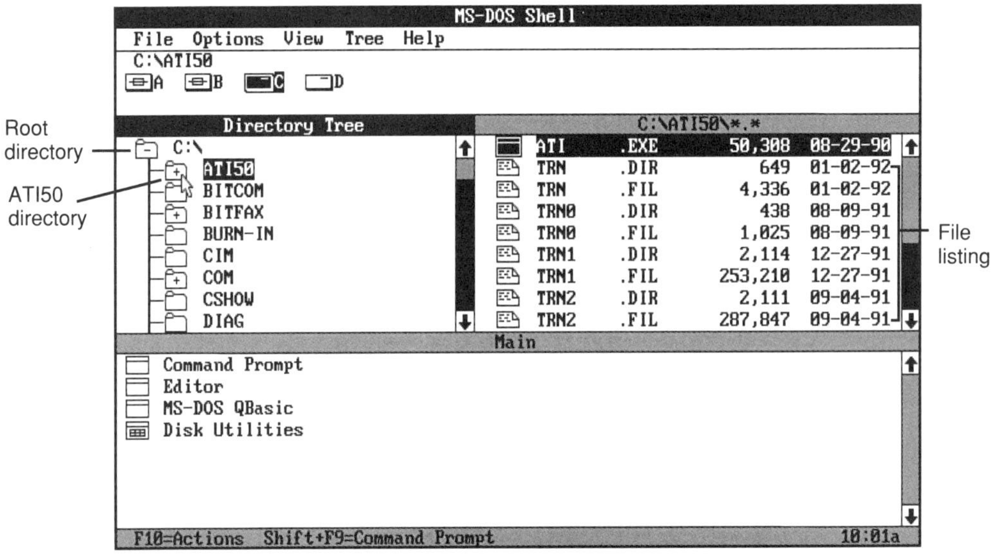

Fig. 5.4. Locating the ATI50 subdirectory.

5. Click the box next to ATI50, or highlight it and press the plus key.

   Two subdirectories appear under ATI50. Like ATI50, these subdirectories also were created when the disk tutor was installed.

6. Notice that a plus sign appears in the box beside the SUB2 directory. Click this box, or highlight it and press the plus key to display its subdirectories.

7. Do the same for SUBSUB2 to display the subdirectory under it.

> A shortcut for displaying all the directories under a given directory is to highlight that subdirectory and press the asterisk (*) key. To display all the subdirectories on a disk, press Ctrl-* at any time. You can accomplish the same with the mouse, of course, but using the keyboard is faster.

Changing How Files Are Displayed

The Shell lists all the files in the current directory (except hidden and system files) alphabetically. To list the files in your directories in a different order, follow these steps:

1. Make sure you are logged on to the root directory of drive C. If you are not, click the C icon and then click C:\ in the directory display. Or press Ctrl-C, press Tab to go to the Directory Tree area, and then highlight C:\ with the arrow keys.
2. Click Options in the menu bar or press Alt-O.
3. Click File Display Options or press F. The File Display Options dialog box appears (see fig. 5.5).
4. Notice the Sort By options. By default, the Shell sorts files alphabetically by name (the first choice), but you can select any of the options described in table 5.1.

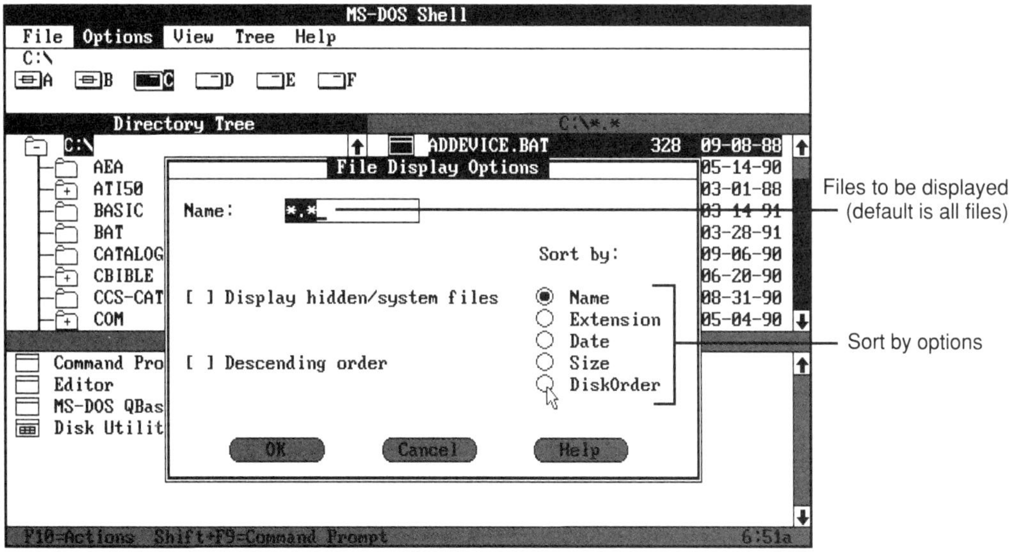

Fig. 5.5. The File Display Options dialog box.

5. Click the DiskOrder option, or press the Tab key three times (the cursor may disappear) and then use the arrow keys to select DiskOrder.
6. Click OK or press Enter.

   The display changes to list the files in the order they were placed on the disk. You also can control whether files are listed in ascending (the default) or descending order.
7. Repeat steps 2-5; then click Descending Order and OK. Or, press Tab twice, press the space bar once (to insert the X), and press Enter.

The files are still listed in the order they were placed on disk, but this time they are listed in descending order; that is, the file most recently placed on the disk is listed first.

8. To return to the default file-sorting option, repeat steps 2-5 once again; then click Name, Descending Order (to delete the X), and then OK.

   From the keyboard, press Tab twice, press the space bar once (to delete the X), press Tab again, press the up- or down-arrow key to select Name, and press Enter.

Table 5.1. File-Sorting Options

Option	Sorting Order
Name	Alphabetical
Extension	By *extension* (the characters to the right of the period in a file name), then by file name, in alphabetical order
Date	By the dates the files were last modified, with the most recent file listed last (the oldest files are listed first)
Size	By file size, from smallest to largest
DiskOrder	By the order files were placed on the disk

You can easily see the options you have for displaying your files. As your experience with the DOS Shell increases, you will find practical uses for many of these options.

Selecting Files

Before you can copy, erase, edit, or work with a file in any way, you must first *tag*, or select, it. Tagging files is easy, as the following steps illustrate:

1. Log on to the DOS directory of drive C by clicking the C icon and then DOS in the directory display. Or, press Ctrl-C, press Tab to go to the Directory Tree area, and then highlight the DOS directory with the arrow keys.
2. Click the file FORMAT.COM or highlight it using the arrow keys. This file is now *tagged*, and you can perform any action on it.
3. To deselect this file, simply choose another file.

Tagging Multiple Files in Sequence

You may want to choose more than one file at a time. You may want to copy a group of files from one place to another, for example. The Shell makes selecting a group of files easy.

To tag two or more files that are in sequence, follow these steps:

1. Click DISKCOPY.COM or highlight it using the arrow keys.
2. Move the mouse to DOSKEY.COM (which is probably the third file down from DISKCOPY), hold down the Shift key, and click the mouse.

   If you are using the keyboard, hold down the Shift key and use the down arrow to highlight DOSKEY.COM.
3. Release the Shift key. You have tagged multiple files in sequence, as shown in figure 5.6.

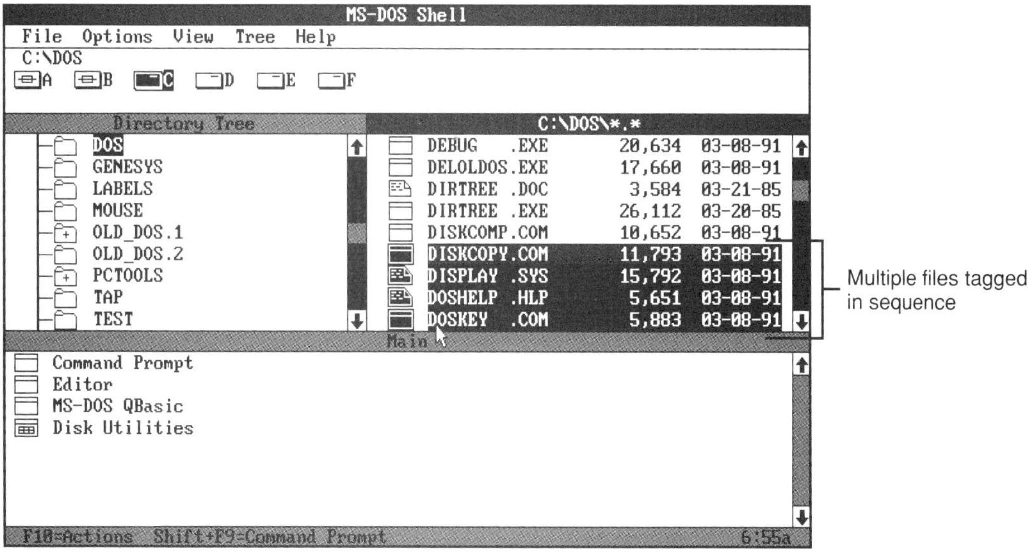

Fig. 5.6. Tagging multiple files in sequence.

4. To deselect a file, press the Ctrl key and then click the file you want to deselect.

If you are using the keyboard, press Shift-F8, highlight the file(s) you want to deselect, press the space bar for each file, and then press Shift-F8.

> To deselect all the files quickly, simply click a single file (which selects that file), or press the up- or down-arrow key. You also can press Ctrl-\ (backslash).

Tagging Multiple Files Not in Sequence

To tag a group of files that are not in sequence, follow these steps:

1. Select DISKCOMP.COM.
2. Hold down the Ctrl key and click DISPLAY.SYS and DOSKEY.COM. Release the Ctrl key.

   If you are using the keyboard, press Shift-F8; notice that the word ADD appears in the bottom right corner of the screen beside the time display. Use the down arrow to go to DISPLAY.SYS and press the space bar. Move to DOSKEY.COM and press the space bar again. Then press Shift-F8 again.

   You now have three non-sequential tagged files, as shown in figure 5.7.

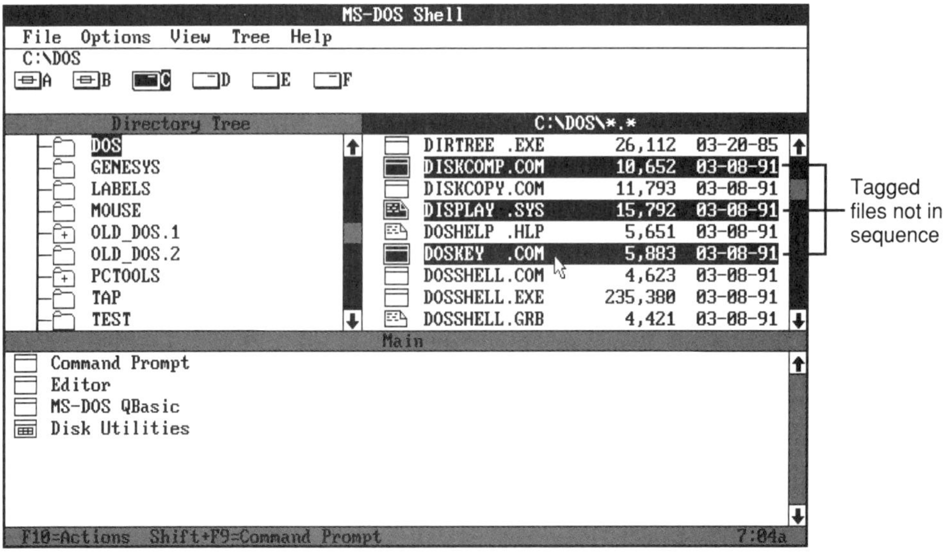

Fig. 5.7. Tagging multiple files not in sequence.

3. To deselect a file(s), follow the same procedure outlined in step 4 of the preceding section.

Tagging All Files in a Directory

To tag all files in a directory, follow these steps:

1. From the File List area, press Ctrl-/ (slash).

   You can use the mouse to click File and Select All, but the keyboard method is faster.

2. To deselect all the files, press Ctrl-\ (backslash). You also can simply click a single file or press an up- or down-arrow key.

You can use the mouse to click File and Deselect All, but the keyboard is faster.

Updating and Repainting the Screen

Sometimes the Shell does not update the screen to reflect files that have been added, deleted, or restored. If you run a word processing program from the Shell (for example, when creating new files), the Shell does not display the files when you return to it. In such a case, you must tell the Shell to update the screen display.

To update the screen, you simply tell the Shell to reread the disk by double-clicking the appropriate drive icon (drive C, for example) or by highlighting the drive icon you want and pressing F5. DOS recounts all the directories and files on the disk.

If you forget to manually update the screen, the Shell updates automatically the next time you start the Shell.

Similarly, you may run a TSR (terminate-and-stay-resident) program that pops up over the Shell; an example of such a program is SideKick. Such a program still may be displayed on-screen even after you exit it, however.

To make the Shell window visible again, repaint the screen by pressing F5. You also can click View and Repaint Screen, but the keyboard method is faster.

Getting On-Line Help

The DOS Shell provides built-in on-line help, which is a quick way to get information about using the program. You can get help by pressing F1, by using the Help button in the dialog boxes, or by using the Help menu (see the following sections).

Using F1

The quickest way to get help is by pressing F1. If you need some help with a menu item, such as the File menu, you can get help by following these steps:

1. Press the Alt key to activate the menu bar.
2. Use the left- or right-arrow key to select the File menu.
3. Press F1. The help screen appears (see fig. 5.8).

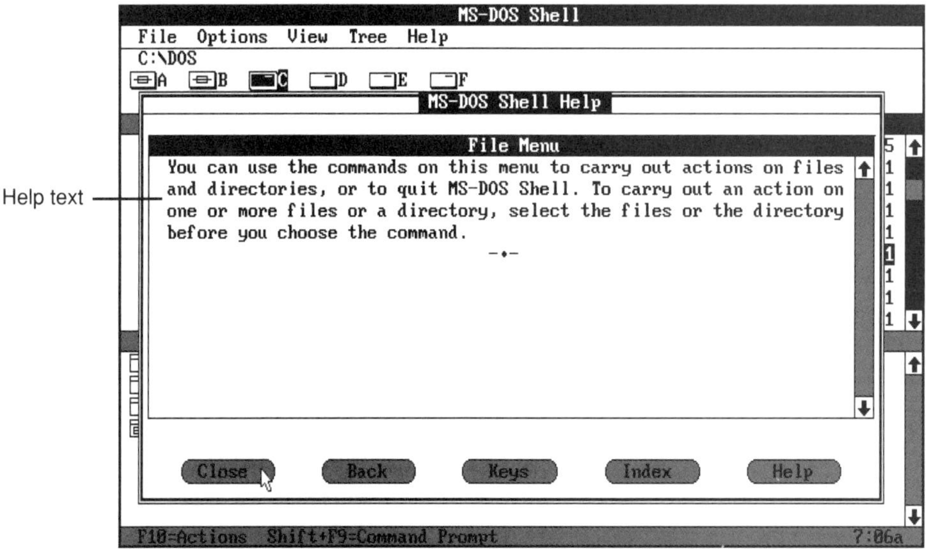

Fig. 5.8. The help screen for the File menu.

4. Click the Close button or press Esc to exit the help screen.

If you want additional help with a command, such as the Search command on the File menu, follow these steps:

1. Click File or press Alt-F.
2. Highlight the Search command using the up- or down-arrow key.
3. Press F1. The Search Command help screen appears (see fig. 5.9).
4. Click the Close button or press Esc to exit the screen.

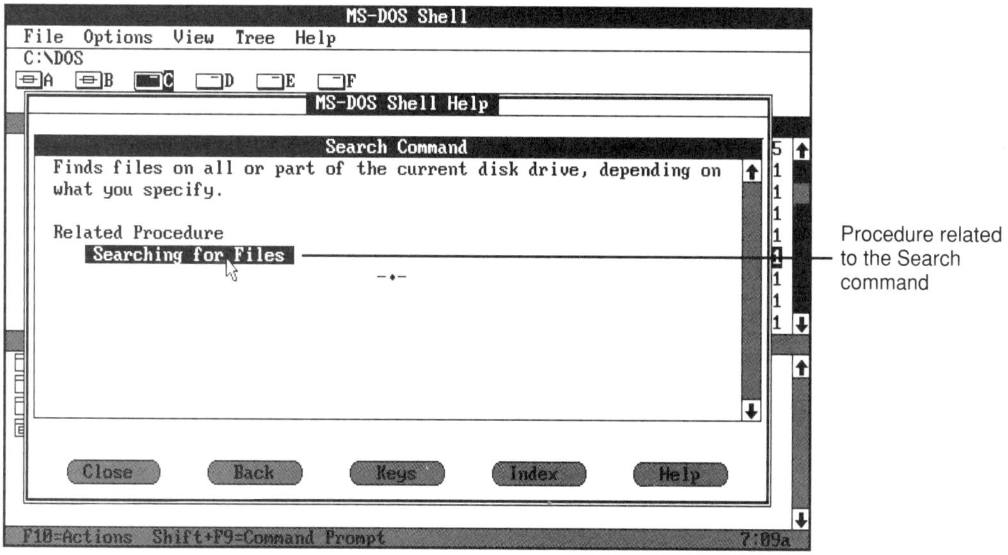

Fig. 5.9. The help screen for the Search command.

If you need help with a dialog box (for example, the dialog box that appears after you choose the Search command), follow these steps:

1. Click File or press Alt-F.
2. Click Search or press H.
3. Press F1 to display the help screen (see fig. 5.10).
4. Click the Close button and then Cancel (click Close from the help screen and click Cancel from the Search dialog box). Or, press Esc twice.

A help screen may refer to a related procedure, as does the screen shown in figure 5.9. In this case, the related procedure is Searching for Files. Related procedures are displayed in a different color or in reverse video, depending on the color scheme you are using. To select a related procedure, follow these steps, using the Search Command help screen shown in figure 5.9 as an example:

1. Double-click the Searching for Files procedure, or press Tab until it is highlighted and press Enter. The help screen shown in figure 5.11 appears.

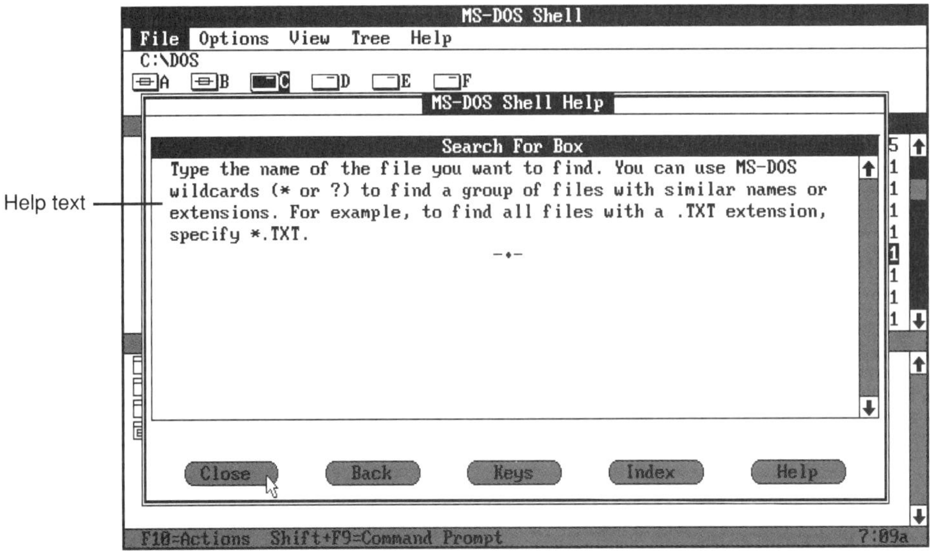

Fig. 5.10. The help screen for the Search dialog box.

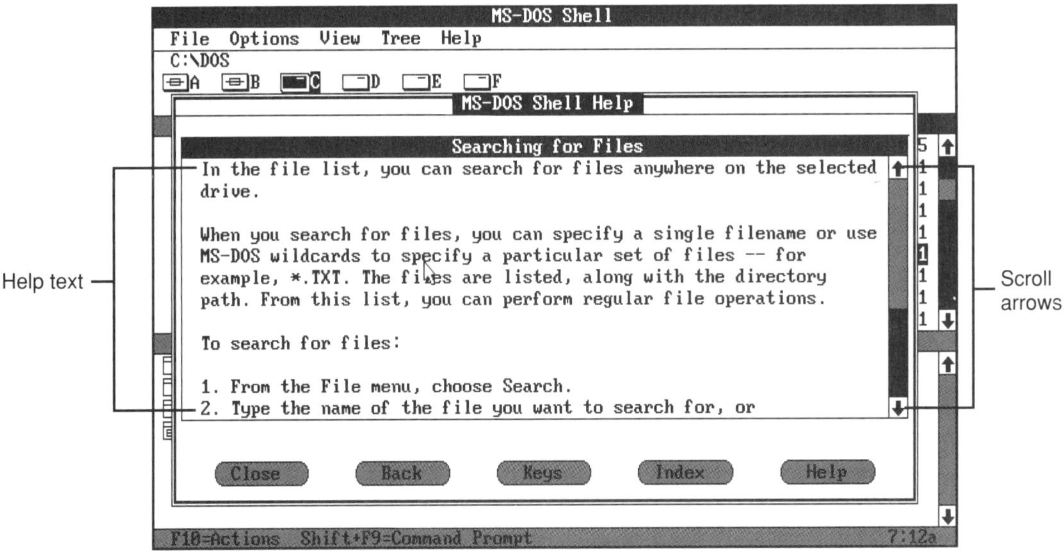

Fig. 5.11. The help screen for the Searching for Files procedure.

2. Use the mouse or arrow keys to scroll through the help text.
3. Click the Close button or press Esc.

Using the Help Button in Dialog Boxes

You also can get help by using the Help button that appears in the lower right corner of a dialog box. To get a help screen similar to figure 5.10, for example, follow these steps:

1. Click File or press Alt-F.
2. Click Search or press H.
3. Click Help or press Tab four times and then press Enter.
4. Click Close and then Cancel, or press Esc twice.

When you are not in a dialog box, choosing the Help button displays general information on using the DOS Shell help system. Follow these steps:

1. Click File or press Alt-F.
2. Highlight the Search command using the up- or down-arrow key.
3. Press F1 to display the help screen shown in figure 5.9.
4. Click Help, or press Tab five times and press Enter.
5. Use the mouse or arrow keys to scroll through the help text.
6. Click Close or press Esc.

Using the Help Menu

Another way to get help is through the Help menu in the menu bar. When you select this menu, an index of help topics appears. Table 5.2 explains the help you can get for each option.

To get help from the Help menu using the mouse, click Help from the menu bar and then click the category you want. Information about that topic or a list of related topics appears.

Table 5.2. Help Menu Options

Option	Effect
Index	Displays a list of all Shell help topics.
Keyboard	Lists keys and key combinations available for use with the Shell.
Shell Basics	Displays an introduction to the Shell.
Commands	Explains each of the Shell's menu options (the same as selecting a command and pressing F1).
Procedures	Displays step-by-step instructions for accomplishing tasks in the Shell.
Using Help	Provides an introduction to using the Shell help system.
About Shell	Displays copyright and version information about the Shell.

To get help from the Help menu using the keyboard, press Alt-H. Press the highlighted letter of the category you want. Information about that topic or a list of related topics appears.

> The help screens that go with each topic covered in *Hands-On MS-DOS 5* are another tool for learning the Shell. You can read these screens as an additional review and accelerate your learning even more.

Lesson Summary

- ☐ Disks, directories, and files can be compared to an old-fashioned file cabinet.
- ☐ To change the current disk drive, click the appropriate icon, or press the Ctrl key and the disk drive letter.
- ☐ To change the current directory, click the appropriate directory, or highlight it with the arrow keys and press Enter.
- ☐ The directory structure common on hard disks can be compared to an upside-down tree, with a root directory at the top and multiple branches, or levels, below the root.

- ☐ Using the File Display Options command from the Options menu, you can sort files by name, extension, date, size, and disk order.
- ☐ Before you can do anything with or to a file, you must tag it.
- ☐ To select a single file, click the file or highlight it using the arrow keys. You also can tag multiple files in or out of sequence.
- ☐ To update the screen (reread the disk), press F5; to repaint the screen, press Shift-F5.
- ☐ You can get help in the Shell in three ways: by pressing F1, by selecting the Help button in dialog boxes, and by using the Help menu.

Key Terms

Current directory	The directory that you are currently in. Also the directory that DOS uses as the default when no other directory is specified.
Directory	An area of the DOS file system that holds information about files and directories. The root directory is the highest directory of the tree structure, and every disk has a root.
Disk	A magnetically coated device used to store electronic data.
File	A named collection of information stored on disk. Usually contains data or a computer program.
File display options	The different ways files can be displayed, including alphabetically by name, by file name extension, or by date.
File selection (tagging)	Choosing a file to perform some action on that file (copying it, for example). In the DOS Shell, you can tag files individually or in sequential or nonsequential groups.
First-level directory	A directory immediately down from the root.
Subdirectory	A directory created within another directory. *Directory* and *subdirectory* often are used interchangeably.
Tree structure	An analogy of an inverted tree that shows how directories are related to each other.

Exercises

To increase your proficiency with the Shell, practice the following:

1. Select the disk drives available on your system: drive A and C, for example (see "Selecting Disk Drives and Directories").
2. Change to the different directories on your hard disk; then expand and collapse the directories that show plus (+) or minus (-) signs (see "Changing Directories" and "Collapsing and Expanding Directories").
3. Select a directory and sort the files in it according to the five options given in table 5.1 (see "Changing How Files Are Displayed").
4. While in the same directory, select a single file; select a few more for practice (see "Selecting Files").
5. Tag a group of files in sequence; then tag a group not in sequence (see "Tagging Multiple Files in Sequence" and "Tagging Multiple Files Not in Sequence").
6. Tag all the files in a directory (see "Tagging All Files in a Directory").
7. Update and repaint your screen (see "Updating and Repainting the Screen").
8. Read the help screens on the following topics (see "Getting On-Line Help"):

   Search command
   View options
   File Display Options command
   Select All command
   Deselect All command

In Lesson 6, you begin working with DOS by learning how to *format* disks, or prepare them for use.

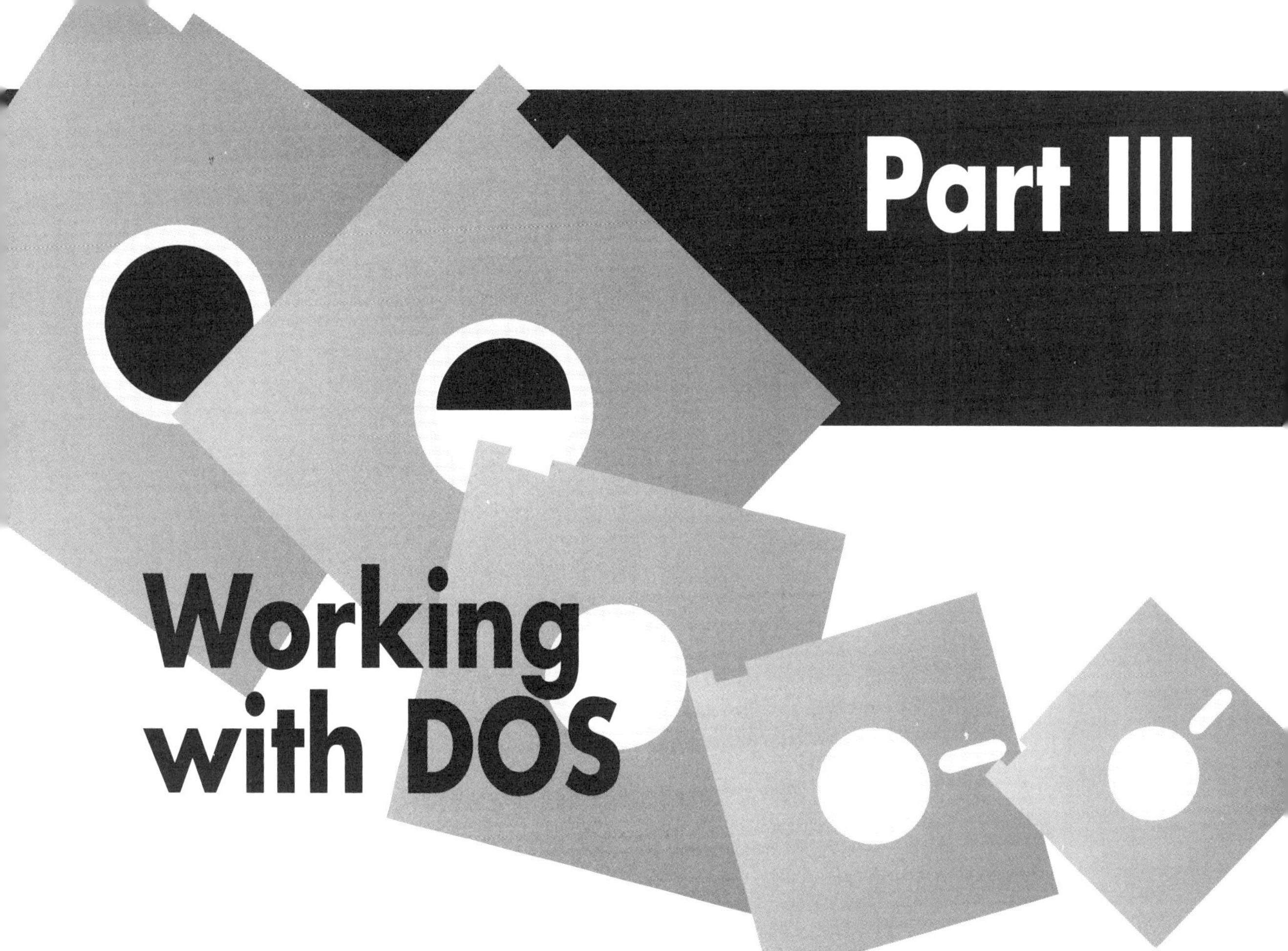

Part III

Working with DOS

The nine lessons in this section present the basic functions and features that every user of a DOS-based personal computer should know:

- How to format disks (Lesson 6)
- How to list disks and directories (Lesson 7)
- How to display and name files (Lesson 8)
- How to copy and compare disks (Lesson 9)
- How to copy files (Lesson 10)
- How to rename, move, and erase files (Lesson 11)
- How to use hierarchical directories (Lesson 12)
- How to use your printer and other devices (Lesson 13)
- How to use BACKUP and RESTORE (Lesson 14)

Lesson 6

Formatting Disks

Now that you have learned how to operate the Shell, you are ready to start working with DOS. In this lesson, you learn the following:

- How to phrase a DOS command
- The difference between internal and external commands
- Why disks must be formatted
- How to format disks in a variety of ways

What you need to complete this lesson: Three blank disks that are compatible with your floppy disk drive

Estimated time to complete this lesson: 35-40 minutes

Phrasing DOS Commands

As you probably have discovered, there are many DOS commands. Learning them will be much easier, however, if you remember that all DOS commands are phrased in the same way.

In DOS language, a DOS command consists of three parts:

commandname	*parameters*	*switches*

The *commandname* simply refers to the command you want to execute. Later in this lesson, for example, you learn about the FORMAT command. The word *format*, therefore, is the command name. When you want to execute a DOS command, you simply type its name and press Enter.

Parameters refer to additional information about the command. In this example, you might add an A: as a parameter to the FORMAT command. This would tell DOS where you want the command to be executed—in this case, on drive A.

Switches give DOS even more information about how you want a command carried out. Again using FORMAT A:, you might add the /S switch. /S tells DOS not only to format the disk in drive A, but to put the system files on it so that it can boot the computer. Many commands have more than one switch, and some enable you to use more than one switch at a time.

There is an easier way to express all this:

	commandname	*parameters*	*switches*
(or)			
	what	*where*	*how*
(or)			
	FORMAT	*A:*	*/S*

This example shows the three main parts of a command: *what* you want to do (format a floppy disk), *where* you want to do it (in drive A), and *how* you want to do it (place the system files on the disk). DOS can be a little confusing sometimes, but if you keep this simple phrasing in mind, it will make DOS much easier to understand and remember.

Think of this phrasing process as what happens when a delivery man delivers a package to you. *What* he wants to do is deliver a package (command), *where* he wants to deliver it is to your address (parameter), and *how* he wants to deliver it is by driving his truck to your address (first switch) and then by walking to your door (second switch).

Understanding Internal and External Commands

To help you understand the concept of internal and external commands, follow these steps:

1. If the Shell is not running, start it by typing **DOSSHELL** and pressing Enter.
2. Choose the DOS subdirectory from the Directory List by clicking on the DOS subdirectory or highlighting it with the arrow keys.
3. Scroll through the file list. You will see many files listed, such as APPEND, ASSIGN, ATTRIB, BACKUP, CHKDSK, DISKCOPY, FIND, FORMAT, and many others.

These files are *external* DOS commands. This simply means that they are separate computer programs, each of which carries out a particular task. An external command must reside on a disk or in a subdirectory where DOS can find it before it can be executed.

Several other commands automatically load into the computer's memory every time you boot DOS. These tiny commands, called *internal* commands, are the most useful and most used DOS commands. The COMMAND.COM program automatically loads these commands into internal memory where they are always available. Because these commands reside in memory, they don't show up in a directory listing. Some of the internal commands you will learn about in later lessons include CD (Change Directory), COPY, DIR, ERASE, MD (Make Directory), RD (Remove Directory), and TYPE.

Understanding Formatting

It is important that you learn how to prepare blank disks to receive your information (spreadsheets, databases, and correspondence files). The process of preparing disks to receive information is called *formatting* or *initializing*.

Before a disk is formatted, it is only a round piece of plastic coated in magnetic material and held in a plastic jacket. You must format a disk before you can use it.

As illustrated in figure 6.1, you can think of blank, unformatted disks as unlined paper. Formatting prepares the disk to store your information. As the lines on paper serve as guides for the writer, the *tracks* and *sectors* on the disk serve as guides for the computer.

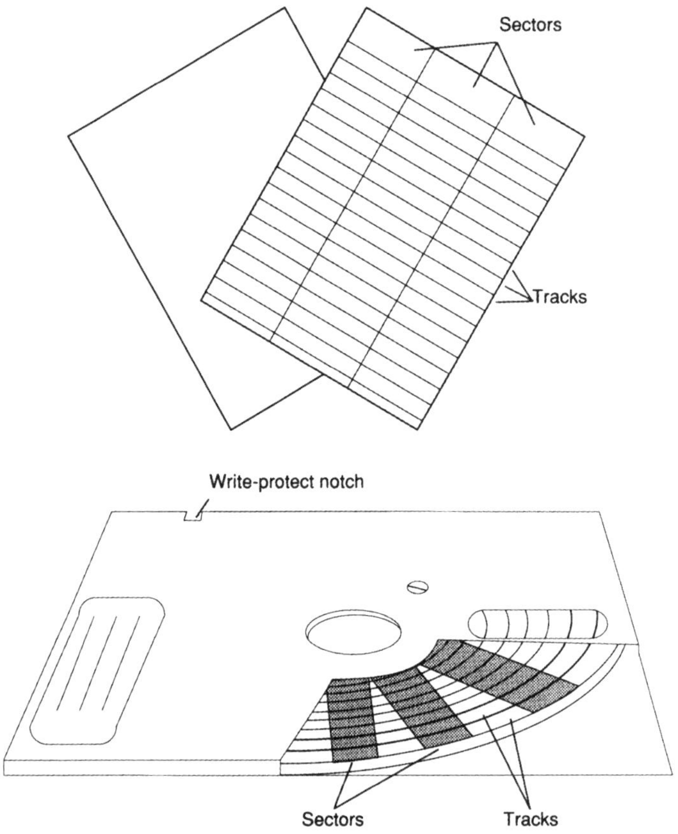

Fig. 6.1. Formatting a disk.

In addition to preparing the disk to accept DOS information and files, formatting also checks the disk for parts that are physically defective and marks those areas so that DOS will not try to write information there. There are actually two kinds of formatting.

Physical formatting simply divides the disk into tracks and sectors. *Logical formatting*, however, does much more. Logical formatting organizes the disk into four main areas: the boot record, the file allocation table (FAT), the root directory, and the data area. See Appendix D for more information on these areas.

Formatting and Erasing Disks

In previous versions of DOS, FORMAT destroyed all information on the disk, which meant that once the disk was formatted, any data that may have been on the disk was gone forever.

But new to DOS Version 5 is DOS's *safe format*. When you format a disk using DOS 5, DOS automatically uses safe format, which enables you to restore the data that was on the disk before the format by running the UNFORMAT command.

If, however, you do want to destroy the data on a disk, you can use the /U switch with FORMAT, which does an unconditional format.

> Never format a disk containing files you want to keep. Make sure that all your disks are labeled clearly.

Formatting a Disk from the Shell

The easiest way to format a disk is to choose the Format command from the Disk Utilities group in the Shell. Follow these steps:

1. Double-click on the Disk Utilities group in the Program List area. Or, press the Tab key to activate the Program List area, use the arrow keys to highlight (select) the Disk Utilities group, and press Enter.
2. Double-click on Format or use the arrow keys to highlight Format and press Enter.

   The Format dialog box appears (see fig. 6.2).
3. Because drive A is the default, click on OK or press Enter.

   The following message appears on your screen:

   ```
   Insert new diskette for drive A:
   and press ENTER when ready...
   ```

   If your computer has two floppy disk drives and you want to format a disk in drive B, you simply type **B:** in place of **A:**.

   To cancel the command at this point, you can press Ctrl-Break or Ctrl-C, which returns you to the Shell.

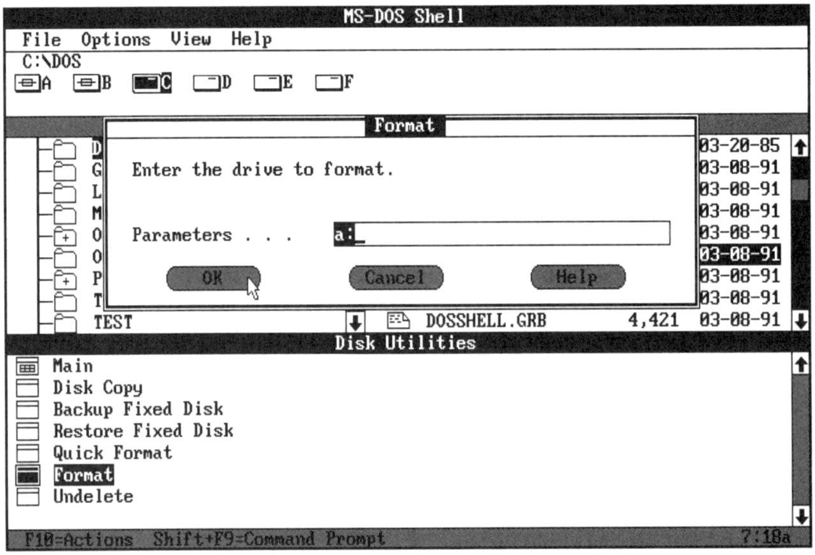

Fig. 6.2. The Format dialog box.

4. Insert a blank disk that is compatible with your system into drive A, close the drive door, and press Enter.

   The light on the drive comes on and the following message appears:

   ```
   Checking existing disk format.
   Saving UNFORMAT information.
   Verifying 1.2M
   ```

   If you use a new disk, you will not see the

   ```
   Saving UNFORMAT information
   ```

   message.

   Also, the

   ```
   Verifying 1.2M
   ```

   message will be different, depending on the disk capacity you are using, such as 360K, 720K, or 1.44M.

   As FORMAT continues, it displays the percentage of the disk that has been completed.

   When formatting is complete, the following message appears:

   ```
   Format complete.

   Volume label (11 characters, ENTER for none)?
   ```

5. Type the name **PRACTICE-1** and press Enter.

   This gives the disk a name. You don't have to give the disk a name, but by doing so, you help identify it. You will learn more about volume labels in Lesson 7.

   Depending on the disk capacity you are using, you now will see something similar to the following:

```
1213952 bytes total disk space
1213952 bytes available on disk

      512 bytes in each allocation unit
      2371 allocation units available on disk

Volume Serial Number is 2A49-14D2

Format another (Y/N)?
```

   Descriptions of these message lines follow:

   - *Bytes total disk space:* Specifies total capacity of the disk.
   - *Bytes used by system (not shown):* Appears if you use the /S switch to transfer the three DOS system files (IO.SYS, MSDOS.SYS, and COMMAND.COM) to the disk. These files enable you to use the disk to boot the computer. You learn about the /S switch in "Using Switches with the FORMAT Command," later in this lesson.
   - *Bytes in bad sectors (not shown):* Appears if physical flaws exist on a disk. FORMAT marks these areas as bad sectors so that DOS will not try to store information in these sectors.

     You may come across a disk that causes the message

     ```
     Invalid media or track 0 bad—disk unusable
     ```

     to appear at the beginning of formatting. This message means that the disk cannot be used at all because it is physically defective.

     If you have a disk with bad sectors, have your dealer replace the disk, or use the disk with less storage space; usually 2048 bytes in bad sectors is acceptable, but that is up to you. You should replace or throw away defective disks with a bad 0 track. Before you do either, however, try to reformat the disk. Some disks do not format properly the first time, but they may format with a second try.
   - *Bytes available on disk:* Indicates the total disk space available on the disk, minus whatever space is taken up by the system files and bad sectors. In the preceding example, this number is the same as the total bytes available.

- *Bytes in each allocation unit:* Refers to how many bytes are in each sector (allocated unit) of the disk. In this case, each sector contains 512 bytes, or .5K.
- *Allocation units available on disk:* Refers to how many sectors are on the disk. Because this disk has 2,371 sectors, and each sector has 512 bytes, this makes a total of 1,213,952 bytes on the disk, which matches the message

  ```
  Bytes total disk space
  ```

- *Volume serial number:* Specifies a unique serial number assigned to the disk. This number does not change unless the disk is formatted again.
- *Format another (Y/N)?:* Gives you the option to format another disk or to exit the FORMAT program.

6. Because you will use this practice disk in later lessons, take it out of the disk drive, label it *Practice Disk 1*, and set it aside.

> Never use a pencil or ball point pen to write on a label that is already on a 5 1/4-inch floppy disk. Pressing on the disk with a pencil or pen will damage the disk's surface. Always use a felt tip pen.

7. Press Y and Enter after the message

   ```
   Format another (Y/N?)
   ```

8. Press Enter at the prompt

   ```
   Insert new diskette for drive A:
   and press Enter when ready...
   ```

9. Format another disk for use in the next section, give it the volume name **PRACTICE-2**, and label it *PRACTICE DISK 2.*
10. Press N and Enter at the message

    ```
    Format another (Y/N)?
    ```

Then press any key to return to the Shell.

> It's a good idea to take the time to format all the disks in a newly purchased box of disks. This way you will always have a formatted disk on hand and you won't have to stop whatever you are doing just to format a disk.

Quick Formatting a Disk

You can greatly speed up the formatting process by doing a *quick format* instead of a complete format. This is useful for quickly erasing a disk. A quick format is faster because it does not format all of the disk; it simply deletes the file allocation table (FAT) and the root directory of a disk. Because a quick format doesn't perform all the other functions of formatting, you can perform quick formats only on disks that have been previously formatted.

To quick format a disk, follow these steps:

1. Double-click on the Disk Utilities group in the Program List area. Or, press the Tab key to activate the Program List area, use the arrow key to select (highlight) the Disk Utilities group, and press Enter.

2. Double-click on Quick Format, or use the arrow keys to highlight Quick Format, and press Enter.

   The Quick Format dialog box appears (see fig. 6.3).

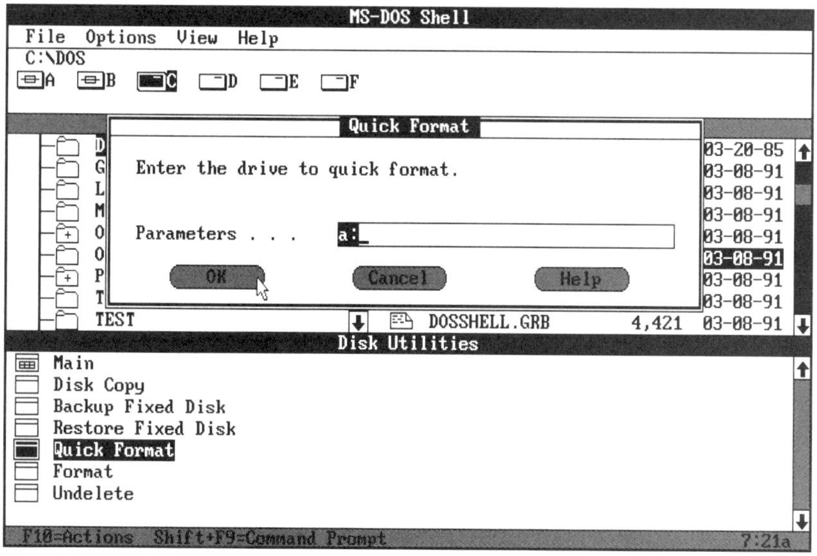

Fig. 6.3. The Quick Format dialog box.

3. Click on OK or press Enter.

4. Insert the Practice-2 disk that you formatted earlier into drive A, close the drive door, and press Enter.

The screen messages will be the same as before, but the process itself will go much faster.

```
Checking existing disk format.
Saving UNFORMAT information.
QuickFormatting 1.2M
Format complete.

Volume label (11 characters, ENTER for none)?
```

5. Type **PRACTICE-2** at this prompt and press Enter. The following information appears:

```
1213952 bytes total disk space
1213952 bytes available on disk

      512 bytes in each allocation unit
      2371 allocation units available on disk

Volume Serial Number is 2A49-14D2

QuickFormat another (Y/N)?
```

6. Press N and Enter after the message

```
QuickFormat another (Y/N)?
```

Put this disk aside for use in future lessons and then press any key to return to the Shell.

Formatting a Disk from the DOS Prompt

There may be times when you want to format a disk from the DOS prompt. This process is identical to formatting a disk from the Shell, except that you have to type the command and parameters. Follow these steps:

1. If you are in the Shell, click on Command Prompt in the Main Program List, or just press Shift-F9.

   This temporarily takes you to DOS and displays the following message and DOS prompt:

```
Microsoft(R) MS-DOS(R) Version 5.00
      Copyright Microsoft Corp 1981-1991.

C:\DOS>
```

   The DOS prompt may display a different directory, such as C:\>, but this doesn't matter for the purpose of this lesson.

2. At the DOS prompt, type **FORMAT A:** and press Enter.

   To cancel the command at this point, you can press Ctrl-Break or Ctrl-C, which returns you to the DOS prompt.

   If you fail to type a drive letter, DOS replies with the message

   ```
   Required parameter missing—
   ```

   If you type **FORMAT C:** or the drive letter of any other fixed disk, DOS replies with the following message:

   ```
   WARNING, ALL DATA ON NON-REMOVABLE DISK DRIVE C: WILL
   BE LOST!

   Proceed with Format (Y/N)?
   ```

   Unless you are purposely reformatting your hard disk, press N and Enter to cancel the command.

> Be extremely careful when you use the FORMAT command. Be sure to specify only drive A or drive B when you format.

3. Insert another blank floppy disk into drive A and proceed with the format as before. All the screen messages will be the same as in the "Formatting a Disk from the Shell" section. There is no need to give this floppy a name, but you certainly may.
4. Press N and Enter after the message

   ```
   Format another (Y/N)?
   ```

5. Type **EXIT** at the C:\> prompt and press Enter to return to the Shell.

Using Switches with the FORMAT Command

As you have learned, a *switch* is an added option that tells a command more precisely how to do something. You can use up to 11 switches with the FORMAT command, but it is unlikely that you will ever need to use more than five of these. You can add each of these switches to the FORMAT command in the Format dialog box or on the DOS command line.

Using the /S Switch

The /S (system) switch is necessary to create a bootable disk that contains the operating system. It accomplishes this by copying the operating system files (IO.SYS, MSDOS.SYS, and COMMAND.COM) to the disk. Without the /S option, you can't boot a formatted disk (that is, use it to start the computer).

Disks without the operating system are used primarily for data storage. On computers with a hard disk, the hard disk is usually the bootable disk, and drive A is used to save the data. Normally, you will not use the /S switch on computers with a hard disk, but you may run into a situation where it is needed. The command used to create a bootable disk in drive A is

```
FORMAT A: /S
```

You can type the complete command at the DOS prompt or simply add the /S switch to the command line in the Shell's Format dialog box. The procedure then continues in the same way as you learned earlier.

You will format a disk with the /S switch in the "Exercises" section at the end of this lesson.

> It is a good idea to have at least one bootable floppy disk available. In case your hard disk fails, you can at least get your computer running by inserting the bootable floppy disk into drive A and restarting the computer.

Using the /V:*label* Switch

Normally, you are prompted for a label after the formatting process is complete, but the /V (volume) switch enables you to specify a label for the disk as you run the command. For example, the command

```
FORMAT A: /V:PRACTICE-1
```

accomplishes what you did in step 5 in the section "Formatting a Disk from the Shell," including automatically inserting the volume label. You can type the complete command at the DOS prompt or simply add the /V:*label* switch to the command line in the Shell's Format dialog box.

You learn more about volume labels in Lesson 7.

Using the /Q Switch

You learned about the Shell's Quick Format command in the section "Quick Formatting a Disk," but you also can perform a quick format from the DOS prompt with the /Q (quick) switch. Type the following command:

FORMAT A: /Q

As you learned earlier, Quick Format is much faster than a complete format because it simply deletes the file allocation table (FAT) and the root directory of a disk; it doesn't perform all the other functions of formatting. Therefore, you can use the /Q switch only on disks that have been previously formatted.

Using the /U Switch

By default, FORMAT does a nondestructive (safe) format of a disk; that is, it does not destroy the data on the disk. You therefore can use the UNFORMAT command to recover data on disks that have been accidentally formatted with the normal FORMAT command.

You can use the /U (unconditional) switch to destroy any data that may be on the disk. Use the command

FORMAT A: /U

if you receive any read/write errors when using a disk. You can type the complete command at the DOS prompt or simply add the /U switch to the command line in the Shell's Format dialog box.

> When formatting a disk that has never been formatted, use the /U switch to reduce the formatting time.

Using the /F:*size* Switch

Since the personal computer first came on the scene, there have been many changes in disk capacity. Very early disks had only one side and could hold only 160K, for example, while double-sided disks that hold 1.2M are common today. Chalk one up for progress.

Suppose that you have a 1.2M drive but need to give data to someone who has a 360K disk drive. Because the formats are incompatible, you need to format a double-density disk for 360K. DOS 5 enables you to do this with the /F:*size* switch. Use the command

FORMAT A: /F:360

to format a double-sided, double-density, 360K floppy disk in a 1.2M, 5 1/4-inch disk drive.

> Because of hardware differences, some 360K drives cannot reliably read disks formatted in a 1.2M drive. This process, therefore, is not always reliable. You can use utility programs such as PC-Tools and Norton Utilities, however, to do this more reliably.

Perhaps you need to format a 720K, 3 1/2-inch diskette in a 1.44M drive. You can do so with this command:

FORMAT A: /F:720

Unlike FORMAT /F:360, this command can be relied on because 720K drives have become more standardized. You can type the complete command at the DOS prompt or simply add the /F:*size* switch to the command line in the Shell's Format dialog box. Table 6.1 shows the values for the size that you can use with each disk drive type.

Table 6.1. DOS 5.0 /F:*size* Switch and Disk Drive/Floppy Combinations

Drive Type	Allowable Values for Size
160K, 180K	160, 180
320K, 360K	All of the 160 and 180 values, plus 320 and 360
1.2M	All of the 160, 180, 320, and 360 values, plus 1200 and 1.2
720K	720
1.44M	All of the 720K values, plus 1440 and 1.44
2.88M	All of the 720K values, plus 2880 and 2.88

Remember, DOS supports a lower density disk in a higher density drive, but it does *not* support a higher density disk in a lower density drive.

Getting On-Line Help from the DOS Prompt

Not only can you get help in the DOS Shell, but you also can get instant help while working from the DOS prompt. This new addition to DOS 5 is one of its most outstanding features.

To see how quickly you can get help in DOS 5, follow these steps:

1. If you are in the Shell, click on Command Prompt in the Main Program list, or just press Shift-F9.
2. At the DOS prompt, type **FORMAT /?** and press Enter.

   This displays the following help message:

```
C:\>FORMAT /?
Formats a disk for use with MS-DOS.

FORMAT drive: [/V[:label]] [/Q] [/U] [/F:size] [/B ¦ / S]

FORMAT drive: [/V[:label]] [/Q] [/U] [/T:tracks / N:sectors] [/B ¦ /S]

FORMAT drive: [/V[:label]] [/Q] [/U] [/1] [/4] [/B ¦ / S]

FORMAT drive: [/Q] [/U] [/1] [/4] [/8] [/B ¦ /S]

        /V[:label]    Specifies the volume label.

        /Q            Performs a quick format.

        /U            Performs an unconditional format.

        /F:size       Specifies the size of the floppy
                      disk to format (such as 160, 180,
                      320, 360, 720, 1.2, 1.44, 2.88).

        /B            Allocates space on the formatted
                      disk for system files.

        /S            Copies system files to the formatted
                      disk.

        /T:tracks     Specifies the number of tracks per
                      disk side.

        /N:sectors    Specifies the number of sectors per
                      track.

        /1            Formats a single side of a floppy
                      disk.
```

`/4`	`Formats a 5.25-inch 360K floppy disk in a high-density drive.`
`/8`	`Formats eight sectors per track.`

You can access help on any DOS command by using the /? switch. Remember this as you progress through this book.

You also can display a one-line description of *all* DOS commands by typing **HELP** and pressing Enter.

3. Type **EXIT** and press Enter to return to the Shell.

Lesson Summary

- ☐ Any DOS command is phrased in the same basic way:

  commandname *parameters* *switches*

  or

  what *where* *how*

- ☐ Before you can use a new disk to store information, you must format the disk by using the FORMAT command.
- ☐ You can use the FORMAT command to erase all information from a used disk.
- ☐ You can use switches with the FORMAT command to add options.
- ☐ The message

  `x bytes in bad sectors`

  tells you that some parts of the disk are bad. The bad sectors will not be used to store information. If you choose to use a disk with bad sectors, it will have reduced storage space.
- ☐ You can access on-line help from the DOS prompt by typing the command and adding the /? switch.

Key Terms

Bootable Disk	A disk (hard or floppy) that contains the DOS system files and which you can use to boot (start) the computer.
Command	An instruction you give to the computer that executes a DOS function or a program.

COMMAND.COM	A special file that contains the instructions needed to activate DOS and make it usable. Also contains the DOS internal commands.
Commandname	Refers to the command you want to execute. Tells DOS *what* you want to do.
External command	A separate computer program that carries out a particular task.
Formatting	Preparing a disk for use by DOS.
Internal command	A tiny program that resides in the computer's internal memory.
Parameter	A value passed to a command which gives the command specific instructions. Most DOS commands have one or more parameters. Tells DOS *where* you want to carry out a command.
Sector	A pie-shaped section of a track that serves as a disk's smallest storage unit.
Switch	A value that gives a command even more specific information about the command. Tells DOS *how* you want a command carried out.
Track	An invisible, electronically produced circle on a disk where data is stored.

Exercises

1. Using the /S switch, format a bootable floppy disk from the Shell or from the command line. Label this disk **BOOT_DISK**. Remember, you can use the /V:*label* switch to specify this label as you run the command (see "Using the /S Switch" and "Using the /V: *label* Switch").
2. Format as many disks as you can acquire. Perhaps you recently bought a box of disks, or perhaps you have some that have been used before. (See "Formatting a Disk from the Shell.")
3. If you have brand new disks, format them with the /U switch. If the disks already have been formatted, use the /Q switch, but make sure there are no files on the disks that you need to keep. Be sure that each disk has a label on it, and then store these disks for future use.

4. If you have a high capacity disk drive (1.2M or 1.44M), and if you have a low capacity disk (360K or 720K), format the disks with the /F switch.

For More Information

For additional beginner-level information, as well as some intermediate information concerning what was presented in this lesson, refer to *MS-DOS 5 QuickStart* (Que Corporation). For a more in-depth handling of these subjects, refer to *Using MS-DOS 5* (Que Corporation). See Appendix E for a description of these Que books.

In Lesson 7, you will learn some foundational principles about how to work with disks and directories.

Lesson 7

Disk and Directory Basics

By this point, you should feel comfortable with a number of the features of DOS, especially those that relate to the Shell. You will find yourself using more and more disks as you become familiar with your system and experienced in expanding and editing the files you create.

With only volume labels on these disks, you may wonder how you will know what files are stored on each disk. The directory-listing capability of the Shell and the directory (DIR) command issued from the DOS prompt are invaluable for this purpose.

In this lesson, you learn how to do the following:

- Display the directory of a disk
- Read and interpret directory information
- Display a directory by using the /P and /W switches
- Clear the screen
- Print a copy of a directory listing
- Name disk drives
- Assign volume labels

Learning how to work with disks and directories (as well as files, covered in Lesson 8) is crucial to your overall understanding of DOS. Make sure that you fully understand these lessons before continuing.

What you need to complete this lesson: Practice disks 1 and 2

Estimated time to complete this lesson: 30-35 minutes

Displaying and Interpreting a Directory

Listing the directories of your disks is the best way to find out what is on the disks. Whether you are working in the Shell or from the DOS prompt, you will often use DOS's directory-listing powers.

Obtaining Directory Listings in the Shell

In Lesson 5, you learned the basic procedures for working with files and directories in the Shell. This section builds on that knowledge.

To obtain a directory listing while in the Shell, follow these steps:

1. Start the Shell, if it is not already running. Make sure that you are logged on to drive C by clicking the C icon or by highlighting C with the Tab key and the arrow keys and pressing Enter. Alternatively, you can press Ctrl-C.
2. Change to the DOS subdirectory by clicking DOS in the Directory Tree area. Or, press Tab to activate the Directory Tree area and highlight DOS with the arrow keys.
3. Change the Shell's display to Single File List by clicking the View menu and then the Single File List option. Or, press Alt-V and S.
4. Scroll down the file listing until the file COMMAND.COM appears. Click COMMAND.COM or press Tab to get to the File List area, and then use the arrow keys to highlight COMMAND.COM. Your screen should look similar to figure 7.1.

Notice the information beside COMMAND.COM. The size of the file (47,867 bytes, or about 48K) is given first, followed by the date the file was created or last changed (03-08-91). The Shell provides this information for each file in the listing.

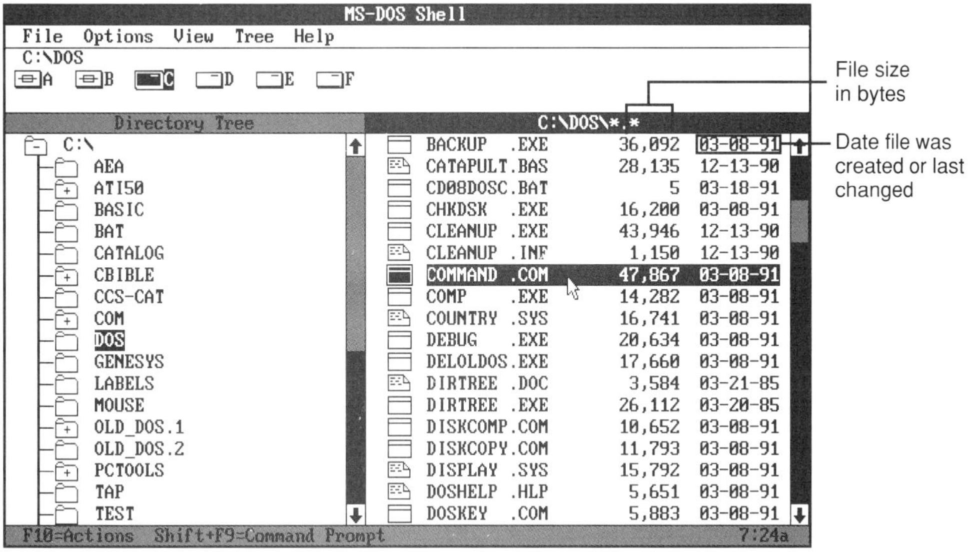

Fig. 7.1. The single file view.

The Single File View option is an excellent way to use the Shell. It provides immediate information about your disks, directories, and files and gives the most complete display. After your programs are loaded and the Task List is defined, you may find yourself using this viewing option more than any other. (For more information on the Task List, see Lesson 15.)

Understanding the Path

You already have some knowledge of the directory structure. To understand how directories relate to one another, you need to understand the concept of the *path* or *pathname*.

DOS uses *paths*, or chains of directory names, to guide itself through directories in order to find the file you want. When you want to find a file stored in a subdirectory, for example, you must indicate the path for DOS to take to locate the file. To indicate the subdirectory and the file, you use the backslash (\) path symbol. The first backslash always indicates the root directory, and subsequent backslashes indicate subdirectories.

This principle is important as you work with your programs. Word processing and spreadsheet programs, for example, demand some knowledge of path names so that you know how to save your files to and retrieve them from directories.

If your hard disk has a directory called 123 that contains the Lotus 1-2-3 spreadsheet program, for example, the 123 directory exists as a subdirectory of the root directory of drive C. Figure 7.2 illustrates this structure.

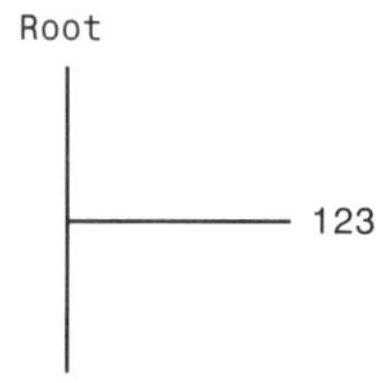

Fig. 7.2. A directory tree of the \123 subdirectory.

Figure 7.3 illustrates the directory structure if you have a DATA subdirectory under 123 containing the file BUDGET91.WK1.

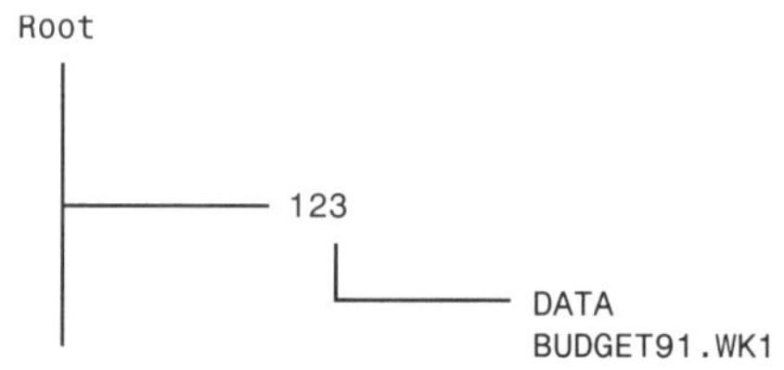

Fig. 7.3. A directory tree of the \123\DATA subdirectory.

The complete *path name* for BUDGET91.WK1 follows:

C:\123\DATA\BUDGET91.WK1

In the same way that you need exact directions to get to a place you have never been to, DOS needs a path to follow to get where it needs to go. Just as you use streets and street names as paths to arrive at your destination, DOS uses the backslash (\) character and directory names as path markers. Figure 7.4 shows the path for BUDGET91.WK1.

Fig. 7.4. The path to BUDGET91.WK1.

Just as you know to turn onto a different street when your directions indicate, DOS knows to "turn" when it sees a backslash (\); the directory name tells DOS which "street" to turn onto as it seeks the destination, BUDGET91.WK1.

Obtaining Directory Listings from the DOS Prompt

At this point, you get your first real taste of working with DOS at the command-line level. As you have seen, working with DOS from the Shell is very easy, but working at the DOS prompt is often faster than working in the Shell.

The COPY command, for example, copies files from one place to another (you learn more about this command in Lesson 10). For many users, it is faster to type the command **COPY *.* A:** (to copy all files in the current directory to drive A) than to tag all these files in the Shell and then issue the Shell's Copy command from the File menu. Other users, however, prefer the simplicity of the Shell even though it is slower at times. As you progress, you will decide for yourself.

The DIR command displays a list (a directory) of the names of the files stored on a disk. This command also displays information about file size, the date and time each file was created or edited, and the amount of space remaining on the disk.

To obtain a listing of the files stored on a disk in a particular disk drive, follow these steps:

1. Exit the Shell temporarily by pressing Shift-F9 or permanently by pressing F3.

2. Place the *Hands-On MS-DOS 5* disk that came with this book into drive A and close the drive door.

> On master disks such as the disk tutor, or disks that come with other software packages you buy, be sure a *write-protect label* (one of the small labels that come with a box of disks) covers the notch on the outside edge of your disk. If you are using a 3 1/2-inch disk, turn the disk over and slide the small notch in the upper left corner to expose the opening for write-protection. Write-protection prevents you from inadvertently changing or writing to your master disks.

3. At the DOS prompt (C:\DOS>), type **DIR A:** and press Enter.

   You have just told DOS to display a list of the files on the disk in drive A. You should see a list similar to the one shown in figure 7.5.

```
 Volume in drive A has no label
 Volume Serial Number is 0453-15E4
 Directory of A:\

ATI      EXE     50308 08-29-90   5:16p
TRN      DIR       649 01-02-92   4:45p
TRN      FIL      4336 01-02-92   4:45p
TRN0     DIR       438 08-09-91   1:08p
TRN0     FIL      1025 08-09-91   1:08p
TRN1     DIR      2114 12-27-91   8:42a
TRN1     FIL    253210 12-27-91   8:42a
TRN2     DIR      2111 09-04-91   2:49p
TRN2     FIL    287847 09-04-91   2:49p
TRN3     DIR       387 01-02-92   9:32a
TRN3     FIL       822 01-02-92   9:32a
ANSWERS  TXT      1339 07-01-91  10:16a
CLIENTS  ADD        64 07-01-91  11:34a
COMMANDS TXT     23035 08-08-91   2:45p
CONTENTS TXT      1307 08-10-91  11:22a
DOSERROR TXT     28224 08-08-91   2:43p
FAMILY   ADD        56 07-01-91  11:37a
FRIENDS  ADD        56 07-01-91  11:36a
GLOSSARY TXT     38660 01-13-92   2:33p
Press any key to continue . . .
```

Fig. 7.5. A directory of drive A.

The first line of this message shows the volume label assigned to the disk during the formatting process.

The second line displays the serial number given to the disk when it was formatted.

The third line tells you which disk drive and directory path are displayed. In this case, you are getting a directory of drive A; the slash tells you that this directory is the root directory. (Lesson 12 presents more information about root directories and paths.)

Below these lines, you see one line for each file on the disk. Each line lists a file name (and extension), the size of the file in bytes, and the date and time the file was created or last updated. Figure 7.6 shows you the information for the first file listed on-screen.

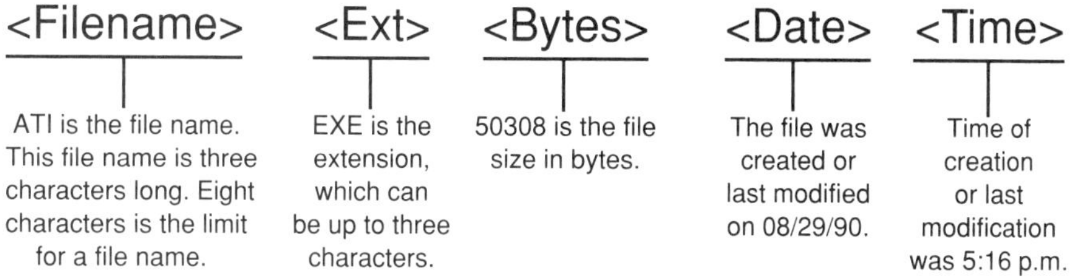
<Filename>
<Ext>
<Bytes>
<Date>
<Time>
ATI is the file name. This file name is three characters long. Eight characters is the limit for a file name.
EXE is the extension, which can be up to three characters.
50308 is the file size in bytes.
The file was created or last modified on 08/29/90.
Time of creation or last modification was 5:16 p.m.

Fig. 7.6. Information on a single file.

The next-to-last line tells you the number of files contained in the directory and the amount of disk space these files consume.

The last line tells you how much space is left on the disk. This information is especially useful in keeping track of your disk's available storage space, for example, when you need to know how much storage space remains on a disk after copying a group of files to it.

4. Now type **DIR** after the DOS prompt and press Enter. The current directory of drive C appears. (Remember, you do not have to specify the drive when issuing a command to take action on the currently logged drive.)

   Because all the file information for the current directory cannot fit on one screen, file names at the beginning of the directory pass out of sight before you can read them, and only the last part of the directory remains on-screen. This phenomenon is called *scrolling*.

   If you didn't notice the scrolling the first time, type **DIR** again, press Enter, and watch the screen.

> If no scrolling took place, type **DIR C:\DOS** and press Enter. Scrolling now should occur.

When you list a directory too large to fit on one screen, you have several options for viewing the entire directory.

Freezing the Screen (Ctrl-S or Pause)

You can stop the lines of text from scrolling off your computer screen, freezing a portion of the information on-screen for as long as you want. The method you use depends on your computer system. On computers without an enhanced keyboard, press Ctrl-S (press and hold the Ctrl key as you press S) as soon as the directory begins to appear on-screen. If you have an enhanced keyboard, press the Pause key. With both keyboards, the scrolling stops until you press any other key to resume scrolling.

To practice freezing the screen, follow these steps:

1. Type **DIR** again (or **DIR C:\DOS** if necessary) and press Enter.
2. As soon as the scrolling begins, press Ctrl-S or Pause. The scrolling stops.
3. Press any key when you want to resume scrolling.

You can press Ctrl-S or Pause as often as you want to stop the scrolling as you examine a long directory. Ctrl-Num Lock also freezes the screen.

> A handy way to control the scrolling is to press and hold down the Ctrl key and then just keep pressing S to stop and start scrolling. You can think of the S as an On/Off switch.

Using the /P and /W Switches

Two *switches* (options) are available for use with the DIR command. The /P (pause) switch displays a set of files and then pauses the screen. When you press a key, the next set of files is displayed, and so on, until you have seen all the file names.

When you use the /P switch with earlier DOS versions, the top few lines containing the volume label, disk drive name, and path scroll off the screen, leaving only the list of files. This small shortcoming was corrected in DOS 5, which displays this information and the first 17 files; each subsequent screen displays the next 22 files. Thus, using the /P switch now is more convenient than pressing Ctrl-S or Pause. On the other hand, Ctrl-S or Pause gives you more control over the files that are displayed at any given time.

The /W (wide) switch produces a wide display of files on-screen. When you use this switch, DOS displays five file names per line (see fig. 7.7). The file size, date, and time, as well as subdirectories, are not displayed. If you don't need all the information that /P provides, /W has the advantage of being faster.

```
 Volume in drive A has no label
 Directory of  A:\

APPEND   EXE    ASSIGN   COM    ATTRIB   EXE    BACKUP   COM    BASIC    COM
BASICA   COM    CHKDSK   COM    COMMAND  COM    COMP     COM    DEBUG    COM
DISKCOMP COM    DISKCOPY COM    EDLIN    COM    FIND     EXE    FORMAT   COM
GRAFTABL COM    GRAPHICS COM    JOIN     EXE    LABEL    COM    MORE     COM
PRINT    COM    RECOVER  COM    RESTORE  COM    SHARE    EXE    SORT     EXE
SUBST    EXE    TREE     COM    XCOPY    EXE    BASIC    PIF    BASICA   PIF
MORTGAGE BAS
       31 File(s)      55296 bytes free
```

Fig. 7.7. A wide directory listing.

You use the /P and /W switches in the same way, typing the switch you want after the DIR command. To get a directory listing that pauses, follow these steps:

1. To make sure you are in the DOS subdirectory, type **CD\DOS** and press Enter. You learn more about the CD (Change Directory) command in Lesson 12.
2. Type **DIR/P** and press Enter.

   Notice the message

   ```
   Press any key to continue ...
   ```

   at the bottom of the screen.
3. Press any key when you are ready to see the next display of files.

   Notice the message

   ```
   (continuing C:\DOS)
   ```

that appears at the top of the screen. DOS 5 adds a number of cosmetic features such as these messages that make it much classier than earlier versions.

4. Continue pressing any key until you return to the DOS prompt.

> When DOS gives you the message
>
> `Press any key to continue...`
>
> it really means *Press almost any key*. If you press the Shift, Ctrl, Alt, Caps Lock, Num Lock, or Scroll Lock key, DOS ignores your action and continues to wait. The space bar is a good key to press when DOS gives you this choice.

To get a wide directory, follow these steps:

1. Type **DIR/W** and press Enter.

   This presents a wide display of the current directory. Occasionally, you may have an unusually large directory. In this case, you can use the /W and /P switches together.

2. Now type **DIR/W/P** and press Enter. (You also could type **DIR/P/W**, because the order of the switches doesn't matter.)

   The first screen of a wide directory display of the DOS subdirectory appears, as shown in figure 7.8.

   The first screen displays 93 files at a time (although only 86 are shown in figure 7.8), not counting the . (current) and .. (parent) directory entries; each subsequent screen displays 110 files.

3. Press any key to continue the listing and return to the DOS prompt.

Printing a Copy of a Directory Listing

For a printed copy (also called *hard copy*, *paper copy*, or *printout*) of the displayed directory, press the Shift and PrtSc keys at the same time (or the Print Screen key only, if you have an enhanced keyboard). You can use these keys whenever you want a copy of what you see on-screen.

Another useful DOS command is CLS, which clears the screen. This command produces a more attractive screen print by erasing unwanted screen clutter. When you type **CLS** and press Enter, the screen clears except for the system prompt in the upper left corner.

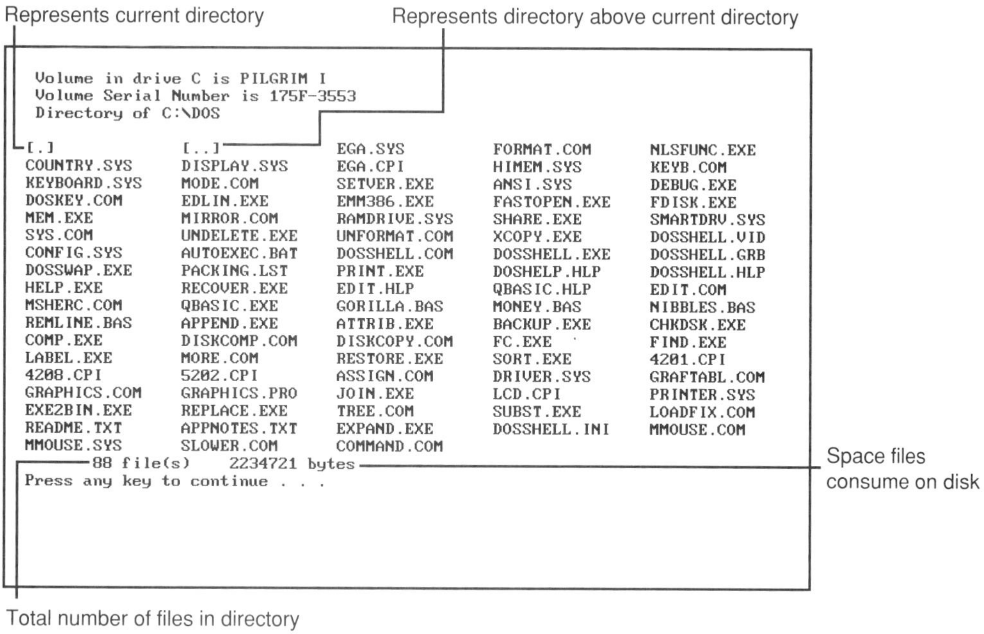

Fig. 7.8. A wide directory listing of files in the C:\DOS subdirectory.

If your printer is connected to the computer and ready to print (with the paper properly loaded), follow these steps to get a clean printout of the C:\DOS subdirectory:

1. Type **CLS** and press Enter. The screen clears and displays the DOS prompt.
2. Type **DIR/W/P** and press Enter.
3. With the directory on-screen, press Shift-PrtSc or the Print Screen key.

   Everything on-screen is sent to the printer.
4. Press any key to display the rest of the listing and repeat step 3.
5. To return to the Shell, type **EXIT** at the DOS prompt and press Enter (if you exited temporarily with Shift-F9), or type **DOSSHELL** and press Enter (if you exited permanently with F3).

> Instead of exiting to the DOS prompt, you can execute a DOS command right from the Shell by selecting the Run command and typing the command in the dialog box that appears. The next section gives you more information.

Issuing DOS Commands From the Shell

Instead of exiting the Shell to issue a DOS command, you can issue the command right from the Shell by selecting the Run command from the File menu. This technique enables you to execute a command quickly.

To issue the DIR command, for example, follow these steps:

1. Click File and then Run. Or, press Alt-F and then R. The Run dialog box appears (see fig. 7.9).

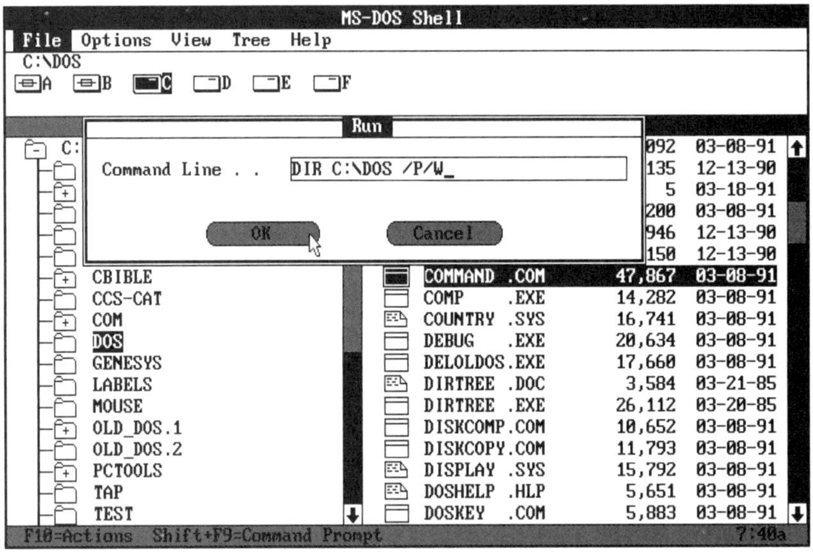

Fig. 7.9. The Run dialog box.

2. Type **DIR C:\DOS /P/W** in the dialog box and press Enter or click OK. The first screen of a wide directory listing of the DOS subdirectory appears.

   Typing **C:\DOS** is necessary only if C:\DOS is not the current directory. A quick glance at the Directory Tree area of File List will tell you the current directory.

3. Press any key to continue the listing and then press any key to return to the Shell.

Naming Disk Drives and Disks

When you know how to boot DOS and copy and format disks, you are ready to create your own files. Although you will usually create files using an applications program (a word processing program such as WordPerfect, a spreadsheet program such as Lotus 1-2-3, or a database program such as dBASE), you also can create files and store information with the DOS text editor, which you learn to use in Lesson 17.

When you create your own files, you need to be familiar with three kinds of names: disk drive names, volume labels, and file names. This lesson explains the principles behind naming disk drives and disks, and naming files is covered in Lesson 8. These two lessons also stress the importance of careful and correct naming. Understanding these principles will enable you to use DOS more fully and help you understand the naming conventions of applications programs.

Understanding Disk Drive Letters

Your disk drives—whether you have two floppy disk drives or one hard disk and one floppy—already have unique names. A disk drive name has two characters: a letter, followed by a colon (:). The colon tells DOS that you are naming a disk drive rather than a file.

If your computer has two floppy disk drives, the first one (on the left or top) is called A, and the second one (on the right, or bottom) is B. If your computer has more than two disk drives, the additional drive names follow the letters of the alphabet: C, D, E, and so on.

If you have one floppy disk drive or one floppy and one hard disk, the floppy drive functions as two drives. In the lessons on copying disks, for example, you will see that a system with one disk drive uses it alternately as drive A and drive B.

Finally, if your system has one floppy drive and one hard disk, the hard disk is drive C. The hard disk drive on an XT, AT, or PS/2, for example, has the drive name C.

When you use the disk drive name before a program name or a file name, you are telling DOS which disk to read to find your program and files. Also, almost any time you specify a file name, the disk drive name precedes the file name. Often, when you tell DOS to run a program from a disk, the program is preceded by the name of the drive.

To practice using different disk drives and shifting drives, follow these steps:

1. Exit the Shell temporarily by pressing Shift-F9 or permanently by pressing F3.
2. Insert a formatted disk (such as Practice Disk 1, which you created in Lesson 6) into drive A and close the drive door.
3. Type **A:** and press Enter. The system prompt changes to A:\>.

> To change the currently logged drive (also called the *default* drive), type the letter of the new drive followed by a colon and press Enter.

4. Type **C:** and press Enter to change the currently logged drive back to C.

   If you have additional disk drives, try changing to a drive other than A or C. But don't try to change to a disk drive you don't have. If you do, you receive an error message such as

   ```
   Invalid drive specification
   ```

   You then will be returned to the DOS prompt, where you must type an acceptable drive.

5. To return to the Shell, type **EXIT** at the DOS prompt and press Enter (if you exited temporarily with Shift-F9), or type **DOSSHELL** and press Enter (if you exited permanently with F3).

These concepts on disk drives are very important and are summarized in the following guidelines.

Guidelines for Naming Disk Drives

- A disk drive must have a two-character name: the first character is a letter, and the second is a colon (for example, B:).
- The first floppy disk drive is A, the second is B, and so on. The first hard disk drive, if you have one, is C.
- When you tell DOS to run a program, the program name may be preceded by the disk drive name.
- When you specify a file name, the name of the disk drive should precede the file name unless the file is in the currently logged drive.
- Be sure to use an existing disk drive. If you name a nonexistent disk drive, DOS displays an error message.

0 0 − +

0 0 + − 6 x 6

− − 0 +

− − 0 −

+ + − 0

− − 0 −

0 − 0 +

0 + 0 −

0 −

− 0

0 +

+ 0

1 2 3 5

1 9 6 8

3 9 10 15

3 9 10 13

2 5 13 17

1112	1121	1122	1211	1212	1221	1222
2111	2112	2121	2122	2211	2212	2221

Understanding Volume Labels

As you learned in Lesson 6, a *volume label* is a name given electronically to a disk for grouping or identifying purposes. As you learned in this lesson, DOS displays the label when you ask for the directory of a disk. It also displays the volume label when you perform other DOS functions, as you will see in other lessons.

When you format a disk in DOS 5, DOS asks for an 11-character maximum volume label after the program has formatted the disk. You also can use the /V:*label* switch with the command to tell DOS what label to place on the disk.

You can check the volume label by using the VOL command; the LABEL command enables you to change or delete the label. Follow these steps to practice using the VOL and LABEL commands:

1. Exit the Shell temporarily by pressing Shift-F9 or permanently by pressing F3.

   Or, you can issue the VOL command directly from the Shell by choosing Run from the File menu and typing the command in the dialog box that appears.

2. Insert Practice Disk 1, which you created in Lesson 6, into drive A and close the drive door.

3. Type **VOL A:** and press Enter. DOS displays a message similar to the following:

   ```
   Volume in drive A is PRACTICE-1
   Volume Serial Number is OF16-11FA
   ```

4. Repeat steps 2 and 3 for Practice Disk 2. A similar message appears:

   ```
   Volume in drive A is PRACTICE-2
   Volume Serial Number is 1941-16F9
   ```

5. Now type **LABEL A:** and press Enter. A display similar to the following appears:

   ```
   Volume in drive A is PRACTICE-2
   Volume Serial Number is 1941-16F9
   Volume label (11 characters, ENTER for none)?
   ```

6. Type any new label and press Enter.

7. Repeat steps 5 and 6 to change the label back to PRACTICE-2.

8. To return to the Shell, type **EXIT** at the DOS prompt and press Enter (if you exited temporarily with Shift-F9). Or, type **DOSSHELL** and press Enter (if you exited permanently with F3).

If you simply want to erase this label without entering a new one, you simply press Enter. Then answer Yes to the prompt

```
Delete current volume label (Y/N)?
```

and press Enter.

Guidelines for Volume Labels

- A disk can have only one volume label.
- You can assign the volume label as part of the formatting process or by using the LABEL command in DOS Versions 3.0 and later.
- You can use any of the following characters in volume labels (no other characters are allowed):

  The letters A-Z and a-z

  The numerals 0-9

  These special characters:

  ~ ! @ # $ ^ & ( ) - _ { } ‘

  A space (only in an 11-character label)

Lesson Summary

- ☐ The single file view in the Shell is a good way to view disks, directories, and files.
- ☐ To change from the currently logged disk drive to any other drive, type the letter of the new drive followed by a colon (for example, **C:**).
- ☐ To handle a directory too long to fit on one screen, use Ctrl-S or the Pause key to stop the scrolling motion of the screen, /P to get a directory that pauses, or /W to get a wide listing of file names.
- ☐ You can quickly get a printed copy of the screen by pressing Shift-PrtSc (or the Print Screen key on enhanced keyboards).
- ☐ The CLS command erases the contents of the screen.

- ☐ A disk drive must have a two-character name. The first character is a letter and the second character is a colon.
- ☐ You can assign a volume label of 1 to 11 characters to a disk when you format it. The volume label helps you group and identify disks.

Key Terms

CLS	Clears (erases) the computer screen.
DIR	Displays a list (or *directory*) of the names of the files stored on a disk and information about those files.
Hard copy	Paper printout of computer data. (Also called printout or paper copy.)
LABEL	Changes or deletes the volume label of a disk.
Path	List of directory names, separated by a backslash (\\), that defines the location of a specific directory or file. For example, C:\\123\\DATA\\BUDGET.WK1.
Root directory	Main directory in a hierarchy of directories that DOS creates on every disk. The first backslash (\\) in a path represents the root directory.
Scrolling	Moves information on your computer screen. Controlled with the /P switch in the DIR command, by pressing Pause, or by pressing Ctrl-S.
Shift-PrtSc or	Prints contents of the computer screen on the printer. Print Screen
VOL	Displays the volume label of a disk.
Volume label	Name given electronically to a disk for grouping or identifying purposes.

Exercises

To become proficient in listing your files, practice these procedures:

1. Get directory listings in the Shell by changing to the various subdirectories on your hard disk (see "Displaying and Interpreting a Directory").

2. Insert various disks, such as the disk that came with this book and the disks that came with DOS 5, into drive A and list the files on them.
3. Exit the Shell.
4. Put a practice disk into drive A, close the drive door, and list the files on it using the DIR command. Use the /P switch as needed (see "Using the /P and /W Switches").
5. Issue **DIR /W** (and /P if needed) on the practice disk; then press Shift-PrtSc or the Print Screen key to print the listing (see "Printing a Copy of a Directory Listing").
6. Issue the CLS command to erase the display.
7. Repeat these procedures with different disks.

For More Information

For additional beginner-level information, as well as some intermediate information concerning the concepts presented in this lesson, refer to *MS-DOS 5 QuickStart* (Que Corporation). For a more in-depth discussion of these subjects, refer to *Using MS-DOS 5* (Que Corporation).

In Lesson 8, you continue to learn basic DOS principles by exploring the basic concepts of files.

Lesson 8

File Basics

As a file folder in a file cabinet contains related information, a *file* is a collection of similar data items that are stored together on disk. Understanding files is essential to understanding DOS—and computers in general—because you work with files more than anything else.

This lesson picks up where Lesson 7 left off in presenting concepts that are basic to your understanding of DOS. In this lesson, you learn how to do the following:

- Display the contents of a file
- Use wild-card characters
- Use the CHKDSK (Check Disk) command
- Name files

What you need to complete this lesson: The following lesson files, which were installed with the disk tutor: ANSWERS.TXT, COMMANDS.TXT, CONTENTS.TXT, DOSERROR.TXT, GLOSSARY.TXT, and MESSAGE.TXT

Estimated time to complete this lesson: 20-25 minutes

Displaying the Contents of a File

After you build a list of files on a particular disk, you may want to display the contents of one or more files in the directory. DOS enables you to display the contents of text files without changing to another program, such as a word processor.

Another occasion for displaying text files is displaying text files that are included with software packages. A text file named README.TXT, for example, is included with DOS 5. This text file (TXT) contains additional information that was not included in the printed manual that came with DOS. TXT files always indicate files that you can display easily with the TYPE command.

Files with a DOC (for document) extension are also text files that you can view from DOS. DOC files often are found on disks containing shareware and public domain programs, which you can get from many shareware distributors and electronic bulletin board systems. Some word processors, such as Microsoft Word, also automatically assign this extension to files.

Another type of text file you may see on occasion is a READ.ME file, or even clever ones such as README.1ST and README.NOW. You learn more about file names and extensions in "Assigning File Names," later in this lesson.

Displaying a File in the Shell

You'll learn more about file names and extensions a little later, but for now you'll view a text file in the Shell. Follow these steps:

1. Start the Shell, if it is not already running, and make sure that you are logged onto drive C by clicking on the C: icon or by highlighting C: with the Tab key and pressing Enter. If the disk tutor was installed to a drive other than C, substitute that drive letter.
2. Click on the ATI50 subdirectory or highlight it with the arrow keys.
3. Click on the box next to ATI50 or highlight it and press the + key.
4. Click on the SUB1 directory under ATI50 or highlight it with the arrow keys.
5. Now click on the file MESSAGE.TXT or highlight it with the arrow keys.

6. Click on File and then on View File Contents. Or, just press F9 as a shortcut.

   The personal message from the author in figure 8.1 should appear:

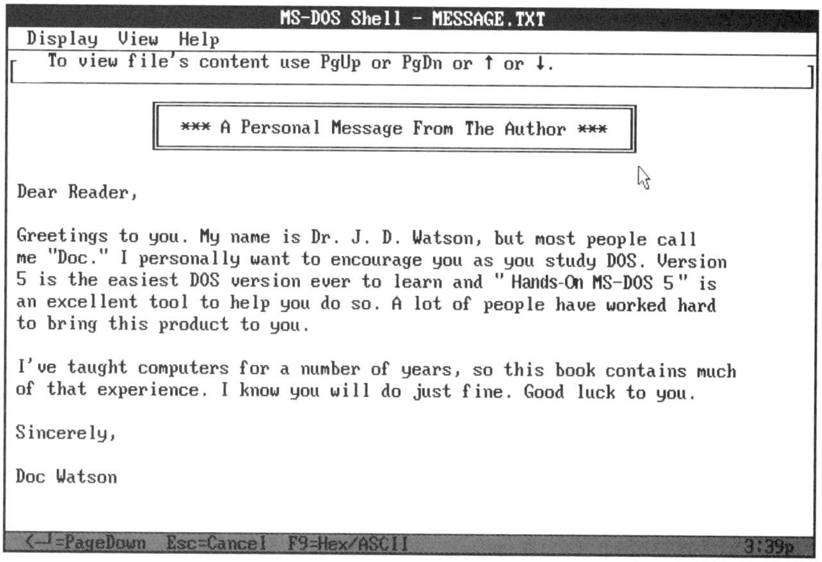

Fig. 8.1. A MESSAGE.TXT file displayed in the Shell file viewer.

7. Press Esc to exit the viewer, highlight the CONTENTS.TXT file, and press F9.

   This text file contains more than one screenful of information. The Shell makes provision for this by enabling you to use the up- and down-arrow keys, as well as the PgUp and PgDn keys to browse through the file.

8. Press Esc to exit the viewer.

Displaying a File from the DOS Prompt

DOS also provides a way of viewing text files directly from the DOS prompt by using the TYPE command. Follow these steps:

1. If you are in the Shell, exit it temporarily by pressing Shift-F9 or permanently by pressing F3.

As described in Lesson 7, you also can issue the TYPE command directly from the Shell by choosing Run from the File menu and typing the command in the dialog box that appears.

2. Type **TYPE C:\ATI50\SUB1\MESSAGE.TXT**.

> If you installed the disk tutor on a drive other than drive C—such as drive D, E, or any other drive—then substitute that drive for C.

Be sure to leave a space between the command (TYPE) and the drive name, but leave no spaces between the colon and the file name. Also, be sure to specify the file's extension (TXT) along with the root name (MESSAGE), if the file has an extension. If you do not type the file name exactly as it is listed in the directory, DOS displays the error message

```
File not found
```

C:\ATI50\SUB1\MESSAGE.TXT is the full *path name* that leads to the text file MESSAGE.TXT. The path name tells DOS precisely where to find the file you want. An alternate way to display the file is to go first to the correct subdirectory by typing **CD\ATI50\SUB1** and pressing Enter, and then type **TYPE MESSAGE.TXT**.

3. Press Enter. The personal message from the author shown in figure 8.2 should appear.

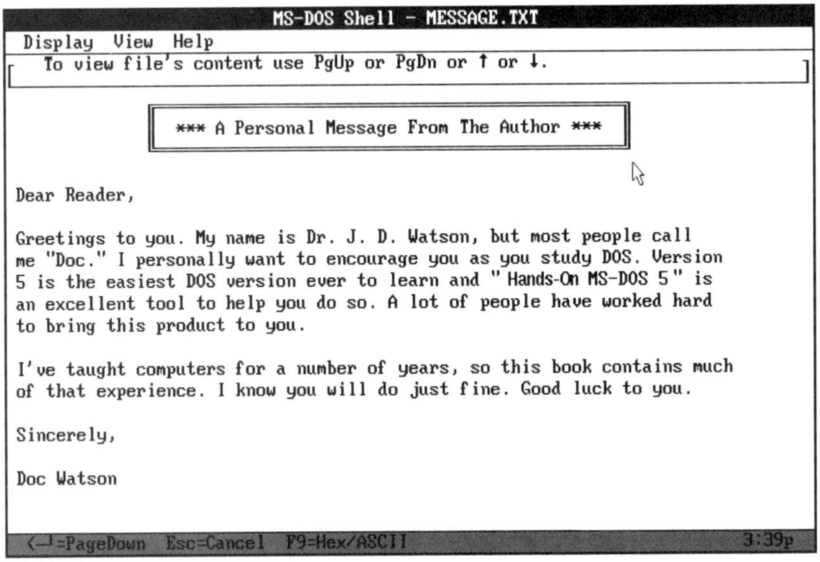

Fig. 8.2. The MESSAGE.TXT file displayed using the TYPE command.

This file is small enough to fit on one screen. Files that are larger than one screen, however, scroll off the screen like a directory listing does with the DIR command. Again, DOS enables you to stop the scrolling.

4. Type **TYPE C:\ATI50\SUB1\CONTENTS.TXT**.

   Again, you also can first go to the correct subdirectory by typing **CD\ATI50\SUB1** and pressing Enter, and then typing **TYPE CONTENTS.TXT**.

   This text file contains the basic contents of this book; it also contains more than one screen of information. So, just as you did with the DIR command, you can use Ctrl-S or the Pause key to pause the scrolling.

5. Press Enter and quickly press Ctrl-S or the Pause key to freeze the screen.

   An alternative similar to the /P switch in the DIR command is the MORE command, which pauses the display with each screenful of information. To see how this command works, first type **TYPE C:\ATI50\SUB1\CONTENTS.TXT | MORE** and press Enter.

   With each full screen, the display pauses and the message

   ```
   — More —
   ```

   appears at the bottom of your monitor.

6. Press any key when you want to start the scrolling; then press Ctrl-S or Pause to freeze the screen again. Continue until you have viewed the entire file.

> A handy way to stop the scrolling is to press and hold down the Ctrl key and then just keep pressing S to stop and start scrolling. You can think of the S as an on/off switch.

7. Repeat steps 4 through 6 until you are proficient.

8. Now type **TYPE C:\DOS\FORMAT.COM** and press Enter.

   Don't be alarmed by what you see on-screen. You have just asked DOS to display a program file. This information looks like nonsense with a few recognizable words thrown in here and there. Thus, as you can see, the TYPE command is most useful with text files.

9. To return to the Shell, type **EXIT** at the DOS prompt and press Enter (if you exited temporarily with Shift-F9), or type **DOSSHELL** and press Enter (if you exited permanently with F3).

Remember that you can issue the TYPE command or any other DOS command from the Shell by choosing the Run command from the File menu and typing the command in the Run dialog box.

Using the CHKDSK Command

Suppose that you want to check the amount of space remaining on a disk, but you don't need the list of files that the DIR command provides. Like the FORMAT command, the CHKDSK (Check Disk) command reports disk storage space and provides the following useful information:

- Volume name and creation date
- Volume serial number
- Total disk space
- Number of bytes used for hidden or system files
- Number of bytes used for directories
- Number of bytes for user files
- Bytes used by bad sectors (if the disk is flawed)
- Bytes available for use (free space)
- Bytes in each allocated unit (each sector)
- Total allocated units (sectors) on disk
- Available allocated units (sectors) on disk
- Bytes of total memory (RAM)
- Bytes of free memory

To issue the CHKDSK command, follow these steps:

1. Exit the Shell temporarily by pressing Shift-F9 or permanently by pressing F3.
2. Type **CHKDSK** and press Enter.

   Because you have not specified a drive, CHKDSK runs on drive C. The number of bytes differs depending on your computer, but information similar to that in figure 8.3 appears.

   After you examine the information, run the CHKDSK command on another drive, as follows.

```
C:\DOS>CHKDSK

Volume PILGRIM I   created 05-03-1991 10:17a
Volume Serial Number is 175F-3553

  33419264 bytes total disk space
     73728 bytes in 2 hidden files
     88064 bytes in 34 directories
  23130112 bytes in 1126 user files
  10127360 bytes available on disk

      2048 bytes in each allocation unit
     16318 total allocation units on disk
      4945 available allocation units on disk

    655360 total bytes memory
    465712 bytes free

C:\DOS>
```

Fig. 8.3. Issuing the CHKDSK command.

3. Insert Practice Disk 1 into drive A and close the drive door.
4. Type **CHKDSK A:** and press Enter.
5. To return to the Shell, type **EXIT** at the DOS prompt and press Enter (if you exited temporarily using Shift-F9), or type **DOSSHELL** and press Enter (if you exited permanently using F3).

Two switches, /F and /V, are available with the CHKDSK command, but they are beyond the scope of this lesson. You do not need the /F switch unless you encounter the following message when running CHKDSK:

```
Errors found, F parameter not specified
Corrections will not be written to disk
```

Appendix C provides additional information about this message. It also describes the very practical use of the /V switch.

Using Wild-Card Characters

When you examine disk directories, you may notice certain similarities among file names. A group of file names may have the same extension, such as EXE, COM, BAT, or 91, for example. Or, a group of files may have similar root names, such as SALES88, SALES89, SALES90, SALES91, and so on.

DOS enables you to work with groups of similar files simultaneously. To use this feature, you must know how to use *wild-card characters*. Just as wild cards are used in many card games to match any other card, DOS uses wild-card characters to represent one or multiple characters. When you specify a file name that includes these special characters, the file name may match more than one file on the disk.

The two wild-card characters that DOS accepts are the question mark (?) and the asterisk (*). DOS interprets the question mark to mean *match any one character in the file name*. DOS interprets the asterisk to mean *match any number of characters in the file name*. The ? and * match places where characters are not specified in a file name. You also can use combinations of ? and *. Table 8.1 illustrates how to specify file names using wild cards and table 8.2 gives examples of wild cards used with the DIR command.

Table 8.1. Wild Cards in the DIR Command

Wild Card	Effect
?	Replaces any single character in a file specification.
*	Replaces every character from the asterisk to the end of the file name or extension.
.	Replaces every character in the root file name and every character in the extension. *.* selects all files in a directory.

If you want to perform an action on all your SALES files from the 1980s, for example, you can use the ? wild card: SALES8?. DOS then matches this ambiguous name with all files on the disk, displaying SALES80, SALES81, SALES82, and so on.

Suppose that you want to work with all files with the extension WK1. You can use the asterisk: *.WK1. DOS matches the asterisk with all files that have the WK1 extension.

Table 8.2. Wild-Card Examples

Specification	Effect
DIR MYFILE.123	Presents directory information for the file MYFILE.123.
DIR *.WK1	Lists each file in the directory with the extension WK1 (a Lotus 1-2-3 worksheet extension).
DIR C*.*	Lists every file with a file name beginning with the letter C.
DIR *.*	Lists all files in the directory.
DIR *.	Lists all files in the directory that have no extension.
DIR ???.BAT	Lists all three-letter file names with a BAT extension.
DIR MYFILE.???	Lists all files named MYFILE that have three-letter extensions.

To practice using these wild-card characters with the DIR command, follow these steps:

1. Exit the Shell temporarily by pressing Shift-F9 or permanently by pressing F3.
2. Change to the DOS subdirectory by typing **CD\DOS** and pressing Enter.
3. Type **DIR *.COM/P** and press Enter.

   In this statement, you are asking for a directory of C:\DOS; you want to see all files that have the COM extension. Your screen should resemble figure 8.4.

   Notice that the /P switch is used because the display does not fit on one screen. Of course, you can use the DIR *.COM/W command to see a wide display of all the COM files.
4. Press any key to continue the listing.
5. Now type **DIR ???.*** and press Enter.

   This command displays only those files with file names of three characters or fewer. Your screen should look like figure 8.5.

```
 Volume in drive C is PILGRIM I
 Volume Serial Number is 175F-3553
 Directory of C:\DOS

FORMAT   COM     32911 04-09-91   5:00a
KEYB     COM     14986 04-09-91   5:00a
MODE     COM     23537 04-09-91   5:00a
DOSKEY   COM      5883 04-09-91   5:00a
MIRROR   COM     18169 04-09-91   5:00a
SYS      COM     13440 04-09-91   5:00a
UNFORMAT COM     18576 04-09-91   5:00a
DOSSHELL COM      4623 04-09-91   5:00a
EDIT     COM       413 04-09-91   5:00a
MSHERC   COM      6934 04-09-91   5:00a
DISKCOMP COM     10652 04-09-91   5:00a
DISKCOPY COM     11793 04-09-91   5:00a
MORE     COM      2618 04-09-91   5:00a
ASSIGN   COM      6399 04-09-91   5:00a
GRAFTABL COM     11205 04-09-91   5:00a
GRAPHICS COM     19694 04-09-91   5:00a
TREE     COM      6901 04-09-91   5:00a
LOADFIX  COM      1131 04-09-91   5:00a
MMOUSE   COM     14668 08-01-88  12:00a
Press any key to continue . . .
```

*Fig. 8.4. Using the * wild card with DIR to find COM files.*

```
C:\DOS>DIR ???.*

 Volume in drive C is A
 Volume Serial Number is 175F-3553
 Directory of C:\DOS

.            <DIR>     05-03-91  10:37a
..           <DIR>     05-03-91  10:37a
TP           <DIR>     07-25-91  10:23p
EGA      SYS      4885 04-09-91   5:00a
EGA      CPI     58873 04-09-91   5:00a
MEM      EXE     39818 04-09-91   5:00a
SYS      COM     13440 04-09-91   5:00a
FC       EXE     18650 04-09-91   5:00a
LCD      CPI     10753 04-09-91   5:00a
RED                  5 07-29-91   7:57a
M        BAT        25 10-05-91   9:05a
M        EXE      2590 10-05-91   9:07a
       12 file(s)     149039 bytes
                     4569088 bytes free

C:\DOS>
```

*Fig. 8.5. Using the ? and * wild cards.*

If you do not specify a file extension, DOS uses * to match all extensions. In step 5, for example, you can just type **DIR ???**. As another example, typing **DIR DOSSHELL** lists the six files used by the DOSSHELL program.

Remember that you can issue the DIR command or any other DOS command from the Shell by choosing the Run command from the File menu and typing the command (**C:\DOS*.COM/P**, for example) in the Run dialog box. If you already are logged on to the DOS subdirectory, you can use the same command given in step 3.

6. To return to the Shell, type **EXIT** at the DOS prompt and press Enter (if you exited temporarily with Shift-F9). Or, type **DOSSHELL** and press Enter (if you exited permanently with F3).

Even though the Shell is good for tagging files, as you learned in Lesson 5, the wild cards still can be handy for quick searches even when working in the Shell. Also, as you can imagine, this wild-card feature can be enormously useful when you want to manipulate more than one file at once.

Wild-card characters can be dangerous when used with certain commands, such as the ERASE command. In the lessons that follow, you learn more about wild-card characters and how to use them cautiously with other commands.

Assigning File Names

This section gets to the heart of what files are all about. As noted at the beginning of the lesson, a *file* is a collection of similar data items. Like a file folder in a file cabinet, a file on a disk contains information about a particular subject, such as names and addresses of clients, financial information, inventory records, or correspondence. Just as files in a file cabinet are labeled and arranged to help you find information easily, files on your computer disks and the information within them can be organized for maximum efficiency.

The key to any filing system is the person in charge of the filing system—in this case, the person entering data onto the disks. You have complete control over the way information is arranged on your disks and how easily that information can be accessed. Careful and correct naming can help you organize and retrieve information efficiently. If you name your files well, the file names will cue you about the type of information contained in each file.

When you create a new file, you give it a name. A file name has two parts:

- A root name, called the *file name*
- A suffix, called the *extension*

A file name can contain from one to eight characters, and the extension can contain from one to three characters. The file name is separated from the extension by a period (.) The period is used only as a separator and is not part of the file name. *Legal* characters (those DOS allows) for file names include the following:

A-Z a-z 0-9 $ # & @ ! ( ) - { } ' ` _ ~

Illegal characters (those DOS does not allow) follow:

[space] + = / [ ] " : ; ? * < > | \ . ,

Notice that the characters ? and * are illegal. As you learned in the preceding section, DOS reserves these characters as wild-card characters. Notice also that the colon (:) is illegal. Whenever DOS sees a colon, it looks for a disk drive, as you learned in Lesson 7.

Consider the following file name stored in the DOS subdirectory:

COMMAND.COM

The first part of the name, COMMAND, is the file name; the second part of the name, COM, is the extension. A period separates the extension from the file name.

> Each file stored on a disk must have a unique name. If you assign the same name to two different files, DOS does not recognize the difference and replaces the previously stored information with the information in the new file.

If you assign a file name longer than eight characters, DOS stores only the first eight characters. If you create two files containing the sales figures from two different years, for example, you may want to name the files PROFITS90 and PROFITS91. These names, however, exceed the eight-character limit for a file name, and if you try to use both as file names on the same disk, you will lose one of the files completely. When you create the first file, PROFITS90, DOS records only the first eight characters (PROFITS9) as the file name. Then, when you create and try to store the file PROFITS91, DOS reads this file name as PROFITS9 and assumes it is a new version of the old PROFITS9. DOS then writes the 1991 information over the 1990 information, completely wiping it out.

You therefore need to be very careful when naming files. If you use eight characters assigned to a previously stored file, you lose the information in the existing file. In this example, the file names can be shortened to PROFIT90 and PROFIT91, or the years can be used as extensions: PROFITS.90 and PROFITS.91.

Fortunately, many applications programs—such as word processors and spreadsheets, and even DOS 5's text editor—display a warning if you attempt to create a second file with a file name that already exists on disk.

Note that an extension is not always required, but it is often useful for distinguishing files. If you choose not to use an extension, you do not need the period. If you choose to use an extension, use one that helps you identify the file.

Table 8.3 gives some common file name extensions. Except for ASC, BAT, DOC, LET, and TXT, however, you should avoid these extensions because they have special meanings or often are generated by DOS or other programs.

Examine the following valid file names. Each file name is phrased correctly and uses legal characters. Notice, however, that although the file names are valid, some are not very descriptive.

$#&@!&().~~~	HALPERN.LET
01234567.890	REQUEST.1
1983.DAT	REQUEST.2
CHAPTER1	SALES84.$
IDEAS	WORKBOOK.TXT
INFO.BAK	ZZZZZ.ZZZ

The importance of using meaningful file names cannot be overemphasized. You may choose to use the LTR extension for letters, the MEM extension for memos, or the RPT extension for reports. Whatever file names and extensions you use, make sure that they describe the contents of the files as much as possible.

Table 8.3. File Extensions

Extension	Meaning
$$$	Temporary or incorrectly stored file
ASC	ASCII text file
ASM	Assembly language source code
BAK	Backup file
BAS	BASIC program file
BAT	Batch file
BIN	Binary file
C	C Source file
COM	Command file
DAT	Data file
DBF	dBASE II, III, III+ and IV
DIF	Data interchange file
DOC	Document or documentation file
EXE	Executable file
HLP	Help file
INI	Start-up files used in Windows 3.0
LET	Letter file
LIB	Program library file
LST	Listing of a program in a file
PAS	Pascal configuration file
SYS	System or device driver file
TMP	Temporary file
TXT	Text file
WK1	Lotus 1-2-3 Release 2.01 and 2.2
WKS	Lotus 1-2-3

Guidelines for Creating File Names

- A file name consists of a root containing one to eight characters, an optional extension (suffix) of one to three characters, and a period between the file name and extension.
- You can use the following legal characters in a file name:

  A-Z a-z 0-9 $ # & @ ! ( ) - { } ' ` _ ~
- You cannot use the following illegal characters in a file name:

  [space] + = / [ ] " : ; ? * < > | \ . ,
- Each file name in a directory must be unique.
- File names and extensions should describe the contents of the file as much as possible.
- A drive name and path name (the position on the disk, discussed in Lessons 5 and 12) often precede a file name (for example, C:\DOS\FORMAT.COM).

Lesson Summary

- To display the contents of a file, issue the TYPE command followed by the exact name of the file you want to display (for example, TYPE MYFILE.1). If you do not type the file name exactly as it appears in the directory, DOS displays the message

  ```
  File not found
  ```

  Alternatively, you can use the File/View command from the Shell.
- You can use the CHKDSK command to get certain information about your disk without obtaining a directory listing. Use CHKDSK, for example, to find out how much storage space is left on a disk.
- The ? wild card tells DOS to match any one character in the file name; the * wild card tells DOS to match any number of characters in the file name.
- A file name has three parts: a root name of one to eight characters, an optional extension of one to three characters, and a period between the file name and the extension.
- Each file stored on the same disk must have a unique name. Assigning descriptive names to your files helps you remember the contents of the files.

Key Terms

CHKDSK	Reports disk storage space and other disk information.
Extension	Optional suffix of one to three characters that helps identify a file more precisely.
File	A collection of similar data items stored together on disk.
File name	A one- to eight-character string that identifies a file. A file must have a file name.
Illegal character	A character that *cannot* be used in a file name or extension.
Legal character	A character that *can* be used in a file name or extension.
TYPE	Displays the contents of a text file.
Wild-card character	Character DOS uses to represent one or multiple characters.

Exercises

Naming your files is one of the most important aspects of using your computer. Follow these steps to develop expertise in assigning names to your files:

1. The following is a list of possible names you can assign to new files. Identify which names are valid and which are invalid. Explain why the invalid file names are incorrect and how DOS would interpret them. (See "Assigning File Names.")

File Name	**Validity (Yes/No)**	**Explanation**
NEW FILE.DOC	________	______________________________
STAFF.MEMO	________	______________________________
.TXT	________	______________________________
DEB.#1	________	______________________________
MS-DOSPCT.CH8	________	______________________________
?4CHRIS	________	______________________________

SALESVOL.BAK	________	______________________________
#83-1542	________	______________________________
$5000+.DAT	________	______________________________
GRADES.89	________	______________________________
B	________	______________________________
25,000.$	________	______________________________
Data[91].WK1	________	______________________________
FUN&GAME.S!!	________	______________________________
MY\FILE.DIR	________	______________________________
DO-TODAY.*	________	______________________________

2. To check your answers, use the Shell's File/View command to view the ANSWERS.TXT file in the ATI50\SUB1 directory (see "Displaying a File in the Shell").

   If you prefer to work from the DOS prompt, use the type command (**TYPE C:\ATI50\SUB1\ANSWERS.TXT | MORE**). If you installed the disk tutor to a drive other than C, substitute that drive letter in the command. (See "Displaying a File from the DOS Prompt.")

3. Now display the following files that were included with *Hands-On MS-DOS 5*:

   C:\ATI50\SUB1\COMMANDS.TXT (Appendix A)
   C:\ATI50\SUB1\GLOSSARY.TXT (Appendix B)
   C:\ATI50\SUB1\DOSERROR.TXT (Appendix C)

These files are the actual text files used to create the listed appendixes. You can use these as a handy reference on your computer. Just issue the TYPE command or use the File/View command in the Shell when you want to look up information from one of these files.

In Lesson 9, you learn about one of DOS's greatest capabilities—making exact copies of entire disks.

Lesson 9

Copying and Comparing Disks

One of DOS's most important features is its capability to copy files. Using the DISKCOPY and COPY commands, you can make backup copies of entire disks, individual files, and combinations of files.

Copying is very important because it provides you with backup copies in case the original becomes damaged or lost. Making backup copies of your disks regularly can save you many hours of work as well as money. If, for example, your DOS system disk is destroyed and you have not made a backup copy, your only option is to purchase another disk.

In this lesson, you learn how to do the following:

- Copy a diskette
- Compare two diskettes
- Cancel a DOS program

What you need to complete this lesson: A 360K or 720K blank disk

Estimated time to complete this lesson: 25-30 minutes

Copying a Diskette with Disk Copy

Whether you are a new or experienced DOS user, you need to make backup copies of your DOS disks, any software that you purchase, and disks on which you store important files.

> Some commercial programs are copy-protected, so you have no choice but to use the original disks. Although copy-protected software is rarely found in today's market, you still may encounter copy-protected programs.

Just as a photocopy machine makes an exact paper copy of a document, the Disk Copy command makes an exact copy of a disk, track by track, sector by sector.

The Disk Copy command requires that *the source and destination disks be the same size and capacity*, however. If, for example, you have a 1.2M (or 1.44M) disk drive and therefore own only 1.2M (or 1.44M) disks, you need to acquire a blank disk with a capacity of 360K (or 720K) in order to follow along with the exercises in this lesson.

Even though Disk Copy automatically formats a disk if it is not already formatted, formatting disks before issuing the Disk Copy command enables you to determine whether a disk contains any bad sectors (in which case you should not use the disk). Running CHKDSK on the disk you want to copy to make sure it has no bad sectors is also a good idea because Disk Copy makes an exact copy of the disk; if the disk you are copying from or the one you are copying to contains bad sectors, Disk Copy may not work properly.

As Lesson 10 explains, using the COPY command is the preferred method for copying files, because it is more efficient and reliable if there are any bad sectors on the disks being used. Disk Copy, however, is faster if the source diskette is full of data.

> Disk Copy is a potentially dangerous DOS command. Because it copies one disk to another, it wipes out any data on the destination disk. Before issuing Disk Copy, use the DIR command to make sure the target disk contains no files that you want to keep.

First you learn how to make a copy of a disk using the Shell and then how to accomplish the same task from the DOS command line. After making copies, store the original diskettes in a vertical or flat position in a sturdy container away from strong magnetic fields and extreme temperatures. If the copy is damaged or wears out, you still have the original, from which you can make another copy. (A diskette's life span, or *spin life*, is approximately 1,000 hours, in contrast to a hard disk's spin life, which is about 50,000 hours.)

Copying a Disk from the Shell

The capability of copying a disk from the Shell is another one of the built-in features of the Shell. You access the Disk Copy command through the Disk Utilities group in the Program List area. Follow these steps:

1. Start the Shell if it is not already running.
2. Make sure that you have the tutor disk that came with this book and a blank, formatted disk. Even though Disk Copy formats a disk, you should use a formatted disk that has no bad sectors.

> Make sure that any master disks such as the disk tutor disk or disks containing other software packages have a *write-protect label* (one of the special small labels that come with a box of disks) over the notch on the outside edge of your disk. If you are using a 3 1/2-inch microfloppy disk, turn the disk over and slide the small notch in the upper left corner to expose the opening for write-protection. Write-protection prevents you from changing or writing to your master disks.

3. Double-click Disk Utilities in the Main Program List area or press Tab to activate the area, highlight Disk Utilities with the arrow keys, and press Enter.
4. Double-click Disk Copy, or highlight Disk Copy with the arrow keys and press Enter. The Disk Copy dialog box appears (see fig. 9.1).

   Notice that the default parameters shown in figure 9.1 are drives A and B. These parameters may not be appropriate for your computer.

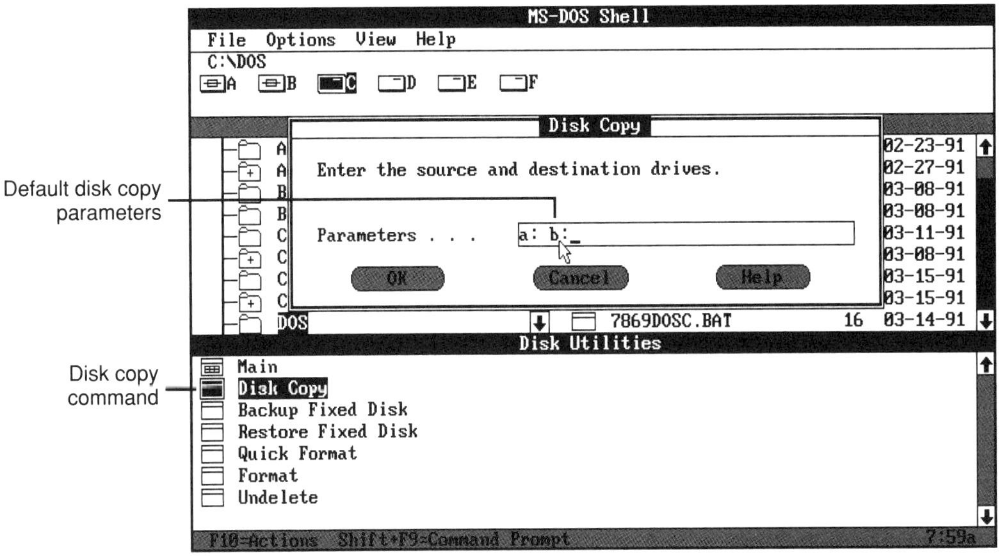

Fig. 9.1. The Disk Copy dialog box.

5. Type the parameters that are correct for your computer. You have three choices:

   - If you have only one floppy disk drive, which is often the case with a hard disk, then you can accept the default parameters or type **A: A:**. DOS prompts you when to put in the original disk and when to replace it with a blank disk, as you will see in a moment.

   - If you have two floppy drives that are the same size and capacity, you can use the default a: and b: parameters. In this case, you insert the original disk into drive A and the blank disk into drive B.

   - If drives A and B are different sizes and/or capacities, you must type **A: A:** or **B: B:**. For example, many computers today have two floppy drives: one 5 1/4-inch, 1.2M drive and one 3 1/2-inch, 1.44M drive. Because you cannot use the Disk Copy command to copy one disk to the other, you must decide which drive to use. Disk Copy then prompts you when to insert the original disk and when to replace it with a blank disk.

   This example gives instructions for copying the disk tutor master (a 5 1/4-inch, 360K disk) in drive A, so you need to have a blank 360K disk. The parameter line in the dialog box should therefore be a: a:.

> If you have only a 3 1/2-inch disk drive, you can use the form in the back of this book to get a 3 1/2-inch disk to use with this book. This disk will be a 720K disk, so you will need to get a blank 720K disk for this procedure.

6. When you are sure the parameters are correct, press Enter or click OK. DOS responds with the following message:

   ```
   Insert SOURCE diskette in drive A:
   Press any key to continue...
   ```

7. Place the disk you want to copy (the *source* disk) into drive A and press any key. The disk drive light comes on and DOS responds as follows:

   ```
   Copying 40 tracks
   9 sectors per track, 2 side(s)
   ```

   If you are copying a 720K disk, the message is the same, except `80 tracks` is substituted for `40 tracks`.

   Similarly, if you were copying a 1.2M disk, the sectors would read `15`; if you were copying a 1.44M disk, the sectors would read `18`.

   After a few seconds, DOS displays the following message:

   ```
   Insert TARGET diskette in drive A:
   Press any key to continue...
   ```

8. Remove the source disk; place the blank, formatted disk (the *target* disk) into drive A and press any key.

   DOS usually copies the entire disk in one pass. On computers with a small amount of memory, however, the messages may reappear. If they do, insert the disks as prompted and press any key.

   If you are copying a 720K disk, DOS asks for the source and target a second time. Similarly, if you copy a 1.2M or 1.44M floppy, DOS asks you for the source and target disks a second and third time because these larger capacity disks contain too much information for DOS to copy the entire disk in one pass. The messages are the same, but they indicate different track and sector values.

> If you choose to have Disk Copy format your disk, you also see the message
>
> ```
> Formatting while copying
> ```
>
> Disk Copy formats the disk and displays the volume serial number before proceeding with the copying.

When done, Disk Copy displays the following message:

```
Copy another diskette (Y/N)?
```

9. Press N; then press any key to return to the Shell.

   If you want to make another copy of the same disk or copy another source disk, press Y and repeat the process.

10. Remove the copy from drive A and label the disk.

    Take one of the blank labels that came with your disks and write *Hands-On MS-DOS 5 Disk* on the label. Place the label on an upper corner of the disk (opposite the permanent label, if one exists) for easy identification.

> If you are working with a 5 1/4-inch disk, use a felt-tip pen (never a ball-point pen or pencil) if you write on the label after putting it on the disk. As you press down, a ball-point pen or a pencil may damage the disk.

11. Set both disks aside for use later in this lesson.

Copying a Disk from the DOS Prompt

Copying a disk from the DOS prompt is exactly like copying a disk from the Shell; you use the same command, but you type it manually on the command line. Much of the procedure that follows is a review of what you have already learned. Follow these steps:

1. Exit the Shell temporarily by pressing Shift-F9 or permanently by pressing F3.
2. Take out the tutor disk that came with this book and a blank, formatted disk. (Follow the guidelines given in step 2 of the "Copying a Disk from the Shell" procedure.)

3. At the command prompt (C:\>, for example), type **DISKCOPY** followed by the correct parameters for your computer. Refer to step 5 of the "Copying a Disk from the Shell" procedure for the correct disk drive(s) to enter as parameters.
4. Follow steps 6, 7, and 8 from the Shell procedure.
5. When the copying procedure is complete, press N to exit the Disk Copy program.

   If you want to make another copy of the same disk or copy another source disk, press Y and repeat the process.
6. If you have followed the Shell procedure for copying this disk, you need not label this copy. Just quickly format it, as you learned in Lesson 6, and reuse it.
7. Set both disks aside for use later in this lesson.
8. To return to the Shell, type **EXIT** at the DOS prompt and press Enter (if you exited temporarily with Shift-F9), or type **DOSSHELL** and press Enter (if you exited permanently with F3).

> If you accidentally insert a disk that contains files in the drive as the target disk, the source disk is copied to the target disk—right over the existing files. All the information you had on that disk is wiped out. To keep this from happening, make sure that all your disks are labeled and that disks you don't want erased are write-protected.

Using the /V Switch with DISKCOPY

In the next section, you learn how to use DISKCOMP, which compares two disks to see if they are identical. But instead of using a separate command, you can use the /V switch with DISKCOPY to verify the target disk as it is being copied.

Whether you are working in the Shell or from the DOS prompt, you need only add the /V switch to the end of the command—for example, type the following:

DISKCOPY A: A: /V

The procedure will be the same as in the previous two sections, except that you will be prompted one or more additional times (depending on the capacity of the disks) to insert the disks into the drive.

The advantage of the /V switch over DISKCOMP is that /V operates while the copying process is going on and is therefore faster than DISKCOMP. The disadvantage of the /V switch is that it slows down the DISKCOPY process.

Comparing Two Diskettes

The DOS command DISKCOMP compares the contents of two compatible diskettes, track by track. You can use DISKCOMP to compare two diskettes to make sure that they are identical, whether or not you used the /V switch with DISKCOPY. If you use /V with DISKCOPY, you probably don't need to use DISKCOMP, but if you have any doubts about your important data, it's better to be safe than sorry. If you have crucial data disks that you have created or master disks that came with a software program, you may want to use DISKCOMP after using DISKCOPY.

DISKCOMP works the same way as DISKCOPY does, except that DISKCOMP does not copy. The following procedure compares the copy of the tutor disk with the master disk to make sure that the copy is an exact one. Follow these steps:

1. From the Shell, click File and then Run, or press Alt-F and then R to display the Run dialog box.

   Alternatively, you can exit the Shell and work from the command line.

2. Type **DISKCOMP** and the same parameters you used for the DISKCOPY procedure, such as **A: A:**.

3. Press Enter or click OK.

   Like DISKCOPY, DISKCOMP prompts you to insert the two disks. When the process is complete and the two disks are the same, your monitor displays a message similar to the message shown in figure 9.2. Depending on the number of mismatches, you may, of course, get more than one compare error.

   If, however, the disks are not exact, DISKCOMP displays a message similar to the one in figure 9.3.

4. Press N to exit the DISKCOMP program.

```
C:\DOS>DISKCOMP A: A:

Insert FIRST diskette in drive A:

Press any key to continue . . .

Comparing 40 tracks
9 sectors per track, 2 side(s)

Insert SECOND diskette in drive A:

Press any key to continue . . .

Compare OK

Compare another diskette (Y/N) ?
```

Disks are identical

Fig. 9.2. The DISKCOMP complete message.

```
C:\DOS>DISKCOMP A: A:

Insert FIRST diskette in drive A:

Press any key to continue . . .

Comparing 40 tracks
9 sectors per track, 2 side(s)

Insert SECOND diskette in drive A:

Press any key to continue . . .

Compare error on
side 0, track 0

Compare another diskette (Y/N) ?
```

Disks are not identical

Fig. 9.3. The DISKCOMP mismatch message.

If you get a mismatch, you need to run DISKCOPY again. Using a different blank disk the second time or reformatting the same one before trying again is a good idea.

Canceling a DOS Program

Suppose that you start the copying process with the Disk Copy command but decide to stop the program before it finishes running. You may need to stop this command for two reasons:

- You realize that you do not have the correct source disk in drive A.
- You realize that you are not using a blank disk as the target disk.

In the first part of this lesson, you learned how to copy disks, and you made a copy of your disk tutor master disk. In the next exercise, you learn how to get out of the Copy mode after issuing the command.

To experiment with copying errors and to stop the program, follow these steps:

1. Begin the Disk Copy procedure as you did before by repeating steps 3, 4, 5, and 6 of the procedure described in "Copying a Disk from the Shell."

   Alternatively, you can issue the command at the DOS command line.

   You see the message

   ```
   Press any key when ready...
   ```

2. Press Ctrl-C or Ctrl-Break.

   On-screen you see `^C`. Ctrl-C and Ctrl-Break tell DOS to stop the program and take control of the system. You know that DOS has taken over when you see the DOS prompt on-screen.

Ctrl-C and Ctrl-Break are "panic buttons." You can use them when things go drastically wrong, such as when you put the wrong disk in a drive, use the wrong file, or invoke the wrong command. These buttons interrupt any DOS command.

> Ctrl-C and Ctrl-Break also work on some programs other than DOS commands. If you get stuck in a program and cannot get out, try Ctrl-C or Ctrl-Break. Additionally, Ctrl-Break sometimes works when Ctrl-C does not.

If neither of these panic buttons works, you may have to reboot by pressing Ctrl-Alt-Del or by turning the computer off and then on again. Many computers have a reset button that acts like the off switch except that the computer isn't physically or manually turned off. This button saves wear on the switch and computer circuitry.

Never interrupt a command while it is writing to a disk unless it is absolutely necessary. Commands such as DISKCOPY and COPY physically write to the disk (see Lesson 10). Interrupting this process can damage the file allocation table and cause you to lose data (see Appendix D).

Lesson Summary

- Using the Disk Copy command, you can copy entire disks to make backup copies of important files.
- The Disk Copy process automatically formats a blank disk before DOS copies information from the source disk to the target disk. The Disk Copy process also destroys all the information on the target disk, so make sure you use a blank disk or one that contains information you no longer want.
- Using DISKCOMP, you can compare two disks to see whether they are identical. This command is most effective for comparing disks that have just undergone a Disk Copy procedure.
- Ctrl-Break and Ctrl-C (^C) are panic buttons that you can use to stop DOS commands and some other programs while they are running.

Key Terms

Ctrl-C (or Ctrl-Break)	Key combination that interrupts and cancels a DOS command
DISKCOPY	Makes an exact copy of a diskette
DISKCOMP	Compares two diskettes to see if they are exactly the same
Source disk	Disk that you want to copy
Spin life	Lifespan of a disk
Target disk	Disk you copy the source disk to

Exercises

To practice what you learned in this lesson, as well as accomplish a very important task, follow these steps:

1. Issue DISKCOPY and DISKCOMP to copy and compare the master disks that came with DOS 5. (See "Copying a Diskette with Disk Copy" and "Comparing Two Diskettes.") Be sure to label all disks properly.
2. Repeat the first exercise with other programs you own, such as WordPerfect or Lotus 1-2-3.

Back up all your applications programs in this way and keep the backup disks in a separate location. Back up all other important disks, such as data disks that you use with your application programs.

In Lesson 10, you learn more about DOS's copying capabilities by learning how to copy individual files.

Lesson 10

Copying Files

One of the most important and often performed tasks is copying individual files. You will do this many times every computing day. In the last lesson, you learned how to make a backup copy of an entire disk by using the DISKCOPY command. At times, however, you do not want to copy a disk, but only a few files on that disk. For example, you may want to reorganize your files by placing all related files together, with word processing on one disk, spreadsheets on another, and databases on still another. You can perform these operations by using the COPY command.

In this lesson, you learn how to do the following:

- Copy a file onto the same disk
- Copy a file onto another disk
- Use wild-card characters to copy several files

What you need to complete this lesson: Practice Disk 1

Estimated time to complete this lesson: 30-35 minutes

Copying Files in the Shell

A tremendously powerful feature of the Shell is its capability to copy files, either individually or in groups. The Shell enables you to easily control which files you want to copy and where you want to copy them.

Copying a Single File in the Shell

Copying a single file using the Shell involves merely selecting the file and choosing Copy from the File menu. Follow these steps:

1. Start the Shell if it is not already running.
2. Click on the DOS subdirectory in the Directory Tree. Or, press Tab to go to the Directory Tree area and use the arrow keys to highlight DOS.
3. Click on the COMMAND.COM file, or press Tab to activate the File List area and highlight the file with the arrow keys.
4. Click on File and then on Copy. Or, press F8 or Alt-F and then C.

   The Copy File dialog box appears (see fig. 10.1).

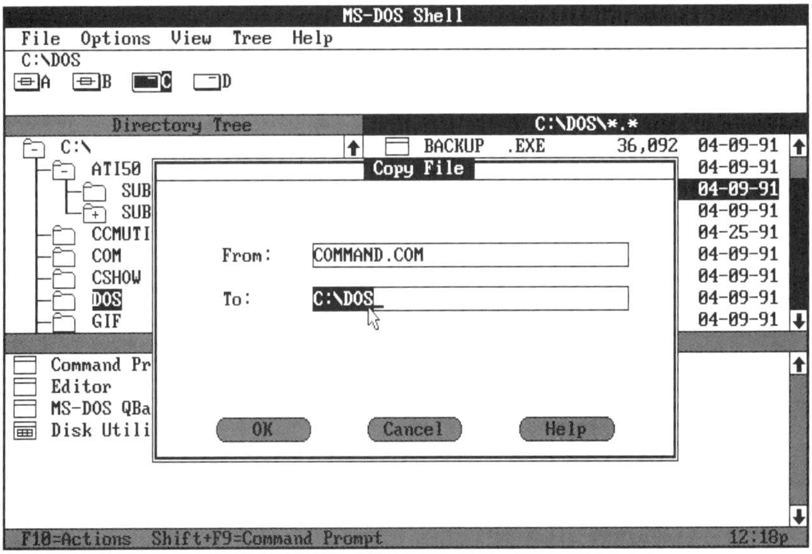

Fig. 10.1. The Copy File dialog box.

5. Press the Backspace key to erase the destination drive/directory (To:) and type **A:**. Insert Practice Disk 1 into drive A and press Enter or click OK.

   The drive light comes on and the selected file is copied onto the diskette.

   As you will learn later, one danger of copying files in DOS is that if the target file already exists on a disk, DOS overwrites that file with the file that you are copying to disk. The DOS Shell safeguards against this, however, by providing a Replace File Confirmation dialog box.

6. Repeat steps 4 and 5.

   Notice that after pressing Enter, the Replace File Confirmation box appears, as in figure 10.2.

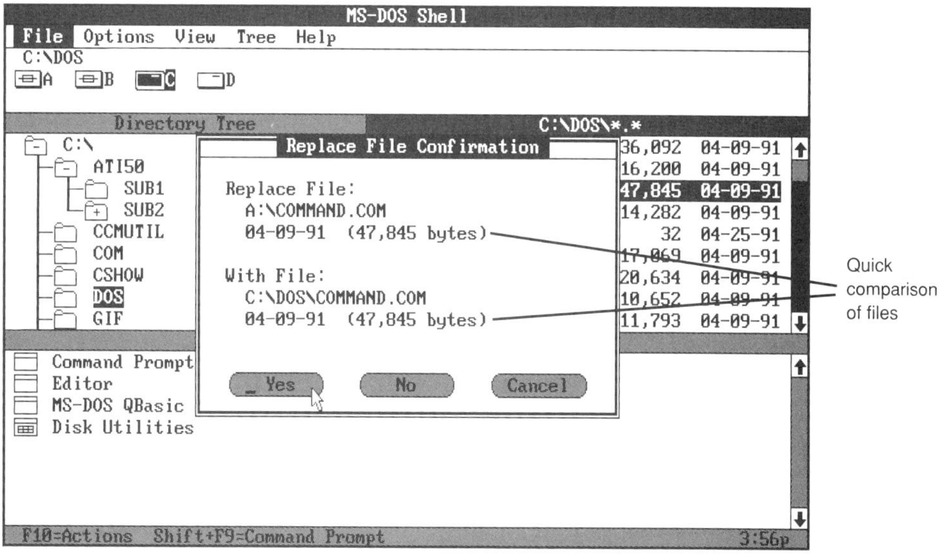

Fig. 10.2. The Replace File Confirmation box.

At this point, you are given a choice. If you want to replace the file that already exists on the disk, click on Yes or press Enter. If you do not want to replace the existing file, click on No or press Tab once and then Enter. For the experience, click on Yes or press Enter.

> A shortcut to canceling file replacement is to simply press the Esc key. You can use the Esc key at other times as a shortcut as well.

Copying Multiple Files in the Shell

As you learned in Lesson 5, one of the great strengths of the Shell is its ability to tag (mark) certain files, either in or out of sequence. By tagging files, you can perform actions on them as a group. For example, follow these steps to copy a group of files from your hard disk to a floppy disk:

1. Go to the DOS subdirectory.
2. Click on the file APPEND.EXE, or press Tab to activate the File List and highlight the file with the arrow keys.
3. Now tag the next five files by moving the mouse pointer to BACKUP.EXE, holding down the Shift key, and clicking the mouse. Or, hold down the Shift key and use the down arrow to highlight BACKUP.EXE. Release the Shift key to complete the tagging procedure.

   Remember: If you want to tag *all* files in a directory, just press Ctrl-/.
4. Press F8 to display the Copy File dialog box, press the Backspace key to erase the destination drive/directory (To:), type **A:**, and press Enter or click OK.

Notice the box that now appears. This lists the files as they are copied and counts them off (1 of 6, 2 of 6, and so on).

There will, of course, be times when you want to tag and copy files that are not in sequence.

To tag and copy files not in sequence, follow these steps:

1. Click on the DISKCOPY.COM file or highlight it with the arrow keys.
2. Hold down the Ctrl key and click on the file named DOSKEY.COM and then on the file DOSSHELL.EXE. Release the Ctrl key.

   If you are using the keyboard instead of the mouse, after choosing DISKCOPY.COM, press Shift-F8; notice that the word ADD appears in the bottom right corner of the screen beside the time display. Use the down arrow to go to DOSKEY.COM and press the space bar. Go to DOSSHELL.EXE and press the space bar again. Now press Shift-F8 again.
3. Copy the files to drive A by pressing F8.

Copying Files by Dragging the Mouse

If you have a mouse, there is another way to copy files that is even faster than tagging. This feature is called *dragging*. What this amounts to is "picking up" one or more files with the mouse and placing them where you want them to go. Follow these steps:

1. Go to the DOS subdirectory.
2. Press and hold down the Ctrl key.
3. Put the mouse pointer on the file MORE.COM and then press and hold down the left mouse button.
4. Now just drag (move) the pointer to the drive A icon.

   Notice how the symbol changes to a document symbol when you arrive at the icon. Also notice that the message

   ```
   Copy files to A:\
   ```

   appears in the lower left corner of the screen. This message would change if you placed the file on some other drive or directory.
5. Release the mouse button and then release the Ctrl key.

   The Confirm Mouse Operation dialog box now appears (see fig. 10.3).

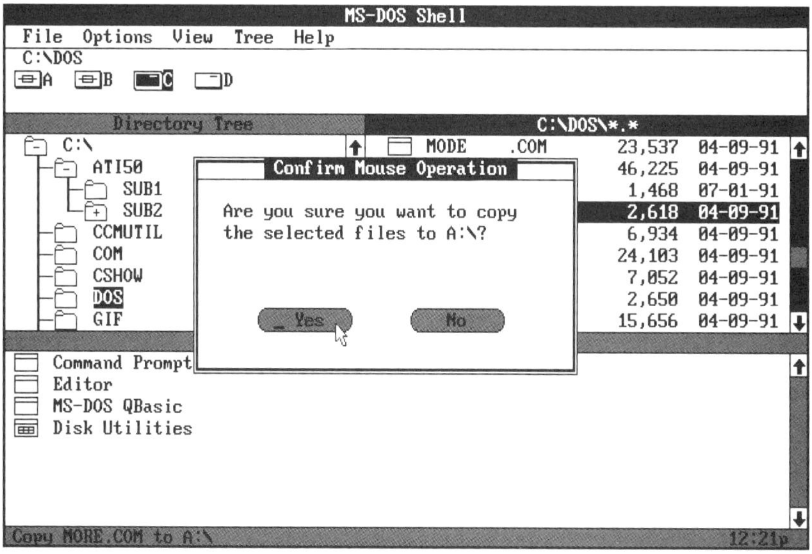

Fig. 10.3. The Confirm Mouse Operation dialog box.

6. Click the Yes button or press Enter to copy the file.

Always be sure the destination directory or drive icon is visible before you begin this operation. Naturally, you also can use this procedure to copy a group of files, as you learned earlier.

Viewing File Information

A powerful feature in the Shell is its ability to instantly display information about a file or even about a group of files. To illustrate this feature, follow these steps:

1. Repeat steps 1, 2, and 3 from the "Copying Multiple Files in the Shell" section.
2. Once the files are tagged, click on Options and then Show Information. Or, press Alt-O and S.

   The Show Information box appears (see fig. 10.4).

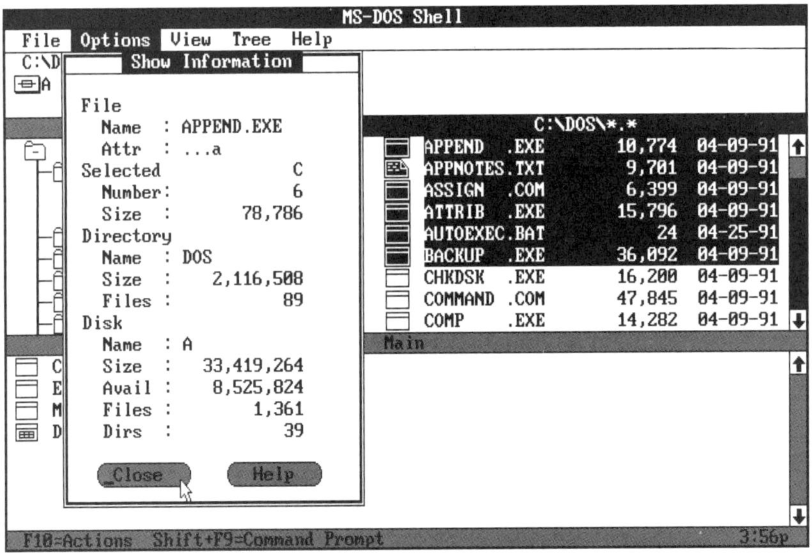

Fig. 10.4. The Show Information box.

This box contains a great deal of information. First, it shows the file name and the *attributes* of the selected file; you'll learn more about attributes in another lesson.

Second, the number of selected files and their total size is shown. This is extremely helpful, for example, when you want to see if a group of files on your hard disk will fit on one floppy disk.

Third, the name, size, and number of files in the selected directory is listed.

Fourth, the name and size of the disk, along with the number of files and directories on the disk is displayed, as well as the available space on the disk.

3. Press Esc and deselect the files by pressing Ctrl-\ (backslash).

Copying Files from the DOS Prompt

Copying files from the DOS prompt requires you to use the DOS command COPY, along with the correct parameters and/or switches. As mentioned in Lesson 9, using the COPY command is the preferred method for copying files, because it is more efficient and reliable if there are any bad sectors on the disks being used. COPY is also superior because it takes better advantage of disk space than DISKCOPY; while DISKCOPY places files on the target disk in exactly the same place they were on the source disk, COPY starts at the beginning of the disk and just fills the disk up with files. One other advantage of COPY is that it doesn't wipe out everything on the target disk, as does DISKCOPY; it adds each file to the disk without affecting the other files on the disk.

Copying a File onto the Same Disk

One use for the COPY command is to copy a file onto the same disk. Suppose that you want to use the CONTENTS.TXT file in the ATI50\SUB1 directory for taking a few notes on this book, but you also want to keep the CONTENTS.TXT file intact. You first have to make a copy of CONTENTS.TXT by using the COPY command. Because you are going to store the copy of the target file on the same disk as the source file (CONTENTS.TXT), you must assign a new name to the copy.

To perform this operation, follow these steps:

1. Exit the Shell temporarily by pressing Shift-F9 or permanently by pressing F3.

> ***Remember:*** You can issue the COPY command, or any other DOS command from the Shell by choosing the Run command from the File menu and typing the command in the Run dialog box.

2. Type **CD\ATI50\SUB1** and press Enter.

   If you installed the disk tutor on a drive other than C, you must log onto that drive first (D, for example) before issuing this command.

3. Type **DIR** and press Enter.

   Before performing a copy operation, you should make sure that

   - You are logged onto the correct drive and/or subdirectory.
   - You know the exact name of the source file.
   - You have enough space left on the disk for another file the same size as or larger than the source file.
   - You do not give the target file the same name as another file on the disk. (If you do, you will lose the contents of the existing file on the target disk.)

   The directory of the ATI50\SUB1 should look similar to the screen shown in figure 10.5.

   When you examine the directory, you can see that the source file (CONTENTS.TXT) is stored in the C:\ATI50\SUB1 subdirectory and that plenty of space remains for another file of the same size or larger. You also can check the new name you have chosen for the target file, CONTENTS.NTS, against the other file names in the directory.

4. Type **TYPE CONTENTS.TXT** and press Enter to display the contents of the source file. Make sure that this file contains the data that you want to copy.

5. Type **COPY CONTENTS.TXT CONTENTS.NTS**.

   This command tells DOS to make a copy of the file CONTENTS.TXT, stored on the disk in the C:\ATI50\SUB1 subdirectory, to name the copy CONTENTS.NTS, and to store the copy in the same subdirectory.

6. Press Enter.

   When the copy operation is complete, you receive the message

   ```
   1 File(s) copied
   ```

   and the DOS prompt returns to the screen.

7. Type **DIR** and press Enter.

   Once the copy operation is complete, check the directory to ensure that the new file name, CONTENTS.NTS, has been added to the directory.

8. Type **TYPE CONTENTS.NTS** and press Enter.

```
Microsoft(R) MS-DOS(R) Version 5.00
             (C)Copyright Microsoft Corp 1981-1991.

C:\ATI50\SUB1>DIR

 Volume in drive C is A
 Volume Serial Number is 175F-3553
 Directory of C:\ATI50\SUB1

.            <DIR>      06-26-91  12:58p
..           <DIR>      06-26-91  12:58p
MESSAGE  TXT        851 03-23-91   1:04p
CONTENTS TXT       1255 06-26-91   1:25p   ← Source file
ANSWERS  TXT       1339 07-01-91  10:16a
LESSON15 DOC        353 07-13-91   9:03a
COMMANDS TXT      22488 07-15-91  11:51a
GLOSSARY TXT      36073 07-15-91  11:51a
DOSERROR TXT      24048 07-15-91  11:54a
        9 file(s)      86407 bytes
                     8730624 bytes free   ← Space available on disk

C:\ATI50\SUB1>
```

Fig. 10.5. The directory of drive C:\ATI50\SUB1.

With this command, you can view the contents of the new file and verify that it is identical to the source file.

You have just created a copy of a file and stored the copy on the same disk under a different name. You now can make changes to one of the files and leave the other intact.

Copying a File onto Another Disk

Now suppose that you want to make a backup copy of the CONTENTS.NTS file you just created and that you want to place the copy on Practice Disk 1.

To copy a file to another disk, as you did in the Shell, follow these steps:

1. Insert Practice Disk 1 into drive A, if it isn't already there.
2. Type **CD\ATI50\SUB1** and press Enter, if you are not in the correct directory.
3. Type **DIR** and press Enter.

   This step enables you to check the name and size of the file that you want to copy.
4. Type **DIR A:** and press Enter.

   This step enables you to make sure that you have enough space for the copy and that the target disk does not contain a file with the same name as the source file.

   If you are using a new disk for the copy, you do not have to be concerned about space or other file names. But when you are trying to copy a file onto a disk that already contains files, you may save time and unnecessary frustration by checking before you copy.
5. Type **COPY CONTENTS.NTS A:** and press Enter.

   You see the message

   ```
   1 File(s) copied
   ```
6. Type **DIR A:CONTENTS.NTS** and press Enter to make sure the file is listed.

You have just copied a file under the same name from one disk to another. If you want to change the name of the file as you copy it, you can do so by following the same steps, with one addition: In step 5, add the new file name to the end of the statement. For example, type **COPY CONTENTS.NTS A:CONTENTS.NEW**.

> The importance of making backup copies of files cannot be overemphasized. Just as you keep a backup copy of a disk to use in case the original is lost or destroyed, you should make backup copies of important files periodically (perhaps every day).

When you issue a full COPY command, you supply the following:

- The source drive
- The source file name
- The destination drive
- The destination file name (only if the name is to be changed)

If you omit one or more of these items, known as *parameters*, DOS makes assumptions. These assumptions are often called the *currents* or the *defaults*. DOS says, *If a parameter is missing, use the current setting.* If you omit the destination file name, for example, DOS assumes that you want the current file name to be specified as the source and names the new copy of the file the same as the source file.

Similarly, if you do not specify the drives and/or subdirectories, DOS uses the defaults. If you do not specify a drive or directory for the file you want to copy, for example, DOS searches the default drive for the source file. If DOS does not find the file, it displays the message

```
File not found
```

Likewise, if you do not specify a drive or directory to which you want the file copied, DOS copies the file onto the default drive.

> A good habit to form is to go to the subdirectory in which you want to perform an action. Doing so eliminates having to type long path names when issuing commands and is often less confusing. Instead of typing **COPY C:\DOS*.* A:**, for example, type **CD\DOS** and press Enter and then type **COPY *.* A:**.

Copying All Files from One Disk to Another

As you know, DISKCOPY works with entire floppy disks, while COPY works with individual files. If you need an exact copy of an entire floppy disk, use DISKCOPY. But if you need to copy an individual file or a group of files, use COPY.

To copy a floppy disk full of files to a directory on your hard disk, for example, follow these steps:

1. Type **MD C:\PD1** and press Enter.

   This command creates a new subdirectory called PD1 on the hard disk. PD1 is an abbreviation of Practice Disk 1.

2. Insert Practice Disk 1 into drive A.
3. Type **COPY A:*.* C:\PD1 /V** and press Enter.

This command tells DOS to copy all files from drive A to the PD1 subdirectory on C. In very little time, all the files are copied.

Remember: The asterisk (*) is a wild-card character. The characters *.* tell DOS to match all characters in the file names—in other words, to copy *all* files.

Also take careful note of the /V switch used in this command. This switch instructs DOS to double-check the files as they are copied in order to verify that the files are transferred correctly. This switch slows down the copying process, but you may want to use it when copying crucial data.

> There is a handy shortcut to typing ***.*** to refer to all the files in a directory or on a disk. Typing a period (.) also means all files. COPY. and COPY *.*, for example, mean the same thing.

As you may have guessed, you can reverse this process to copy a directory of files from a hard disk to a floppy disk. However, you must first make sure that the group of files you want to copy will fit on one floppy disk. If they will, you can reverse the preceding procedure with this command:

COPY C:\PD1*.* A:

Using the preceding shorthand tip, you also can change to the subdirectory by typing **CD\PD1)** and typing the command **COPY. A:**.

Understanding the Potential Danger of COPY

COPY is a potentially dangerous DOS command; it is not as harmless as some users think. COPY has two potential dangers:

1. If the target file already exists on a disk, the COPY command overwrites that file with the source file that you are copying to disk. DOS does not warn you of this fact.

   Granted, if DOS did warn you of this, the warning would slow an often-used function, but many users think that the slowdown would be worthwhile.

2. Even some experienced users are not aware of the second danger. Suppose that you want to copy a file called MYFILE.TXT from drive C to drive A. You should type **COPY C:MYFILE.TXT A:** or just **COPY MYFILE.TXT A:**.

If, however, you forget the colon after the A or mistakenly type a semicolon, DOS ignores the semicolon and copies the file right back to drive C, giving it the new file the name A without your ever knowing it. If you then delete the original, you may never find your data. Always be aware of what you type and double-check your commands before you press Enter.

Lesson Summary

- ☐ The Shell's File Information feature provides a wealth of information about selected files, disks, and directories, such as how much total space a group of files consumes.
- ☐ You can copy a file in the Shell from the File menu or by dragging the file to the destination using the mouse.
- ☐ Using the COPY command from the DOS prompt, you can store a copy on the same disk if you change the name of the copy. Or, you can copy a file to another disk or directory, keeping the same name or changing it.
- ☐ You can use COPY instead of DISKCOPY to copy an entire disk. COPY *.* (or COPY.) copies all files to a destination.

Key Terms

COPY	Makes copies of individual files
Current (or default)	Assumptions that DOS makes about the current or default drive, directory, and file name if these are not specified as parameters in a command
Dragging files	Using the mouse to pick up files and copy them to a destination

Exercises

1. Insert Practice Disk 1 into drive A and close the drive door.
2. While in the Shell, go to your DOS subdirectory and tag the following files:

   APPEND.EXE
   ASSIGN.COM
   ATTRIB.EXE
   BACKUP.EXE
   COMMAND.COM
   DISKCOPY.COM
   DOSKEY.COM
   FIND.EXE
   MORE.COM

   (See "Copying Multiple Files in the Shell.")
3. Copy all these files to drive A.
4. Get a directory listing of drive A to ensure that these files are on Practice Disk 1. Also check to make sure that CONTENTS.NTS is there; you created this file earlier in the lesson. (See "Copying a File onto the Same Disk.")
5. Set this disk aside; you'll learn how to delete all the files on this disk in Lesson 11.

Now that you know how to copy files, you are ready to learn how to erase, move, and rename files in Lesson 11.

Lesson 11

Erasing, Moving, and Renaming Files

Erasing, moving, and renaming are three DOS operations that help you manage your files. With RENAME (or REN), you can change the names of your files. ERASE (or DEL) enables you to remove files from a directory. Both commands give you greater control by enabling you to manipulate your files in much the same way as when you use the COPY command.

The DOS Shell also has the capability to move a file from one place to another. Instead of using two steps by copying a file to a destination and then deleting it from its original location, the Shell enables you to do the task in one step. DOS 5 also has the capability to undelete a file that you have erased accidentally.

In this lesson, you learn how to do the following:

- Erase (or delete) files
- Undelete files
- Move files
- Rename files

What you need to complete this lesson: Practice Disks 1 and 2

Estimated time to complete this lesson: 30-35 minutes

Erasing Files

Just like you can erase a whole disk by using the FORMAT command, you can delete individual files that you no longer need by using ERASE. DOS "throws away" disk files with ERASE like you throw unwanted paper into a waste basket. Although ERASE helps you to free space on your disks, the command also is dangerous because if you apply the command carelessly, you can erase the wrong file.

An erased file is difficult to recover. You may be able to "unerase" the file, but only if you have written no new information to the disk. To retrieve erased files, you must use the UNDELETE command, which this lesson explores later. Be extremely careful when using ERASE.

Preparing for the Lesson

Before you continue, make sure that certain files are on Practice Disk 1. In Lesson 10, you copied the following files onto the disk:

APPEND.EXE	CONTENTS.NTS
ASSIGN.COM	DISKCOPY.COM
ATTRIB.EXE	DOSKEY.COM
BACKUP.EXE	FIND.EXE
COMMAND.COM	MORE.COM

Insert Practice Disk 1 into drive A and get a directory listing by pressing Ctrl-A while in the Shell or by typing **DIR** and pressing Enter at the DOS prompt. This way, you can see whether these files are there, because you will delete them during this lesson. If all these files are not listed, copy them as discussed in Lesson 10. (***Note:*** Practice Disk 1 may list other files too, which is okay.)

Erasing Files in the DOS Shell

When you erase a file while working in the Shell, you select the file and then choose Delete from the File menu or press the Del key. To delete a file from Practice Disk 1, follow these steps:

1. Start the Shell, if it is not already running.
2. Insert Practice Disk 1 into drive A.

3. Click the drive A icon or press Ctrl-A.
4. Click the file DISKCOPY.COM.

   From the keyboard, press Tab until the File List area is activated and highlight DISKCOPY.COM with the arrow keys.
5. Click File and Delete. Or, press Del.

   The Delete File Confirmation dialog box appears (see fig. 11.1).

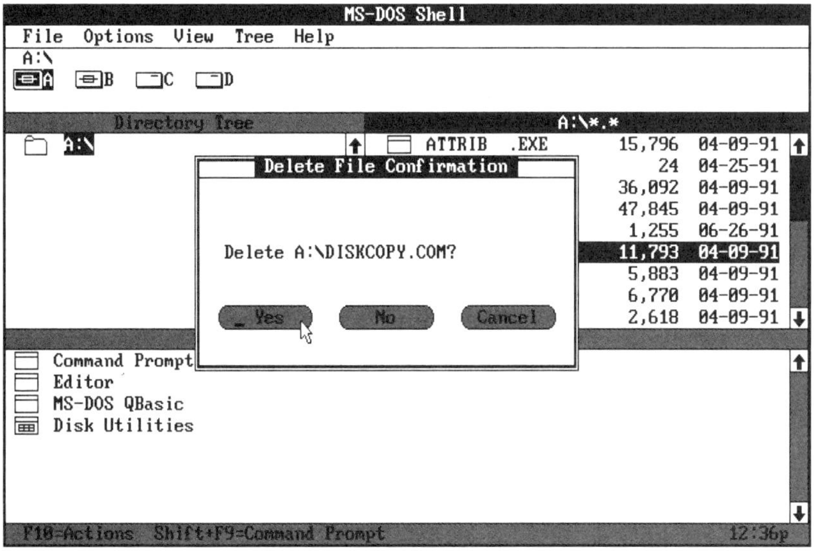

Fig. 11.1. The Delete File Confirmation dialog box.

6. Click Yes or press Enter.

   The file, now erased, disappears from the File List window.

Alternatively, if you change your mind and don't want to delete the file after all, click No and press Enter or choose Cancel. You also can press Esc as a shortcut.

Undeleting a File

Erasing a file does not delete its contents immediately. Instead, DOS marks the entry in the directory as not in use, erases the first letter of the file name, and frees the space occupied by the file.

For this reason, you can recover a mistakenly erased file by using the UNDELETE command, but you must do so immediately.

> Writing any data to disk may overwrite the deleted file area. Some DOS commands, such as MORE, also create temporary files that can replace the deleted file area. Therefore, undelete a file immediately after deleting it.

To emphasize this urgency, run the UNDELETE command right from the Shell and try to recover the file you just erased. Follow these steps:

1. Double-click Disk Utilities and then double-click Undelete. Or, highlight each option with the arrow keys and press Enter.

   The Undelete dialog box appears (see fig. 11.2).

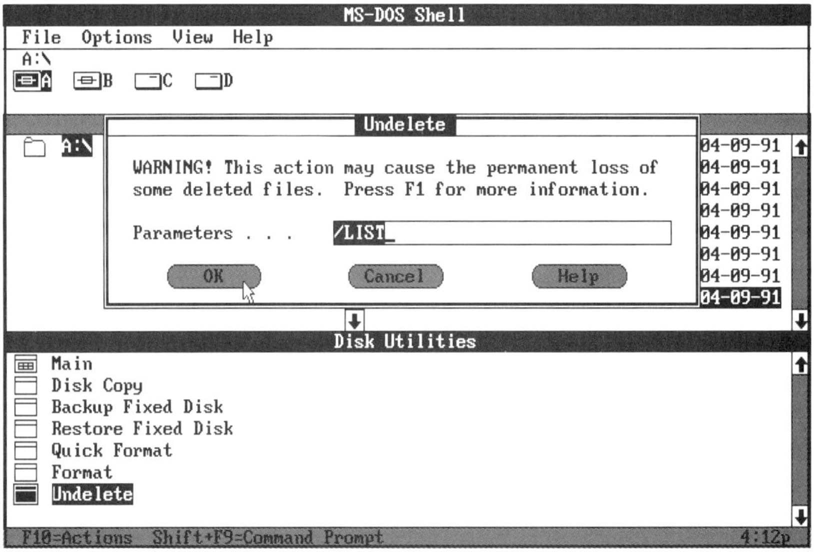

Fig. 11.2. The Undelete dialog box.

   Notice the /LIST switch on the command line. This switch displays all the files that have been deleted on drive A. If you are not logged onto drive A, insert a drive letter and a path (if necessary) in front of the /LIST switch.

2. Click OK or press Enter.

   Note that DISKCOPY.COM can be undeleted.

A message similar to the following appears on your screen showing that the file can be recovered:

```
Directory: A:\
File Specifications: *.*

Deletion-tracking file not found.

  MS-DOS directory contains    1 deleted files.
  Of those,    1 files may be recovered.

Using the MS-DOS directory.

  ?ISKCOPY COM     11793  4-09-91  5:00a  ...A
```

> If two asterisks (**) appear in front of a file name, you cannot undelete the file.

3. Press any key to return to the Shell, and then repeat step 1.
4. Press Backspace once to erase /LIST and press Enter.

   A message similar to the following appears:

```
Directory: A:\
File Specifications: *.*

Deletion-tracking file not found.

  MS-DOS directory contains 1 deleted files.
  Of those, 1 files may be recovered.

Using the MS-DOS directory.

?ISKCOPY COM  11793  4-09-91  5:00a ...A  Undelete
(Y/N)?
```

   Deletion-tracking file refers to a special file utility that you can install to help keep track of deleted files. (You learn how to install this device in Lesson 17.)

5. Press Y to undelete this file.

   The following message appears:

```
Please type the first character for ?ISKCOPY.COM:
```

6. Press D.

   The following message should appear:

```
File successfully undeleted.
```

7. Press any key to return to the Shell.

   Notice that DISKCOPY.COM still is not listed, although it has been undeleted.

8. Double-click the drive A icon or press F5 to reread the disk.

   DISKCOPY.COM now should be listed.

If this were a real situation, you would probably sit back in your chair and breathe a sigh of relief, thankful that your important file was recovered. Once again, be careful when erasing files. There may be a time when you are not so lucky.

Erasing Multiple Files in the Shell

To erase more than one file in the Shell, tag the files you want to delete and then carry out the deletion procedure. Follow these steps:

1. Make sure that you are logged onto drive A and that Practice Disk 1 is still in the drive.

2. Click the file named APPEND.EXE or highlight it with the arrow keys (you must be in the File List area before highlighting).

3. Hold down the Shift key and click the file named BACKUP.EXE (which is probably the second or third file down from APPEND.EXE).

   With the keyboard, hold down the Shift key and use the down arrow to highlight BACKUP.EXE.

4. Release the Shift key and notice that you have tagged multiple files in sequence.

5. Click File and then Delete. Or, press the Del key.

   The Delete File dialog box appears, which lists the files tagged to be deleted (see fig. 11.3).

6. Click OK or press Enter and answer Yes to each confirmation that appears (by clicking Yes or pressing Enter). The tagged files are deleted.

7. Choose the DISKCOPY.COM file.

8. Hold down the Ctrl key and click the file named FIND.EXE. Release the Ctrl key.

   From the keyboard, press Shift-F8. (Notice that the word `ADD` appears in the bottom right corner of the screen beside the time display.) Use the down arrow to find FIND.EXE and press the space bar. Press Shift-F8 again.

   You now have two nonsequential tagged files.

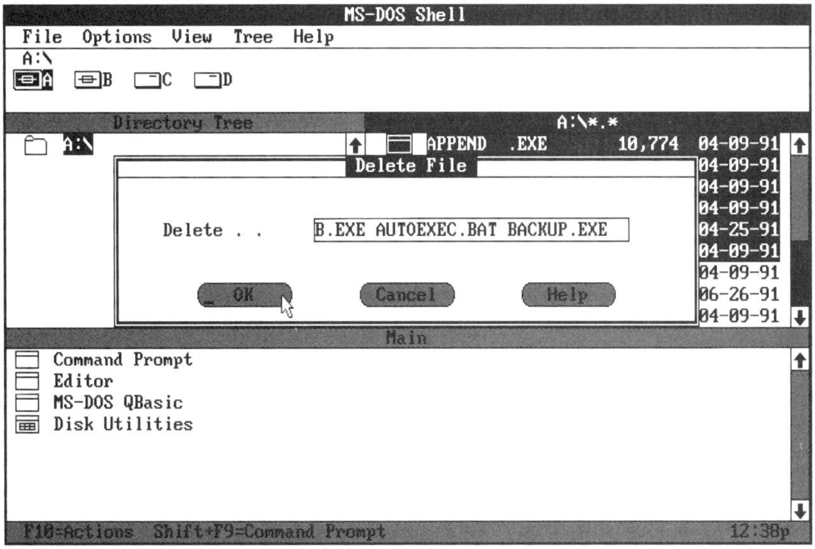

Fig. 11.3. The Delete File dialog box.

9. Delete these files as you did in step 5.

10. Press Ctrl-/ (slash) to tag all the files that remain and delete them also.

11. You now must undelete these files. Double-click Disk Utilities and then double-click Undelete. Or, highlight each option with the arrow keys and press Enter. At the Undelete dialog box, press Backspace, and then press Enter.

    DOS now reports the number of files that you can recover, in a message similar to the following:

```
Directory: A:\
File Specifications: *.*

Deletion-tracking file not found.

  MS-DOS directory contains   10 deleted files.
  Of those,   10 files may be recovered.

Using the MS-DOS directory.

  APPEND EXE       11774  4-09-91  5:00a  ...A
```

12. Undelete these files as you did earlier by pressing Y after each inquiry and supplying the first letter of each file:

A for ?SSIGN
A for ?TTRIB
B for ?ACKUP
C for ?OMMAND
D for ?ISKCOPY
D for ?OSKEY
F for ?IND
M for ?ORE
C for ?ONTENTS

13. Press a key to return to the Shell, but notice that no files are listed in the File List area.
14. Double-click the drive A icon or press Tab to highlight the File area and then press F5 to reread the disk.

All of your undeleted files now are listed.

Erasing Files from the DOS Prompt

Erasing a file from the DOS prompt is simple. As always, you must type the proper command and parameters at the prompt and press Enter. The format of the command follows:

ERASE *d:filename*

or

DEL *d:filename*

Obviously, typing DEL is quicker than ERASE, so you probably should choose to use DEL.

The statements consists of three parts:

- *ERASE* or *DEL* is the command.
- *d:* is the disk drive containing the file to be erased.
- *filename* is the complete name (root name and extension) of the file you want to erase.

To erase DISKCOPY.COM from Practice Disk 1, follow these steps:

1. Exit the Shell temporarily by pressing Shift-F9 or permanently by pressing F3.

   Remember: You can issue DEL or any other DOS command from the Shell by choosing the Run command from the File menu and typing DEL in the Run dialog box. In this case, however, you must include a full path name.
2. Insert Practice Disk 1 into drive A.
3. Log onto drive A by typing **A:** and pressing Enter.

> Logging onto a drive or changing to the correct directory before issuing the DEL command reduces errors, such as typing the wrong path name with the command. If you log onto the correct drive and directory first, the DOS prompt verifies that you are where you should be.

4. Check the exact name of the file you want to erase in the directory by typing **DIR** or **DIR DISKCOPY.COM** and pressing Enter.
5. Type **DEL DISKCOPY.COM**, but don't press Enter yet.

> Double-check what you have typed to ensure that the file you are about to delete is the correct one. You also should check for typing mistakes when deleting files. Suppose that you have files named PROFITS.88 and PROFITS.89 and you want to delete PROFITS.88. If you type an 89 instead of an 88 with the DEL command, you will erase the wrong file.

6. After you're sure you have specified the correct file name, press Enter. The file is deleted.
7. Type **DIR** or **DIR DISKCOPY.COM** and press Enter.

   Notice that DISKCOPY.COM is no longer listed.
8. Type **DEL MORE.COM /P** and press Enter.

   The /P switch, new to DOS 5, is a wise safeguard against accidentally erasing your files. The switch prompts you to confirm your decision with this message before deleting the file:

   ```
   A:\MORE.COM, Delete (Y/N)?
   ```
9. Press Y to delete the file.

Using Wild-Card Characters with ERASE

You can use wild-card characters with the DEL or ERASE commands to erase files with the same extension or even all files in a directory. Do so carefully, however. Follow these steps:

1. Make sure you are still logged onto drive A. This is very important, because you don't want to erase files on other drives accidentally.
2. Type **DEL *.COM**. Don't press Enter yet.

Because all file names with the specified extension are erased, be sure that you don't need any of those files before you issue the command.

Alternately, you can use the /P switch (DEL *.COM /P) for individual confirmation. If you don't want to delete a particular file, press N for No and DOS moves on to the next file to be deleted and prompts you again.

3. Press Enter.
4. Type **DIR** and press Enter to make sure that no files with the COM extension are on the disk.
5. Type **DEL *.*** and press Enter.

> There is a handy shortcut to typing *.* to refer to all the files in a directory or on a disk. Typing a period (.) also means all files. For example, DEL. and DEL *.* mean the same thing. The period simply refers to the current directory.

> The del *.* command is very destructive. DOS displays the prompt
>
> ```
> All files in directory will be deleted!
> Are you sure (Y/N)?
> ```
>
> and deletes no files unless you press Y and Enter. This prompt is the only case where DOS asks for confirmation with wild-card use (unless you use the /P switch).

Again, you can add the /P switch so that DOS prompts you before deleting each file. You usually use the DEL. command for speed when you know that you want to delete all the files in the directory. Press Y and Enter to delete all files.

6. Type **DIR** and press Enter.

Because all the files on the disk are deleted, you should see this message:

```
File not found
```

7. Type **UNDELETE A:** and press Enter; undelete all the files as you did in step 12 of the "Erasing Multiple Files in the Shell" section.

   You can type **UNDELETE A:/LIST** to see a list of the files that you can undelete.

8. To return to the Shell, type **EXIT** at the DOS prompt and press Enter (if you exited temporarily with Shift-F9). Or, type **DOSSHELL** and press Enter (if you exited permanently with F3).

Moving Files

When working at the DOS prompt, the only way to move a file from one place to another is first to copy the original to a destination and then delete the original. The Shell, however, enables you to move files in one quick and easy step.

The procedure is very similar to copying files. Follow these steps:

1. Start the Shell, if it is not already running.
2. Insert Practice Disk 1 into drive A.
3. Log onto the drive where the ATI50\SUB1 subdirectory resides. This drive probably is C, but may be different, depending on which drive you have installed the disk tutor to.
4. Access the ATI50\SUB1 subdirectory by clicking it or highlighting it with the arrow keys.
5. Click the CONTENTS.TXT file.

   From the keyboard, press Tab to activate the File List area and highlight the file with the arrow keys.

6. Click File and then Move. Or, press F7 as a shortcut.

   The Move File dialog box appears (see fig. 11.4).

7. Press the Backspace key to erase the destination drive/directory, type **A:**, and press Enter.

   The drive light comes on, the selected file moves onto the diskette, and the file disappears from the file list.

8. Log onto drive A and notice that the file now is listed there.
9. Reverse this procedure to move the file back to where it was before. In the Move File dialog box, you must type **C:\ATI50\SUB1** in the To text box (unless your drive letter is different) and press Enter.

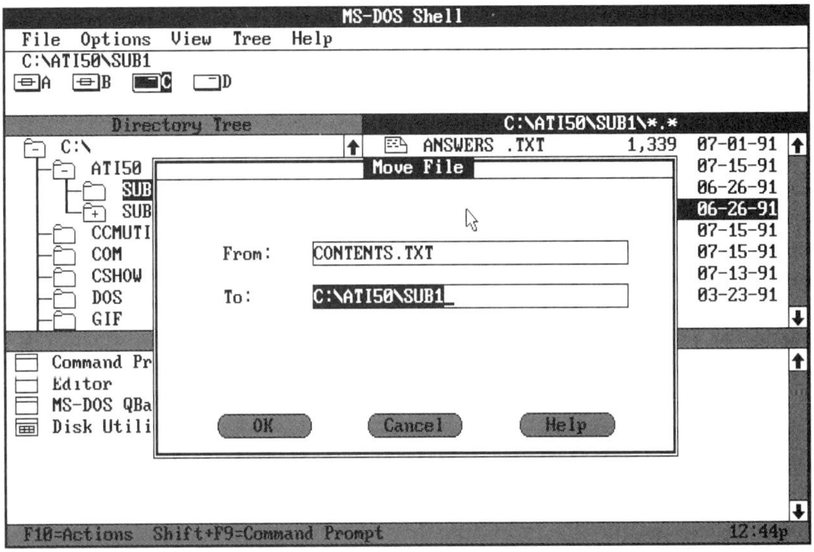

Fig. 11.4. The Move File dialog box.

In the same way that you can copy multiple files simultaneously, you also can move multiple files simultaneously. You must tag only the files you want to move (in or out of sequence) or an entire directory, and then carry out the moving procedure, as in steps 1 through 9. See Lesson 10 for more information on copying files, if needed.

Likewise, you can move files by "dragging" them with the mouse, as you did in copying files. The only difference is that when you copy files, you hold down the Ctrl key and then drag them. To move a file, however, you drag it without holding down any key. Again, review this technique in Lesson 10, if needed.

> Remember whether you have actually moved files, or just copied them. If you confuse the two procedures, you can end up moving files when you actually must leave them in the original location.

Renaming Files

The RENAME (or REN) command enables you to assign different names to files. You have several options with the REN command:

- You can change the root name or the extension.
- You can change the file name and the extension.
- You can add or remove an extension.

Renaming Files in the DOS Shell

Renaming a file in the Shell is extremely easy. Follow these steps:

1. While still in the C:\ATI50\SUB1 subdirectory, click the MESSAGE.TXT file.

   From the keyboard, press Tab to activate the File List area and highlight the file with the arrow keys.

2. Click File and then Rename. Or, press Alt, F, and N.

   The Rename File dialog box appears (see fig. 11.5).

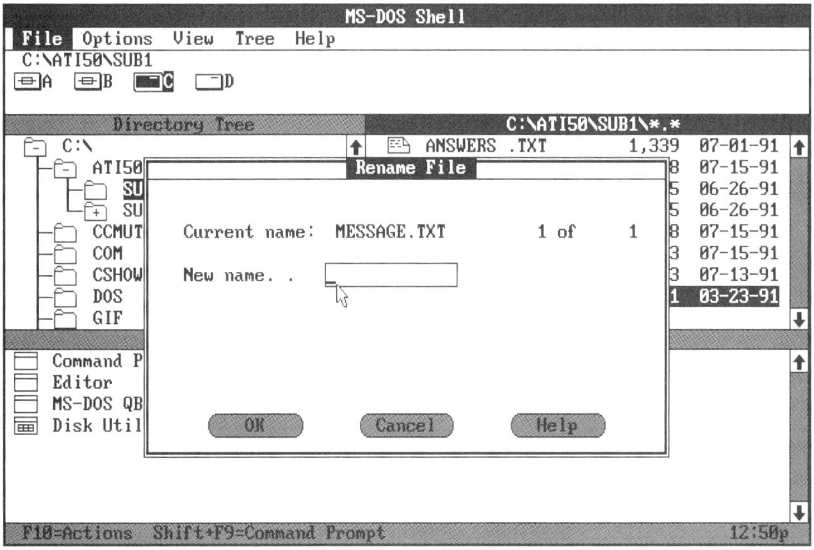

Fig. 11.5. The Rename File dialog box.

3. Type **MESSAGE.DOC** and press Enter. Notice the change in the File List area.

4. To set things right, rename the file back to its original name (MESSAGE.TXT).

If you try to rename a file using an existing file name in the directory, DOS displays an

```
Access Denied
```

message.

> You can change the names of multiple files in the Shell by tagging them first and then issuing the Rename command. The Rename File dialog box then appears and prompts you for a new name for each file.

Renaming Files from the DOS Prompt

Renaming a file from the DOS prompt is almost as easy as renaming one in the Shell. You must type the command and the parameters. The format for the RENAME command follows:

RENAME (or REN) *d:oldfile newfile*

This statement consists of the following parts:

Parameter	Definition
RENAME (or REN)	Command
d:	Name of the drive containing the file with the name you want to change. Specifying the disk drive is optional if the file you want to rename is on the current disk drive or directory. If you are renaming a file not on the currently logged drive, you must specify the drive. If you don't, DOS searches the wrong directory and displays an error message when it cannot find the old file name. On the other hand, if DOS finds the same file name in another directory, DOS renames that file—whether or not you want that file renamed.
oldfile	Complete name (root name and extension, if the name has an extension) of the file you want to change.
newfile	Complete new name you want to assign to the file.

As in the Shell, DOS does not enable you to rename a file using an existing file name in the directory. If you try to rename a file with a file name already in use, you receive the message

```
Duplicate file name
```

or

```
File not found
```

To rename a file from the DOS prompt, follow these steps:

1. Exit the Shell temporarily by pressing Shift-F9 or permanently by pressing F3.

   Remember: You can issue RENAME or any other DOS command from the Shell by choosing the Run command from the File menu and typing the command in the Run dialog box. In this case, however, you must include a full path name.

2. Type **CD \ATI50\SUB1** and press Enter.

   If you have installed the disk tutor to a drive other than C, you must log onto that drive before issuing this command.

3. Type **DIR** or **DIR MESSAGE.TXT** and press Enter.

   Check the directory to be sure that you know the exact name of the file you want to change. Determine also that no file in the directory has the same name as the new file name you have selected.

4. Type **REN MESSAGE.TXT MESSAGE.DOC** and press Enter.

5. Type **DIR** and press Enter.

   Check the directory for the old and new names. Notice that the old file name is no longer listed—the new file name has taken its place.

   After you change the old file name, DOS recognizes only the new file name because the old name no longer exists. If you type **DIR MESSAGE.TXT**, you get the message

   ```
   File not found
   ```

6. To set things right, rename the file back to its original name (MESSAGE.TXT). Type **REN MESSAGE.DOC MESSAGE.TXT**.

Using Wild Cards with RENAME

You can use wild-card characters to rename groups of files. Suppose that several text files in the current directory have the DOC extension. You want to change DOC to PRN, however, so that you can import these files into the popular spreadsheet program Lotus 1-2-3. You easily can perform this task with the command

REN A:*.DOC *.PRN

Lesson Summary

- ☐ ERASE, or DEL, enables you to delete files, thus freeing up storage space on a disk. Use this command carefully, however, because after you delete a file, recovery can be difficult or even impossible.
- ☐ With the Shell, you can move files in one step instead of first copying them to the destination and then deleting them from the original location.
- ☐ With RENAME (or REN), you can change the name of a file by specifying after the command the old file name followed by the new file name.
- ☐ You can use wild-card characters with ERASE to delete more than one file at a time or with RENAME to change the names of several files at once.

Key Terms

ERASE (or DEL)	Removes a file from a disk
RENAME	Changes the name of a file, an extension, or both
UNDELETE	Restores an erased file

Exercises

To practice the important procedures you learned in this lesson, follow these steps:

1. Delete all files on Practice Disk 1. (See "Erasing Multiple Files in the Shell.")
2. Copy all files that reside in the ATI50\SUB1 subdirectory onto Practice Disk 1, and then repeat this for Practice Disk 2. (See "Moving Files.")
3. While working in the Shell, rename every file on Practice Disk 1 to something different; the choices are yours. (See "Renaming Files.")
4. Delete all the files on Practice Disk 1.

5. From the DOS prompt, rename every file on Practice Disk 2 to something different; again, the choice is yours. Use DIR to verify that the files are renamed. (See "Renaming Files from the DOS Prompt.")
6. Finally, delete all the files on Practice Disk 2.

For More Information

For more beginner-level and some intermediate information concerning this lesson, refer to Que's *MS-DOS 5 QuickStart*. For a more in-depth handling of these subjects, refer to Que's *Using MS-DOS 5*. See Appendix E for a description of these books.

In Lesson 12, you learn more about the directory structure of your disks and how to manage your directories.

Lesson 12

Managing Your Directories

In a previous lesson, you learned how to create and name files. Building on this knowledge, you can place 112 files on a double-density (DD) minifloppy disk and 224 files on a high-capacity (HC or HD) disk. For easy access, floppy disks can be sorted and organized by different tasks or functions.

You can arrange, for example, these disks by function (such as word processing, database, and spreadsheet), by topic (such as letters, memos, and sales figures), by year, by company, or by any other logical grouping. When you want to know what files are stored on a disk, you can ask for a directory and view the file names within.

Most computers today, however, have a hard disk, which can store thousands of files. Searching a hard disk containing thousands of files is not only time-consuming, but also impractical. To solve this problem, DOS enables you to use *hierarchical directories*, which make organizing your files easy.

You have already learned a great deal about directories, due primarily to the work you have done with the DOS Shell, but in this lesson, you learn more about managing your directories. You learn to organize hierarchical directories by doing the following:

- Creating directories
- Changing directories
- Removing directories
- Renaming directories
- Using the TREE command

Estimated time to complete this lesson: 25-30 minutes

Using Hierarchical Directories

Hierarchical directories enable hard disk users to organize files on a hard disk in much the same way that floppy disk users organize their disks. Instead of having several disks (each disk with its own purpose or topic) however, the hard-disk user organizes files into subdirectories.

Each disk, whether hard or floppy, starts with one directory, called a *root directory*. The root directory is not named. Instead, the root directory is identified by the backslash (\), a symbol shown often in previous lessons. The root directory holds programs or data files and stores the names of other directories, called *subdirectories*.

For the sake of review, look again at the upside down tree analogy of DOS's directory structure in Lesson 5 (see fig. 12.1).

In simple form, the directory resembles an inverted tree. The root directory is the topmost directory. The numbered boxes in figure 12.1 represent directories (also called subdirectories) on branches of the tree. Directories 1, 2, and 3, for example, are on the same branch of the tree.

The tree-structure analogy loses some of its neatness, however, when it is expanded to cover the hierarchical-directory structure, because any directory, except the root, can have as many subdirectories as space on the disk permits.

As you move from the root directory to a subdirectory, you are moving to a further subdivision of the disk. The inverted tree is similar to a family tree or an organizational chart. In this case, you can compare the root directory to the oldest generation or the most senior person in an organization.

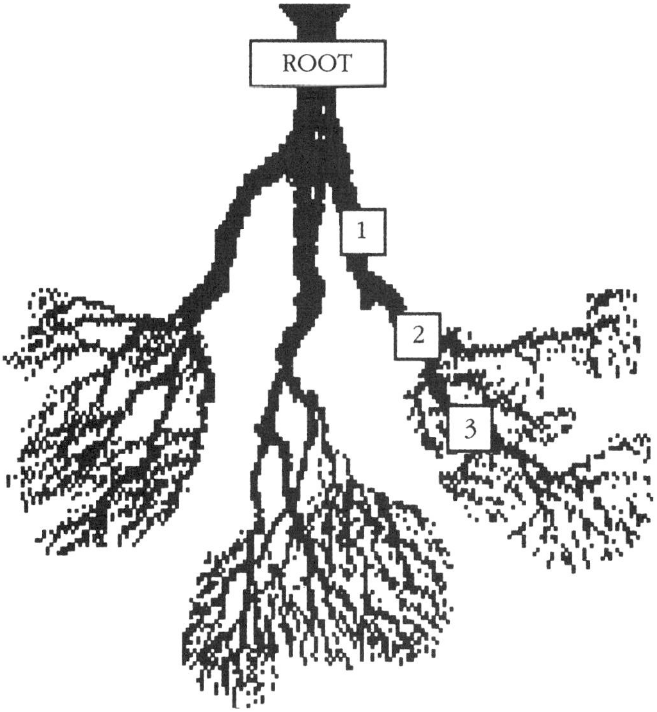

Fig. 12.1. A diagram of a directory tree.

Disk directories are frequently referred to as *parent* and *child directories*. First, consider the analogy of a family tree, as shown in figure 12.2.

In figure 12.2, the family patriarch can be compared to the root directory—the directory from which all other directories come. One child beneath the root is in turn a parent of the one below it, but the other is only a child, having no other offspring. Similarly, the first child has three children, one of which becomes the parent of still another child.

Subdirectories can store the names of files and other information; they also can store the names of other subdirectories. With all these directories and subdirectories, you may think that finding an individual file stored in the subdirectory of a subdirectory of a subdirectory is difficult.

In truth, however, finding a file is not as difficult as it seems. DOS uses *paths*, or chains of directory names, to guide itself through directories to find the file you want. When you want to find a file stored in a subdirectory, you must indicate the path DOS takes to locate the file. To indicate the subdirectory and the file, you use the path symbol—the backslash (\). The first backslash always indicates the root directory, and subsequent backslashes are used as delimiters (or separators) between subdirectories.

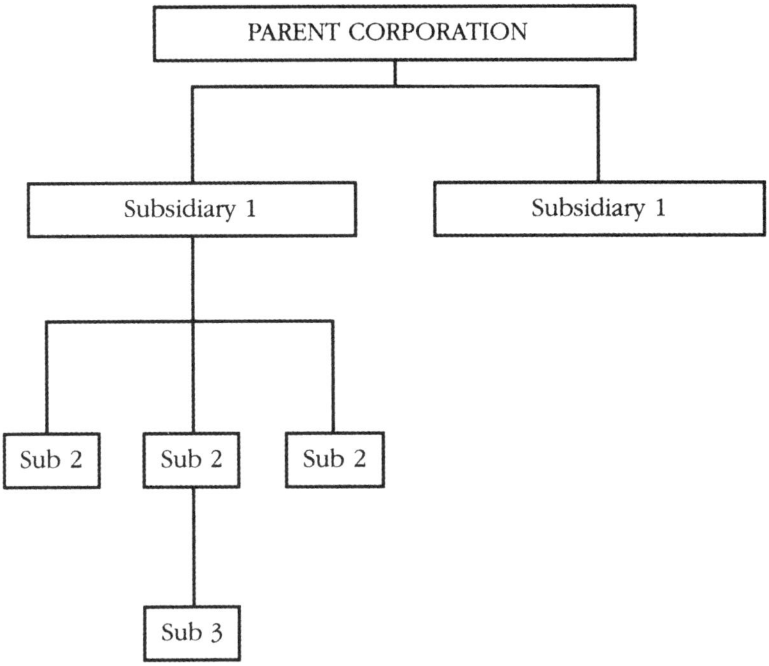

Fig. 12.2. A diagram representing parent and child directories.

To illustrate the important role of paths, DOS can be compared to a corporate empire that has an extremely strict chain of command. All communications must go through channels. Thus, as shown in figure 12.3, if a subsidiary at level 3 wants to communicate with the parent corporation, the message must go through both subsidiary 2 and 1. In DOS, this routing is called the *path*, and looks like this:

\PARENT CORPORATION\SUBSIDIARY1\SUB2\SUB3

To further understand the concept of directory paths in DOS, notice the simple directory setup shown in figure 12.4. Each subdirectory in this example is a subdirectory of the root directory. One subdirectory, \LOTUS, has a data file, MYFILE.123. Another subdirectory, \TEMP, has a file called TAXFORMS.DOC.

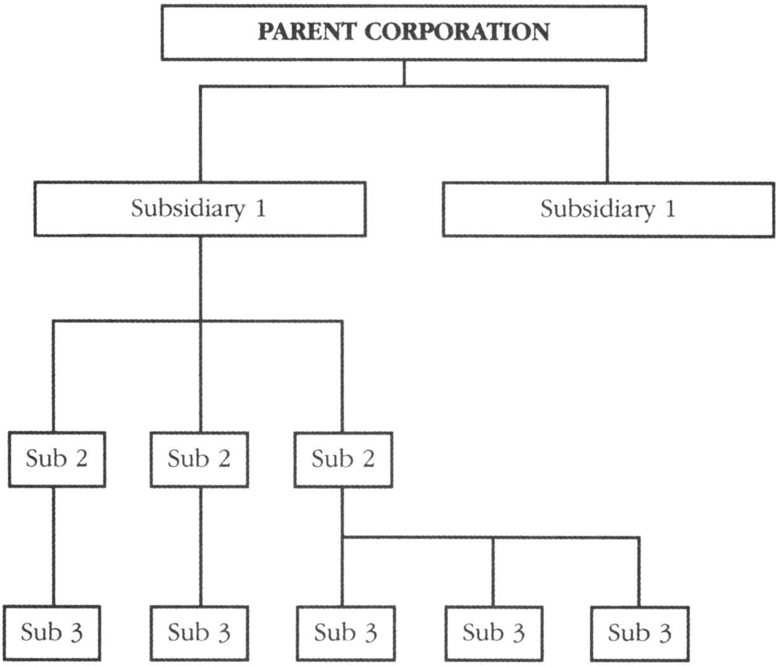

Fig. 12.3. A diagram of a path in a multilevel directory tree.

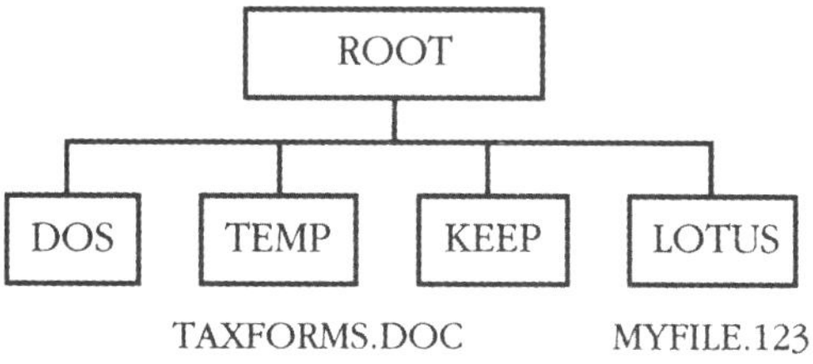

Fig. 12.4. A simple directory setup.

In figure 12.5, MYFILE.123 is a data file in the LOTUS subdirectory. The complete path name for this file is the chain of directories that tells DOS how to find MYFILE. In this case, the chain consists of just two directories: the root (C:\ROOT) and \LOTUS. Figure 12.5 also shows the path name for the TAXFORMS.DOC file.

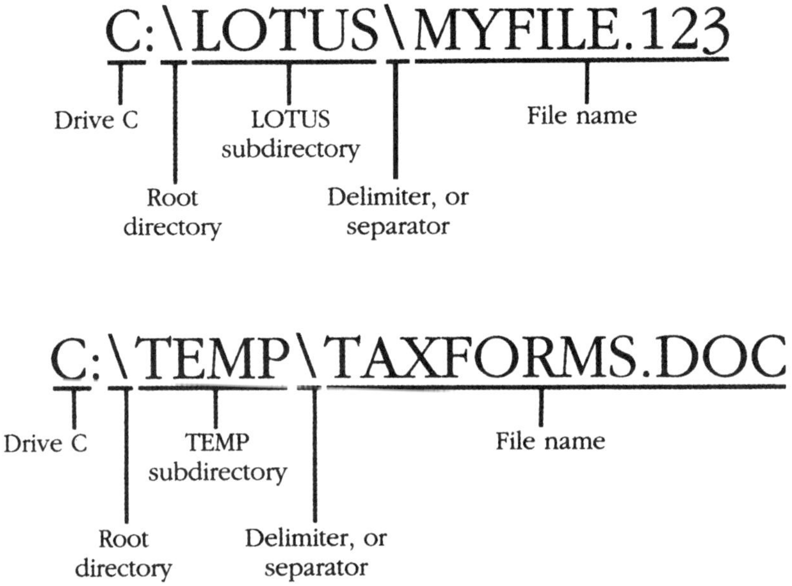

Fig. 12.5. Path-name examples.

With this foundation, you are ready to learn more about managing your directories. Look over the following guidelines and then continue with the lesson; as you continue, these guidelines become second nature.

Guidelines for Path Names

You can refer to these guidelines as you work with path names:

- A path can contain from 1 to 63 characters.
- A path consists of directory names separated by backslashes (\).
- A drive name may precede a path name.
- Generally, a file name follows a path name. In this case, the path name must be separated from the file name by a backslash.
- Each drive has its own path, which DOS keeps in memory.
- To start with the root (uppermost) directory, precede the path name with a backslash (\).
- If you do not start with the root directory, DOS starts with the current default directory of the disk.

Guidelines for Hierarchical-Directory Names

- A hierarchical-directory name has a root name of one to eight characters, an optional extension of one to three characters, and a period separating the root name from the extension.
- Valid characters for hierarchical-directory names are the same characters that are valid for file names: the letters A to Z; the numbers 0 to 9; and the following special characters:

  $ # & @ ! ( ) - { } ' _ ; ^ ~

- The characters that you *cannot* use in hierarchical-directory names are the same characters that are not valid in file names:

  + = / [ ] " : ; , ? * \ < > | . [space]

- You cannot assign the single period (.) and double period (..) to a directory as a name. These names are reserved for the current directory and the parent directory, respectively, and are assigned by DOS.

Managing Directories in the Shell

The Shell provides the easiest way to manage your directories. Using the Shell, you can create, change, delete, and rename directories quickly and efficiently. You already know how to change directories. To learn some other directory-management skills, follow these easy steps:

1. Start the Shell if it is not already running.
2. Log onto drive C by clicking on the C: icon or by pressing Ctrl-C.
3. Make the root directory the current directory by clicking on C:\ or by pressing Tab to activate the Directory Tree area and highlighting C:\ with the arrow keys.

   You want to create a directory under the root, so make the root the current directory by highlighting it. Obviously, if you want to create a directory under some other directory, highlight that directory instead.

4. Click File and then click Create Directory. Or, press Alt, F, and E.

   The Create Directory dialog box appears (see fig. 12.6).

Be sure you are in the correct directory before creating another directory.

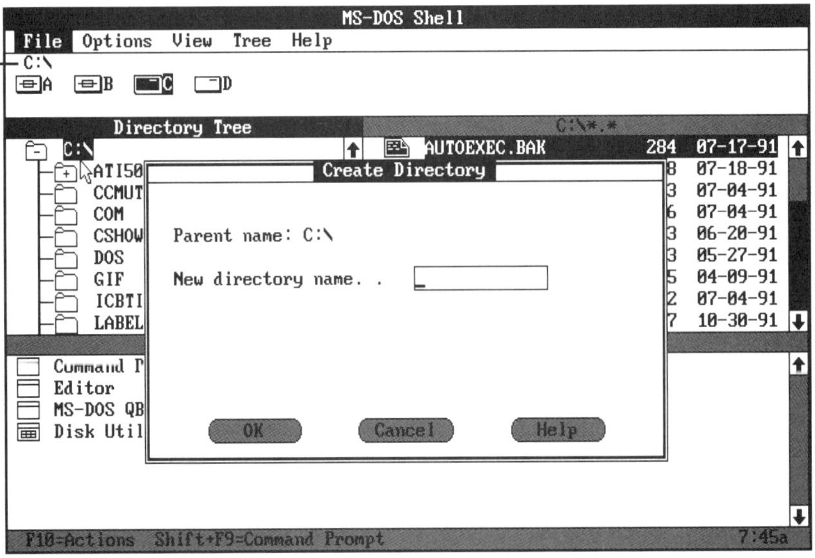

Fig. 12.6. The Create Directory dialog box.

5. Type **BUSINESS** in the dialog box.

   If this directory already exists under the root, choose another name.

> Notice how important it is to be in the correct directory before creating another directory (as in fig. 12.6). When you type a single directory name, that directory is created under the currently highlighted directory. Therefore, step 3 is very important.

6. Press Enter or click OK and scroll down the list to see whether the new directory exists under the root.

   If you want to create a directory under BUSINESS, highlight BUSINESS and create a directory beneath it. You can use this procedure to create as deep a directory structure as you want.

   What if you change your mind and want to name this directory something else? If you are working from the DOS prompt, you first must delete the old directory and then create a new directory. This would be a big inconvenience if the directory were full of files; you would first have to create a new directory, copy the files to the new directory, and then delete the old directory.

The Shell, however, enables you to easily rename a directory, even if it contains files.

7. Highlight the BUSINESS subdirectory you just created; then click on File and then Rename. Or, press Alt, F, and N.

   The Rename Directory dialog box appears (see fig. 12.7).

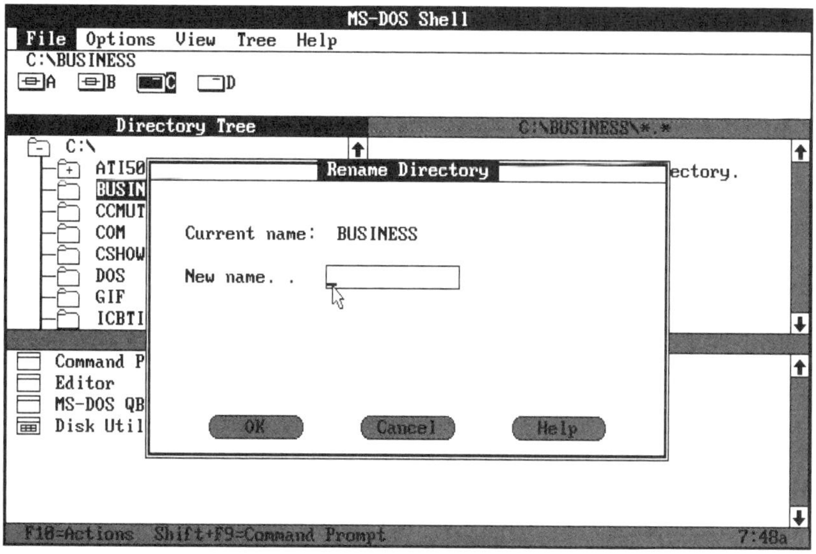

Fig. 12.7. The Rename Directory dialog box.

8. Type the new directory name, **BUSINESS.MY**, and press Enter.

   Notice the name change in the Directory list. Also notice that you used eight characters in the file name and two in the extension. Actually, a directory is simply another type of file as far as DOS is concerned, so all the rules for file names apply to directory names.

   If you discover that you don't really need this new directory, you can remove it easily.

9. Highlight the BUSINESS.MY directory, click File, and click Delete (or press the Del key).

   The Delete Directory Confirmation dialog box appears (see fig. 12.8).

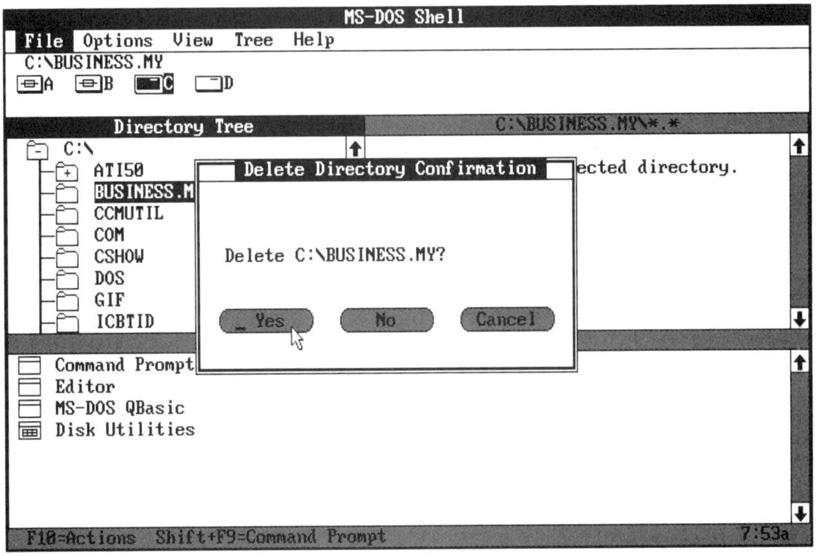

Fig. 12.8. The Delete Directory Confirmation dialog box.

10. Click on Yes or press Enter. The BUSINESS.MY directory disappears from the Directory Tree area.

> You can remove only a directory that is empty. If you try to remove a directory that contains files, the Shell displays a reminder that you must first delete all files before deleting the directory.

Managing Directories from the DOS Prompt

To manage directories from the DOS command line, you must learn three simple commands:

- CD (or CHDIR) tells DOS to change directories.
- MD (or MKDIR) tells DOS to make a new directory.
- RD (or RMDIR) tells DOS to remove a directory.

To learn how to use these commands in setting up hierarchical directories, work through these simple steps:

1. Exit the Shell temporarily by pressing Shift-F9. To exit the Shell permanently, press F3.
2. At the DOS prompt, type **CD** and press Enter.

   The CD command means *change directory* and moves to any directory on your disk. In this case, the command just tells DOS to go to the root directory, which is always the first backslash (\) in a path name.
3. Type **MD\BUSINESS** and press Enter. This command creates a new subdirectory, called BUSINESS, under the root directory.
4. Type **DIR** and press Enter.

   Notice the new subdirectory in the listing (of course, the date and time are different on your screen):

   ```
   BUSINESS      <DIR>  04-13-91      12:07p
   ```
5. Type **MD\BUSINESS\OFFICE** and press Enter. This creates a subdirectory called OFFICE under BUSINESS.
6. Now type **MD\BUSINESS\OFFICE\LETTERS** and press Enter. This makes still another subdirectory under OFFICE.

   You can go as deep in a directory structure as you want, with one restriction: a path name can contain no more than 63 characters.

> For all practical purposes, a directory structure shouldn't go deeper than three levels under the root; two levels is even better. Deep directory structures require typing long paths with the CD command—an activity that soon becomes tiresome.

   You now can use the CD command to change to the subdirectories you have created.

7. Type **CD\BUSINESS\OFFICE\LETTERS** and press Enter.

   The DOS prompt now reflects the current directory:

   ```
   C:\BUSINESS\OFFICE\LETTERS>_
   ```

   Similarly, you can use the CD command to change to any directory on the current drive. Just as BUSINESS was listed as a directory under the root when you used the DIR command, OFFICE would be listed as a directory of BUSINESS, and LETTERS would be listed under OFFICE.

> If the directory you want to change to is directly above the current directory, you can type **CD..** and press Enter to go to that directory. This command takes you one level up in the structure because .. indicates the parent directory of the current directory. As you may recall from Lesson 11, you can use the single period with DEL to delete all files in a directory (DEL.).

8. To get back to the root, type **CD** and press Enter.
9. Now type **RD\BUSINESS\OFFICE\LETTERS** and press Enter.

   You use the RD command to remove subdirectories that you created. Three safety features are built into this command to prevent you from accidentally erasing files that you want to keep:

   - You cannot use RD on the current directory.
   - You cannot use RD on the root directory.
   - You cannot use RD on a directory that is not empty.

   If you try to remove the LETTERS subdirectory while you are in that subdirectory or if files exist in the subdirectory, DOS refuses to delete the directory and displays this message:

   ```
   Invalid path, not directory, or directory not empty
   ```

   Try to remove a subdirectory by typing **RD \DOS** and pressing Enter. DOS refuses to remove this directory because it contains files.

10. Type **RD\BUSINESS\OFFICE** and press Enter; then type **RD\BUSINESS** and press Enter.
11. Use the DIR command again to see that the BUSINESS subdirectory is no longer listed.

As noted in the preceding section, you cannot rename a directory directly from the DOS prompt. You first must create a new directory, then copy the files into the new directory and delete the old directory. Bypassing these steps is another good reason to use the Shell for much of your work.

Using the TREE Command

The Directory List area in the Shell makes navigating a directory structure quick and easy because of the graphic representation it displays. DOS Version 5 also can help you navigate from the DOS prompt, however. The helpful command DOS 5 provides is the TREE command. The DIR command helps a little, but TREE helps much more. TREE graphically displays the directory structure and lists the names of files in each directory. The format of the TREE command follows:

TREE D: PATH /F /A

This statement consists of the following parts:

Specification	Description
TREE	Command
d:	Disk drive from which you want a tree to be displayed.
path	Directory at which you want TREE to begin its display.
/F	Switch that tells DOS to display the files in each directory.
/A	Switch that tells TREE to use text characters in drawing the tree instead of graphics characters. Use /A for monitors and printers that cannot properly handle graphics characters.

When you use the TREE command, DOS displays one directory or one file per line. As a result, a large directory structure or directory listing can scroll off the screen. To prevent scrolling, use the Pause key, Ctrl-S, or the MORE filter to pause the display. To understand how TREE operates, follow these steps:

1. Go to the root directory of drive C by typing **CD** and pressing Enter.
2. Type **TREE** and press Enter. You do not need to type a drive letter because DOS assumes the current drive.

   Your screen displays a graphic tree similar to the one in figure 12.9.

   If you want the display to pause automatically with each full screen, use the command TREE | MORE.

   If this command does not produce a graphic display on your screen as in figure 12.9, use the command TREE /A, which produces a text display such as the one in figure 12.10.

```
C:\>TREE
Directory PATH listing
Volume Serial Number is 207 -15F3
C:.
├───ATI50
│   ├───SUB1
│   └───SUB2
│       ├───SUBSUB1
│       └───SUBSUB2
│           └───SSS1
├───BUSINESS
│   └───OFFICE
│       └───LETTERS
├───DBASE
│   └───DATA
├───DOS
├───123
│   └───DATA
└───UTILITY

C:\>
```

Fig. 12.9. Using the TREE command.

```
C:\>TREE /A
Directory PATH listing
Volume Serial Number is 207C-15F3
C:.
+---ATI50
|   +---SUB1
|   \---SUB2
|       +---SUBSUB1
|       \---SUBSUB2
|           \---SSS1
+---BUSINESS
|   \---OFFICE
|       \---LETTERS
+---DBASE
|   \---DATA
+---DOS
+---123
|   \---DATA
\---UTILITY

C:\>
```

Fig. 12.10. Using the TREE /A command.

You may need to use the /A switch when printing the tree on your printer. Try both commands to see which works best for your system.

TREE also can display the directories under a specific directory other than the root.

3. To display just the directories under ATI50, type **TREE C:\ATI50** and press Enter.

   Alternatively, you can change to the ATI50 subdirectory first and then type **TREE** only.

   Your screen should look similar to the one in figure 12.11.

```
C:\>TREE C:\ATI50
Directory PATH listing
Volume Serial Number is 207C-15F3
C:\ATI50
├───SUB1
└───SUB2
    ├───SUBSUB1
    └───SUBSUB2
        └───SSS1

C:\>
```

Fig. 12.11. Using the TREE command.

4. Type **TREE /F** and press Enter. The directory structure of the disk is listed, as well as the files in each directory.

   To make the display pause automatically with each full screen, use the command TREE /F | MORE.

   An even better use for the /F switch is using it to print a paper copy of the directory for easy reference. You may want to print a new tree after you back up your hard disk. (Procedures for hard disk backup are covered in Lesson 14.)

   You don't need to print a hard copy now, but to print out a hard (paper) copy of the entire tree of drive C on your printer, type the command **TREE C:\ /F > PRN**. If your printer cannot handle graphics characters, add the /A switch after the /F switch. This command redirects output to the printer instead of the monitor screen.

> You can issue the TREE command or any other DOS command from the Shell by choosing the RUN command from the File menu and typing the command in the Run Dialog box. Doing this, however, demands that you type the starting directory, such as **TREE C:**.

5. To return to the Shell, type **EXIT** at the DOS prompt and press Enter if you exited temporarily with Shift-F9. If you exited permanently with F3, type **DOSSHELL** and press Enter.

Understanding How Path Names Affect Commands

In Lesson 10, you learned to use the COPY command with DOS. You can copy files between disks or to a new position on the same disk. Now that you are more familiar with path names, you can use the full form of the COPY command. The syntax of the command follows:

COPY *d1:\pathname1\sfile d2:\pathname2\dfile*

This statement contains the following parts:

Specification	**Definition**
COPY	Command
d1	Source drive
d2	Destination drive
pathname1	Path name for the source file
pathname2	Path name for the destination file
sfile	File name for the source file
dfile	File name for the destination file

The only difference between the full version of the COPY command and its use in Lesson 10 is the addition of the path name. Remember that if DOS is not given a particular parameter, the *rule of currents* applies—that is, if you omit the path for the source file, DOS assumes that the current path is to be used.

The addition of a path name does not apply only to the COPY command. Separating your files into different subdirectories on any disk, particularly on a computer with a hard disk, makes the files much easier to find. You can use path names with many DOS commands to explicitly indicate the file of interest.

> A good habit to form is to go to the subdirectory in which you want to perform an action. Going to the subdirectory often is less confusing because it eliminates having to type long path names when issuing commands. Instead of typing **COPY C:\123*.WK1 C:\123\DATA**, for example, type **CD\123** and then **COPY *.WK1 C:\123\DATA**.

Lesson Summary

- ☐ Hierarchical directories are powerful tools for organizing your files. This system is especially useful for hard disk users because of the large number of files that can be stored on a hard disk.
- ☐ The starting directory, or main directory, of every disk is called the *root directory*. The root directory can hold program or data files, but more importantly, the root directory contains the names of additional directories, called subdirectories.
- ☐ *Subdirectories* are files similar to the root directory. Subdirectories can store the names of files and other information, as well as the names of other subdirectories.
- ☐ The *backslash* (\) has two functions associated with hierarchical directories: it is the symbol for the root directory, and it is the path symbol that separates directory names.
- ☐ A *path* is a chain of directory names that tells DOS how to find the directory or file you want.
- ☐ The Shell is ideal for directory management, but you can use MD (Make Directory), CD (Change Directory), and RD (Remove Directory) from the command line.
- ☐ The *path name* is used in many DOS commands to explicitly describe a location on the disk.

Key Terms

CD (CHDIR)	Tells DOS to change directories
Child directory	Another name for a subdirectory
Hierarchical directory	An organized, multilevel structure of directories
MD (MKDIR)	Tells DOS to make a new directory
Parent directory	Another name for a subdirectory that contains other subdirectories
Path	The list of directory names, separated by a backslash (\), that defines the location of a specific directory or file
RD (RMDIR)	Tells DOS to remove a directory
Rule of currents	Assumptions DOS makes about the current drive, directory, and file name if these are not specified as parameters in a command.
TREE	Graphically displays the directory structure and optionally lists the names of files in each directory

Exercises

For more practice on managing your directories, follow these steps.

1. Using the Shell, create on your hard disk the following subdirectory path:

   C:\MEMO\DEPT1\JOHN

   If you prefer, you may substitute another drive for drive C (such as drive D, E, and so on). See "Managing Directories in the Shell."

2. Copy the following files from the \ATI50\SUB1 directory to the JOHN directory:

   FRIENDS.ADD
   FAMILY.ADD
   CLIENTS.ADD

3. Change to the JOHN directory and delete these files.

4. Remove the new directories.

5. If you want, repeat the above steps while working at the DOS prompt. (See "Managing Directories from the DOS Prompt.")

If you have a printer and several sheets of continuous-feed paper, print a hard copy of the entire tree of drive C by following these simple steps:

1. Make sure that your printer is turned on and properly loaded with paper.
2. At the DOS prompt, type **TREE C:\ /F > PRN**. If your printer cannot handle graphics characters, type **TREE C:\ /F /A > PRN**.

This command redirects output to the printer instead of the monitor screen. (See "Using the TREE Command.")

For More Information

For additional beginner-level information, as well as some intermediate information concerning what was presented in this lesson, refer to *MS-DOS 5 QuickStart* (Que Corporation). For a more in-depth handling of these subjects, refer to *Using MS-DOS 5* (Que Corporation, Chapter 9). See Appendix E for a description of these Que books.

In Lesson 13, you learn more about using your printer.

Lesson 13

Using Your Printer

A *peripheral device* is a piece of hardware that is attached to your computer and used for input, output, and data storage. Your disk drives, printer, and display are all peripherals. DOS enables you to control these devices.

Your printer is one of the most useful peripheral devices, so it is important that you learn how to control it. In this lesson you learn how to do the following:

- Quickly print what is on-screen
- Print entire files
- Control the width and spacing of printer output

If you do not have a printer connected to your computer, you cannot do the following examples, but you can learn how to use a printer by continuing to read.

If you have a printer attached to your computer, make sure that the paper is properly loaded, the power is on, and the printer is on-line (most printers have a light that indicates this).

What you need to complete this lesson: Several sheets of paper for your printer.

Estimated time to complete this lesson: 25-30 minutes

Printing Quickly What Is On-Screen

Sometimes you may need to print quickly what is displayed on your monitor screen. DOS provides two ways of doing this. The first way to print your screen is to press Shift-PrtSc (hold down the Shift key and press the PrtSc key). On 101-key enhanced keyboards, you need to press only the Print Screen key. To print the information on your screen using this method, follow these steps:

1. Make sure the paper is loaded properly in your printer. Also make sure that the printer is turned on and is on-line.
2. Exit the Shell temporarily by pressing Shift-F9 or permanently by pressing F3.
3. Type **CD\DOS** and press Enter.
4. Type **DIR/P** and press Enter to see a directory listing of your disk.

   You should see a partial directory listing similar to the one shown in figure 13.1.

```
 Volume in drive C is A
 Volume Serial Number is 175F-3553
 Directory of C:\DOS

.            <DIR>     05-03-91  10:37a
..           <DIR>     05-03-91  10:37a
EGA      SYS      4885 04-09-91   5:00a
FORMAT   COM     32911 04-09-91   5:00a
NLSFUNC  EXE      7052 04-09-91   5:00a
COUNTRY  SYS     17069 04-09-91   5:00a
DISPLAY  SYS     15792 04-09-91   5:00a
EGA      CPI     58873 04-09-91   5:00a
HIMEM    SYS     11552 04-09-91   5:00a
KEYB     COM     14986 04-09-91   5:00a
KEYBOARD SYS     34697 04-09-91   5:00a
MODE     COM     23537 04-09-91   5:00a
SETVER   EXE     12007 04-09-91   5:00a
ANSI     SYS      9029 04-09-91   5:00a
DEBUG    EXE     20634 04-09-91   5:00a
DOSKEY   COM      5883 04-09-91   5:00a
EDLIN    EXE     12642 04-09-91   5:00a
EMM386   EXE     91742 04-09-91   5:00a
FASTOPEN EXE     12050 04-09-91   5:00a
Press any key to continue . . .
```

Fig. 13.1. A partial directory listing of C:\DOS.

Alternatively, you can issue the DIR/P command from the Shell by choosing the Run command from the File menu and typing the command in the Run Dialog box.

5. Press Shift-PrtSc (or just press Print Screen if you have a 101-key enhanced keyboard).

   Your printer should print the partial directory listing.

> If you want to stop printing for any reason, the only way to do so is to shut off your printer.

6. Press any key to display the next screenful of files, and then press Shift-PrtSc to print that screen.
7. Repeat Step 5 until the entire listing is printed (probably three more times).

You now have a complete printed copy of the DOS subdirectory, but notice that it isn't very presentable. The words

```
Press any key to continue . . .
```

and

```
(continuing C:\DOS)
```

clutter the printout, and the last printed screen contains some of the same files as the preceding screen.

You also can print the contents of the screen by pressing Ctrl-PrtSc (or Ctrl-Print Screen)—that is, holding down the Control key and pressing PrtSc (or Print Screen). There is an important difference between this method and using Shift-PrtSc. Shift-PrtSc prints only what is *currently* on-screen. Ctrl-PrtSc, once activated, prints *everything* the screen displays (that is, what scrolls off the screen) until you press Ctrl-PrtSc again. To use the Ctrl-PrtSc method, follow these steps:

1. Make sure the paper is loaded properly in your printer. Also make sure that the printer is turned on and is on-line.
2. Press Ctrl-PrtSc.

   Nothing happened, did it? Actually, something did. You just turned on screen printing, even though you didn't see or hear anything.
3. Type **DIR** and press Enter.

   Your printer prints the lines of the entire directory listing as they are displayed on-screen.
4. Now type **DIR/W** and press Enter to make sure Ctrl-PrtSc stays in effect until you turn it off.
5. Press Ctrl-PrtSc again to turn off printing.

Using the COPY Command To Print Files

One way of printing a file is to use the COPY command, which you learned about in Lesson 10. Using COPY to print a file simply means that you are going to copy a file from a disk to the printer.

> Files that you have created with an application program—such as a word processor—should be printed with that program. You use the COPY and PRINT commands for printing *pure ASCII text files*—files that contain only text without special embedded codes that word processors create. A word processor that underlines text, for example, does so with a special "invisible" code that is embedded in the document; such a document will not print properly from DOS. DOS 5, however, provides its own text editor (mini-word processor) with which you can create ASCII text files. You learn how to use the Editor in Lesson 17.

To print a file using the COPY command, follow these steps:

1. Make sure the paper is loaded properly in your printer. Also make sure that the printer is turned on and is on-line.
2. Exit the Shell, if necessary—either temporarily by pressing Shift-F9 or permanently by pressing F3.
3. Type **CD\ATI50\SUB1** and press Enter.
4. Type **COPY CONTENTS.TXT PRN** and press Enter.

   The following message appears:

   ```
   1 File(s) copied
   ```

   This message means that DOS copied the file from one place to another—in this case, from a disk to the printer.
5. Type **COPY *.ADD PRN** and press Enter.

   Your screen displays the following file names:

   ```
   CLIENTS.ADD
   FAMILY.ADD
   FRIENDS.ADD
   1 File(s) copied
   ```

   and your printer prints their contents.

Notice that DOS reports that only one file was copied. This is not a mistake because, in effect, only one output file was created—the printed copy of the disk files.

6. To return to the Shell, type **EXIT** at the DOS prompt and press Enter (if you exited temporarily with Shift-F9). Or, type **DOSSHELL** and press Enter (if you exited permanently with F3).

Using the COPY command to print a file does have a drawback, however. It ties up your computer so that you cannot do anything else while files are being printed. The next section presents a solution to this problem.

Using the PRINT Command

The PRINT command enables you to print files while you're using the computer to do other things. This is a primitive form of what is called *multitasking*: the capability of a computer to perform two or more functions (tasks) simultaneously. PRINT keeps track of which files are to be printed in a list called the *print queue* and prints each file in the order in which it is listed. To use the PRINT command, follow these steps:

1. Exit the Shell permanently by pressing F3.

> Do not perform the rest of this procedure if you have exited the Shell temporarily; doing so could *hang* your computer, which halts computer activity. You will need to reboot your system, which could result in data loss.

2. Make sure the paper is loaded properly in your printer. Also make sure that the printer is turned on and is on-line.
3. Type **CD\ATI50\SUB1** and press Enter.
4. Type **PRINT CONTENTS.TXT ANSWERS.TXT MESSAGE.TXT** and press Enter.

   The first time you use the PRINT command, the computer asks for the name of the printer it should use, as follows:

   ```
   Name of list device [PRN]: _
   ```

   You can enter any of the following device specifications:

LPT1	COM1
LPT2	COM2
LP3	COM3
AUX	COM4
PRN	

If you press Enter, PRINT automatically accepts PRN. If you have more than one printer or if you have a serial printer, you may need to use one of the preceding list device names.

If you have only one parallel printer, press Enter. You see the following message:

```
Resident part of PRINT installed

C:\ATI50\SUB1\CONTENTS.TXT is currently being printed
C:\ATI50\SUB1\ANSWERS.TXT is in queue
C:\ATI50\SUB1\MESSAGE.TXT is in queue
```

DOS loads the PRINT utility into memory (which takes about 5K of memory), begins printing the first file, and puts the other files in line to await their turn.

5. While the files are printing, type **DIR** and press Enter; then type **CHKDSK** and press Enter.

   This example illustrates how you can do other things while printing is taking place.

   You also can run other DOS commands, back up files, format disks, or even run your applications programs while PRINT works in the background.

> If you want to cancel the printing of a file that is presently in the print queue, use the /C switch (PRINT MESSAGE.TXT /C, for example). To cancel all the print jobs currently in the queue, use the PRINT /T command.

6. Restart the Shell by typing **DOSSHELL** and pressing Enter.

You can print files even more easily by using the Shell. Follow these steps:

1. Change to the ATI50\SUB1 subdirectory, which is on drive C (unless you installed the disk tutor on a different drive).
2. Make sure the paper is loaded properly in your printer. Also make sure that the printer is turned on and is on-line.
3. Tag (select) the following files:

   CONTENTS.TXT
   ANSWERS.TXT
   MESSAGE.TXT

   Using the mouse, click the first file. Then hold down the Ctrl key, click the other files, and release Ctrl. Using the keyboard, press

Shift-F8, highlight each file with the arrow keys, press the space bar, and press Shift-F8 again.

4. Click File and Print. Or, press Alt, F, and P.

   The tagged files begin printing, and you can continue to work.

5. While the files are printing, click File and Run. Or, press Alt, F, and R. Then type **CHKDSK** and press Enter.

Once again, you are free to do other things while your printer works in the background.

> The PRINT command *must* be loaded before you can print from the Shell. If you choose the Print option without issuing the PRINT command first, you receive an error message. Additionally, you must issue the PRINT command *before* you start the Shell. In Lesson 17, you learn how to tell DOS to issue the PRINT command automatically each time you turn on your computer.

Controlling Print Width and Spacing

You can use the MODE command in a number of ways to control your computer's hardware. Only one use of MODE is important for the beginning DOS user, however: controlling printer output.

Normally, a printer prints 80 characters on a line and six lines per inch, but you can change this with the MODE command.

To print 132 characters on a line (condensed type) and 8 lines per inch, follow these steps:

1. Exit the Shell temporarily by pressing Shift-F9 or permanently by pressing F3.
2. At the DOS prompt, type **MODE LPT1:132,8** and press Enter.

> If your printer is attached to LPT2, type **MODE LPT2:132,8** and press Enter.

The only two lines with which you need to be concerned are

```
LPT1: set for 132
Printer lines per inch set
```

3. Insert the disk that came with this book into drive A and close the drive door.
4. Type **DIR A:/W** and press Enter.
5. Make sure that the printer has paper, is turned on, and is on-line.
6. Press Shift-PrtSc to print the screen contents. Notice the condensed type.
7. To reset your printer (return it to its default width and spacing), type **MODE LPT1:80,6** and press Enter.

Lesson Summary

- ☐ You can quickly print your screen display by pressing Shift-PrtSc (or Print Screen, if you have a 101-key enhanced keyboard); this key combination prints only the current contents of the screen.
- ☐ You can quickly print your screen display by pressing Ctrl-PrtSc (or Ctrl-Print Screen); this key combination prints everything that is displayed on-screen until you press Ctrl-PrtSc (or Ctrl-Print Screen) again.
- ☐ You can use the COPY command to copy files from a disk to the printer, thereby printing them.
- ☐ You can use the MODE command to control the width and spacing of printed characters.

Key Terms

Ctrl-PrtSc or Ctrl-Print Screen	Once activated, prints *everything* the screen displays until pressed again (acts as a toggle switch).
MODE	Used in a number of ways to control the computer's hardware.
Multitasking	The capability of a computer to perform two or more functions (tasks) simultaneously.
Peripheral device	A piece of hardware (a printer, for example) that is attached to your computer and is used for input, output, and data storage.
PRINT	Enables you to print files while you use the computer to do other things.

Print queue	A list of files that the PRINT command prints in the back ground while the computer does other things.
Print Screen	Prints what is *currently* on-screen.
Pure ASCII text file	A file that contains text only, without special embedded codes that a word processor creates.
Shift-PrtSc	Prints what is *currently* on-screen.

Exercises

This section presents a project of great practical value. It creates disk sleeve inserts to store with your disks. You must have a printer attached to your computer to do this project. Follow these steps:

1. Make sure that your printer is turned on and that paper is loaded properly.
2. Go to the DOS prompt, type **MODE LPT1:132,8**, and press Enter. This command causes your printer to print in condensed print with eight lines per inch. (See "Controlling Print Width and Spacing.")
3. Insert a disk containing files into drive A.
4. Type **DIR A:/W** and press Enter to display a wide directory listing. (See "Printing Quickly What Is On-Screen.")
5. Press Shift-PrtSc (or Print Screen) to print the screen contents. Notice the condensed type.
6. Cut out this listing and insert it into the disk sleeve with the disk.
7. Repeat the procedure for as many of your disks as you want.
8. Be sure to reset your printer to 80 characters and 6 lines per inch when you're finished by typing **MODE LPT1:80,6** and pressing Enter. (See "Controlling Print Width and Spacing.")

For More Information

For additional beginner-level information and some intermediate information concerning what was presented in this lesson, see Que's *MS-DOS 5 QuickStart*. For a more in-depth discussion of these subjects, refer to Que's *Using MS-DOS 5*. See Appendix E for a description of these Que books.

In Lesson 14, you learn about one of the most neglected tasks of personal computers—making a backup copy of the hard disk.

Lesson 14

Using BACKUP and RESTORE

As you know, to *back up* files means to make copies of them for storage, in case the originals are damaged or lost. In previous lessons, you learned how to back up whole disks and individual files stored on disks by using the DISKCOPY and COPY commands. You also learned that this is important to do in case one copy of a file or disk is damaged. In this lesson, you learn how important it is to back up your entire hard disk. This job is not one that most experienced users enjoy because it is boring, but those same users also know the dangers they face if they don't back up.

To be dramatic for a moment, the price for backing up your hard disk is *time*; the price for not backing up your hard disk is *tears*. All hard disks fail sooner or later. The day may come when you have a hard disk failure or some other problem damages or destroys your data. If you don't have a backup, countless hours of work may be lost forever.

Hard disks present certain problems, one of which is how to back them up. How do you back up a hard disk, which can hold thousands of files? Originally, it was very clumsy and time-consuming to back up hard drives with DOS; many commercial programs were written to do the job.

Such programs are much faster than DOS (even DOS 5), so you still may want to purchase a program such as PC Tools Backup, Norton Backup, or FASTBACK. Starting with Version 3.3, however, DOS provides a BACKUP command that is at least usable; it may be slow, but it's still free. DOS's BACKUP command makes copies of files and records their directory locations. You then use DOS's RESTORE command to return the files to the subdirectories from which they were copied.

Why not just use the COPY command to make backup copies of all your files? For one thing, using COPY to back up an entire hard disk would be extremely time-consuming. In addition, if a file is too large to fit on one disk, BACKUP can spread it over more than one disk, prompting you to insert new disks. BACKUP also links a set of disks together to form a set.

One disadvantage to using BACKUP, however, is that your files are no longer accessible to you as they were before. BACKUP puts them in a special format that can be read by only the RESTORE command. This should not cause any problems in the long run, however, because hopefully, you will not have to use RESTORE very often.

In this lesson, you learn how to do the following:

- Prepare the correct number of disks for a backup
- Use the BACKUP command to back up a hard disk
- Use the RESTORE command to restore files to a hard disk

Obviously, backing up and restoring are two opposite parts of the same process. *Backing up* means copying the files stored on your hard disk onto floppy disks; *restoring* means copying the files from the floppy disk backups onto the hard disk. Although you should use BACKUP frequently, you need to use RESTORE only when you lose all or some information from your hard disk. You should not have to use RESTORE often.

What you need to complete this lesson: If you intend to do the exercises at the end of this lesson, you will need a large number of blank disks. You can determine how many disks you need by reading the "Preparing the Disks" section, later in this lesson.

Estimated time to complete this lesson: 20-25 minutes

Backing Up the Hard Disk

Successfully backing up a hard disk is a somewhat more complex and time-consuming process than backing up a floppy disk, but it is well worth the time and effort. To make the procedure more manageable, divide it into three phases:

1. Prepare the disks.
2. Type the BACKUP command statement at the DOS prompt (or execute it from the Shell).
3. Execute the BACKUP command statement.

Preparing the Disks

In earlier versions of DOS, the BACKUP command was not as sophisticated as it is now. Beginning with Version 2.0 and before Version 3.3, you need to format the disks that hold the backup data before starting the backup. If you don't format sufficient disks, you must stop the backup, format disks, and restart the process from the beginning.

Beginning with DOS 3.3, however, BACKUP formats the disks during the backup process if you invoke the BACKUP command with the /F switch. DOS 5 is even more intuitive; it automatically formats a disk if needed, so the /F switch is not necessary. Allowing DOS to format disks during backup slows down the procedure, but you would have to take the time to format them anyway.

The first phase in the backup process is determining how many disks you will need and preparing them to store information from the hard disk. Before you begin to back up, you need enough disks to hold all the information stored on your hard disk.

The easiest way to determine how many floppy disks you will need to back up your hard disk is to use table 14.1.

Table 14.1. Number of Disks Required for Backup

Bytes To Back Up	Number of Disks Needed				
	360K	720K	1.2M	1.44M	2.88M
5M	15	8	6	5	3
10M	29	15	10	8	5
15M	44	22	14	12	7
20M	59	29	18	15	8
25M	72	36	22	19	10
30M	86	43	26	22	12
35M	100	50	31	26	14

continues

Table 14.1. continued

Bytes To Back Up	Number of Disks Needed				
	360K	**720K**	**1.2M**	**1.44M**	**2.88M**
40M	114	57	35	29	15
45M	128	64	39	33	17
50M	142	71	43	36	19
55M	156	78	47	40	21
60M	170	85	51	43	22
65M	184	92	56	47	24
70M	200	100	60	50	26
75M	212	106	64	54	28
80M	226	113	68	57	29
85M	240	120	72	61	31
90M	252	126	76	64	33
95M	266	133	81	67	34
100M	280	140	85	71	36

The formula to calculate these values follows:

# of bytes to back up ÷ disk capacity = # of disks

To arrive at the number of bytes, run CHKDSK and use the number in the `Bytes in user files` line. Add to that number the number in the `Bytes in hidden files` line, but only if this number is over 150,000. Divide the total by the capacity of the disk in order to find the number of disks required. It's a good idea to add at least one disk (perhaps even two) to the total because BACKUP stores a little more than just the files from your hard disk. The numbers in table 14.1 add one to the total.

Suppose that you want to back up your entire hard disk—drive C. If the command

CHKDSK C:

reports `27049984 bytes in 999 user files`, and the number of bytes in hidden files does not exceed 150,000, you divide 27,049,984 by the capacity of your disk (1,200,000 for a 1.2M disk) and add 1, as follows:

27,049,984/1,200,000 = 22.5 (23) + 1 = 24

Perhaps you want to back up only one directory or just a few files in a directory. Instead of using CHKDSK, list the directory with the DIR command or with the Shell. Add the number of bytes for the files you want to copy (or look at the directory total that DIR provides at the end of the listing), and then divide by the capacity of your floppy disk as before.

After you determine how many disks you will need for the backup, you should label the disks. You can put anything on the labels you want, but one efficient method is shown in figure 14.1.

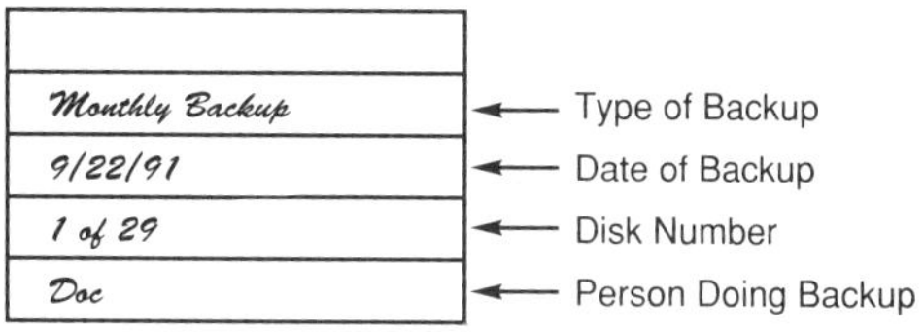

Fig. 14.1. A disk label for a full hard disk backup.

This label tells you the type of backup (full or partial, monthly or daily, and so on), the date the backup was done, the disk number and total number in the set, and the person who did the backup (which is a good idea to include if more than one person uses the computer).

Remember: Never use a ball-point pen or a pencil on labels placed on 5 1/4-inch floppy disks. Always use a felt-tip marker.

Once your disks are prepared, you're ready to write the BACKUP command statement.

Writing the BACKUP Command Statement

Whether you choose to run the BACKUP command from the Shell or from the DOS prompt, the format for the command is the same:

> BACKUP *d1:path\filename.ext d2:*/S/M/A/D:*mm-dd-yy*/T:*hh:mm:ss*
> /F:*size*/L:*d:path\filename.ext*

This statement really isn't as complex as it looks. It consists of these parts:

Parameter	Definition
BACKUP	Command
d1	Disk to be backed up
path	Directory path you want to back up

Parameter	Definition
filename.ext	Name(s) of the file(s) you want to back up. Wild cards are accepted. Suppose that you have one large data file or a group of files that will not fit on one disk; BACKUP divides it for you and places it on two or more disks.
d2	Name of the disk drive to receive the backup files.
/S	Switch that tells DOS to back up all subdirectories, starting with the current or specified directory on the hard disk and working downward. If you start with the root directory, DOS backs up all subdirectories; in other words, if you use /S and start with the root directory, you can back up the whole disk. If you start with a subdirectory rather than the root directory, you back up only the files in that subdirectory and the subdirectories beneath it—not the whole hard disk.
/M	Switch that backs up all files modified since they were last backed up. Use this switch to choose which files you want backed up. /M tells DOS to back up only files that have been changed. Unchanged files on the backup disks are erased unless you use the next switch: /A.
/A	Switch that adds the file(s) to be backed up to the files already on the specified disk drive. This switch is essential when using /M if you don't want unmodified files erased.
/D:*mm-dd-yy*	An alternative switch to those already listed. This switch enables you to specify a date, and it tells DOS to back up any file that has been changed on or after that date. You always should answer the date and time prompts when you boot DOS (unless your computer automatically keeps track of these) so that you can use this feature.
/T:*hh:mm:ss*	Similar to /D. /T backs up files created on or after a specified time.
/F:*size*	Format switch. BACKUP automatically formats a disk if the disk is not formatted. You can use the /F:*size* switch, however, to format the disk to a different capacity, and it operates just like the /F switch in the FORMAT command.

Parameter	Definition
/L:*d:\path\filename.ext*	A switch that creates a log file containing the date and time of the backup and puts the file in the specified directory of the specified drive. If you don't use this switch, BACKUP automatically creates a log file named BACKUP.LOG and puts it in the root directory of the source drive (C:\ if you are backing up drive C, for example).

Executing the BACKUP Command Statement

Once your disks are prepared and you have decided what command statement to use, you are ready to execute the BACKUP command. If you want to use the Shell, which simplifies using BACKUP, follow these steps:

1. Go to the DOS Shell by typing **EXIT** and pressing Enter (if you temporarily left the Shell with Shift-F9). Or, type **DOSSHELL** and press Enter (if you permanently exited with F3).
2. Double-click the Disk Utilities group in the Program List area. Or, press Tab to activate the Program List area, highlight Disk Utilities with the arrow keys, and press Enter.
3. Double-click Backup Fixed Disk or highlight it with the arrow keys and press Enter.

   You see the Backup Fixed Disk dialog box, shown in figure 14.2. Notice the command that appears:

   C:*.* A:/S

The command that appears in the dialog box is the default command in the Shell and should be used the first time you back up your hard disk. This command tells DOS to back up the files in the root directory and all subdirectories. The files are backed up on floppy disks in drive A. In addition, BACKUP.LOG will be created automatically in the root directory of drive C.

When you execute this command, DOS displays the following message:

```
Insert backup diskette 01 in drive A:

WARNING: Files in the target drive A:\ root directory
will be erased

Press any key to continue . . .
```

After you press any key to continue, DOS prompts you to change disks as the backup proceeds.

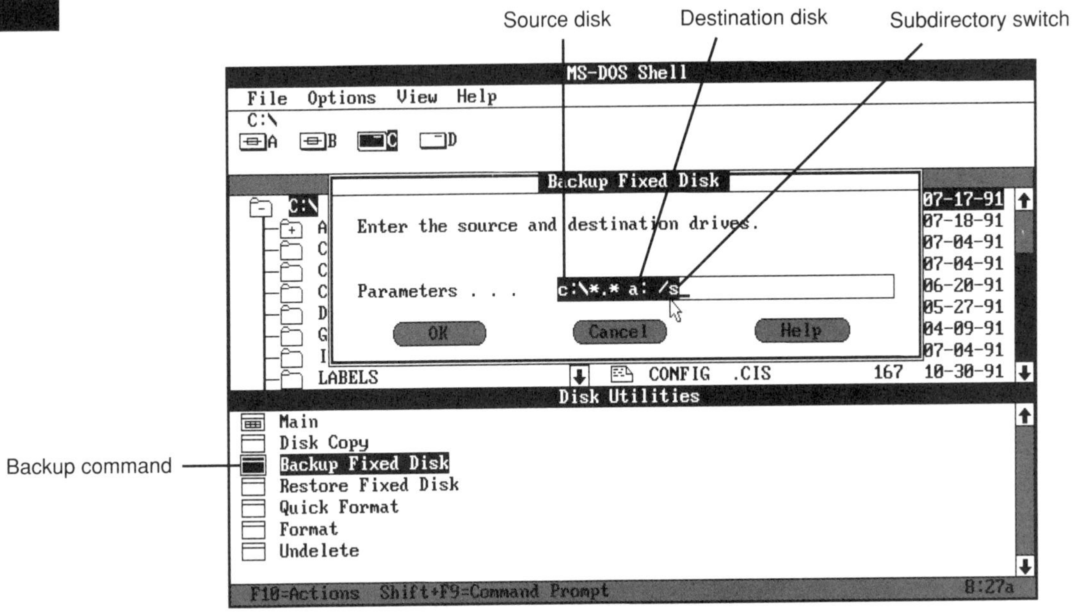

Fig. 14.2. The Backup Fixed Disk dialog box.

> If you prefer to work from the DOS prompt, type the backup command at any C prompt, such as C:\>.

Suppose that you want to keep a separate backup of your DOS subdirectory (which isn't a bad idea, because if some files became damaged, you don't have to go through the long process of reinstalling them from the original DOS disks). You should keep a copy of RESTORE on a separate floppy so that you have access to it. You should copy RESTORE by using COPY command. In this case, the command to back up your DOS directory to floppies is

```
BACKUP C:\DOS\*.*  A:/S
```

Suppose that there are many large Lotus 1-2-3 worksheet files in your 1-2-3 directory on drive C that you want to back up. The command to use follows:

```
BACKUP C:\123\*.WK1  A:
```

Now suppose that you have a large data file named INFO.DAT in your C:\DATABASE subdirectory that is too large to fit on one floppy. BACKUP will spread the file over two or more disks with this command:

```
BACKUP C:\DATABASE\INFO.DAT  A:
```

The /D (date) and /T (time) switches give you even more control over which files are to be backed up. The following command, for example, backs up only those files created on or after March 25, 1992:

```
BACKUP C:\*.* A: /S /D:3-25-92
```

The /T switch enables you to be even more specific. You can, for example, combine the /D and /T switches to back up the files that were created after noon on March 25, 1991 with this command:

```
BACKUP C:\*.* A: /S /D:3-25-92 /T:12:00
```

> Notice that the previous examples have referred to drive C. But what if you have more than one hard disk *partition* (division)? The easiest way to find this out is to just type **D:**, **E:**, **F:**, and so forth until you receive the `Invalid drive specification` error message. This will tell you which hard disk(s) need to be backed up. You then may use any of the previous commands with the proper drive letter.

> To add extra insurance to a critical backup, issue this command at the DOS prompt (or from the Shell) before running BACKUP: **VERIFY ON**. DOS will verify each sector as it is written to the backup disks, double-checking to make sure that your data is backed up correctly. Be aware, however, that this process will double the backup time. After the backup is complete, type **VERIFY OFF**.

Backup Strategies

Perhaps you are wondering why it is necessary to back up your entire hard disk. Why not just back up files you create or change? Why back up application programs that never change?

One good reason for backing up your entire hard disk is that many application programs are configured a certain way when you install them. Therefore, instead of having to go back and reinstall them with the original program disks, you have a totally configured backup copy. Another reason is that if you have a disk crash or failure, you will have a complete copy of your disk, including the complete directory structure, which you can use to restore the disk easily and quickly.

On the other hand, backing up the entire hard disk is time-consuming and requires a great many disks if you have a large hard disk. Some users therefore choose to back up only the files they create or change, either by using BACKUP or COPY.

A hard disk user must decide on a system for backing up files. Following are two strategies for backing up your hard disk. You should decide which is better for you.

Strategy 1

The first strategy can be called the *monthly strategy*. It simply entails making a complete backup of the hard disk once a month—say, the last Friday of the month—and daily backups between. Strategy 1 involves four steps:

1. With a new set of formatted disks, perform a full backup with this command:

   ```
   C:\>BACKUP C:\ A: /S
   ```

   Each disk should be labeled in a similar way to figure 14.1. When the backup is complete, put the set of disks in a safe location.

2. Prepare another set of disks for backup—a quarter to half the disks needed for the full backup. After doing a month or two of backups, you will learn how many disks you need.

3. Each day for the rest of the month, using the second set of disks, perform a backup with this command:

   ```
   C:\>BACKUP C:\ A: /A /S /M
   ```

   The /M switch tells DOS to back up only those files that have changed or were created since the last backup was performed. The /A switch adds the file(s) to be backed up to the files that already exist on drive A. This switch is essential when using /M if you don't want unmodified files erased. Label this set as in figure 14.1, but call it *daily backup* instead of *full* or *monthly*. The date is not crucial, because you will use these disks every day.

   Remember: DOS 5 automatically creates a log file called BACKUP.LOG and places it in the root directory of the source drive (C:\ in this case). This log contains a list of the files it backs up along with the disks on which they reside. You can specify a new name and location of this file by using the /L switch. For added security, you may want to put the file on a floppy by adding this switch: type **/L:A:\BACKUP.LOG**. You can view this log file with the TYPE command (TYPE BACKUP.LOG | MORE) or print it with the COPY command (COPY BACKUP.LOG PRN).

4. You should take one more precaution. Suppose that you are in the middle of a full monthly backup and your hard disk fails. You don't have a backup because the disk failed before you finished. So, what should you do each month? That's right, use another full set of disks and alternate the two sets each month. This way, if you have a hard disk failure in the middle of your backup, you still have a set to fall back on.

Strategy 2

The second strategy is meant to be a compromise for those users mentioned earlier who want to back up only those files they create or change.

So that you will have a full set of backup disks in case of hard disk failure or other problems, you should do a full backup once every three to six months, or at least once a year. You can manually back up the files you create or change by using COPY. The advantage of this method is that it saves time. One disadvantage, however, is that it produces a greater number of unlinked disks to manage. Another disadvantage is that even though there is a backup set, the directory structure will not be up to date and many individual files will have to be copied as well.

Restoring Backup Files

The RESTORE command is the opposite of the BACKUP command. RESTORE transfers the files from your backup disks to your hard disk. The format of the RESTORE command is similar to that of the BACKUP command:

RESTORE *d1: d2:path\filename.ext* /S/P/B:*mm-dd-yy*/A:*mm-dd-yy*/M /N /L:*hh:mm:ss*/E:*hh:mm:ss*

This statement consists of these parts:

Parameter	Definition
RESTORE	Command
d1	Disk drive holding the backup.
d2	Disk drive to restore to—if the disk drive is the current drive, you can omit this part.
path	Optional path to the directory to receive the restored files. The current directory for the hard disk is used if you don't specify a path.

Parameter	Definition
filename.ext	Name(s) of the file(s) you want to restore. If you don't specify a file name, all files are restored.
/S	Switch that restores files in this directory and all other subdirectories beyond it. This switch is identical to BACKUP's /S switch.
/P	Switch that displays a prompt asking whether a read-only file or a file that has been changed since the last backup should be restored.
/B:*mm-dd-yy*	Switch that restores files created or modified on or before a specified date.
/A:*mm-dd-yy*	Switch that restores files created or modified on or after a specified date.
/M	Switch used to restore files modified or deleted since the last backup.
/N	Switch used to restore files that no longer exist.
/L:*hh:mm:ss*	Switch used to restore files saved or altered on or later than a specified time.
/E:*hh:mm:ss*	Switch used to restore files that were saved or altered on or earlier than a specified time.

To use RESTORE to restore a full backup using the Shell, which does simplify using RESTORE, follow these steps:

1. Double-click the Disk Utilities group in the Program List area. Or, press Tab to activate the Program List area, highlight Disk Utilities with the arrow keys, and press Enter.
2. Double-click Restore Fixed Disk or highlight it with the arrow keys and press Enter.

   You see the Restore Fixed Disk dialog box, shown in figure 14.3.

   Notice that no command or parameters are displayed, as in the Backup Fixed Disk dialog box.
3. Type **A: C:\ /S**.

All you need to do is type the parameters because the Shell knows that it is executing the RESTORE command. This command tells DOS to start at the root directory of the hard disk and restore all the files in this directory and all subdirectories from drive A.

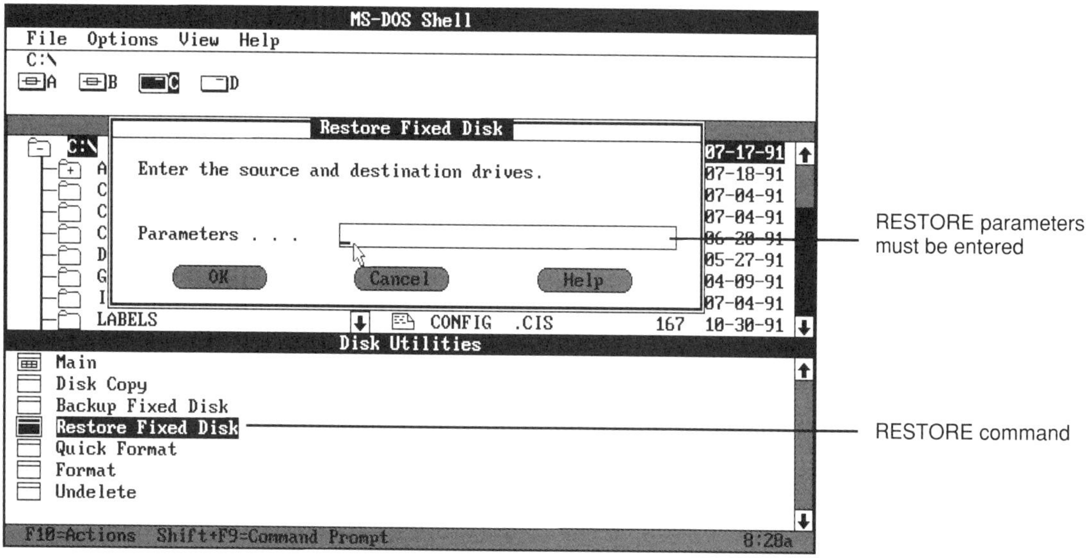

Fig. 14.3. The Restore Fixed Disk dialog box.

If you execute the command, RESTORE displays the following message:

```
Insert backup diskette 01 in drive A:
Press any key to continue . . .
```

When you are restoring files, you must always start with the first backup disk of the set and work sequentially through the set, even if you are restoring only a few files. DOS prompts you when you need to change disks.

After pressing any key to continue, DOS prompts you when to change disks as the restore progresses.

> If you prefer to work from the DOS prompt, type the command at any C:\ prompt, such as C:\DOS>.

> For even more protection, use COPY to copy the RESTORE.EXE program to a bootable floppy disk (one formatted with the /S switch) so that you can get to it in case of a hard disk failure. Label this disk *Disaster Disk*. You then would execute the RESTORE command from the A> prompt.

If you want to restore the DOS directory as noted earlier in the section on the BACKUP command, you use this command:

RESTORE A: C:\DOS*.*

To restore only one file (the FORMAT.COM file, for example) that was accidentally deleted and could not be undeleted, you use this command:

RESTORE A: C:\DOS\FORMAT.COM

To restore the set of Lotus 1-2-3 worksheet files discussed earlier, you use this command:

RESTORE A: C:\123*.WK1

To restore the large data file discussed earlier, you use this command:

RESTORE A: C:\DATABASE\INFO.DAT

Perhaps you are wondering if you easily can restore one or two directories, or even a single file, from the disks on which you did a full backup. The answer is yes. If any of the previous examples were part of a full backup, you could allow RESTORE to look for the proper files on each backup disk, or you could manually look up the proper disk number in the BACKUP.LOG file (which you learned about in "Strategy 1," earlier in this lesson).

The /A (after) and /B (before) switches give you even more control over which files are to be restored. To restore only those files created *on* or *before* March 25, 1992, you use this command:

RESTORE A: C:*.* /B:3-25-92

Similarly, to restore only those files created *after* this date, enter this command:

RESTORE A: C:*.* /A:3-25-92

You also may choose to add the very useful /P (pause) switch to a RESTORE command; this switch displays the following message if RESTORE detects that it is about to overwrite a file that was changed after the original backup:

```
WARNING!  File <filename.ext>
was changed after it was backed up
Replace the file (Y/N)?
```

Appendix D contains some additional information about BACKUP and RESTORE and some special occasions for using them.

Lesson Summary

- ☐ BACKUP and RESTORE are complementary commands that enable hard disk users to create on floppy disks backup files of the hard disk (BACKUP), and then to replace the files from the backup copies to the hard disk (RESTORE).
- ☐ You should have a systematic method of backing up your disk so that information is not lost.

Key Terms

Backup	To make copies of files for storage, in case the originals get damaged or lost.
BACKUP	Makes a special copy of files and their directory locations, usually onto floppy disks.
Monthly backup strategy	A systematic way of backing up the entire hard disk once a month and modified files once a day.
RESTORE	Places files that have been copied with BACKUP back onto the hard disk.

Exercises

Use the principles, step-by-step guidelines, and tips you learned in this lesson to do a complete backup of your hard disk. Take special note of whether your system has more than one hard disk or whether your single hard disk has more than one partition (division). The easiest way to find this out is to type **D:**, **E:**, **F:**, and so forth until you receive the error message

```
Invalid drive specification
```

This tells you which hard disk(s) need to be backed up.

For More Information

For additional beginner-level information, as well as some intermediate information concerning what was presented in this lesson, refer to *MS-DOS 5 QuickStart* (Que Corporation). For a more in-depth discussion of these subjects, refer to *Using MS-DOS 5* (Que Corporation). See Appendix E for a description of these Que books.

Part IV

Going Beyond the Basics

The three lessons in this final section teach you how to do the following:

- Work with programs in the Shell (Lesson 15)
- Customize the Shell (Lesson 16)
- Customize DOS (Lesson 17)

Lesson 15

Working with Programs in the Shell

One of the most valuable aspects of the MS-DOS Shell is its capability to run (or launch) your programs and even to run two or more programs at once. To make using your programs even easier, you can use the Shell to organize your programs into separate groups, each group containing a number of individual programs.

In this lesson you learn how to do the following:

- View program groups
- Start a program
- Switch between programs
- Exit a program
- Associate files with a program

Estimated time to complete this lesson: 30-35 minutes

Viewing Program Groups

As you know from Lesson 4, the Program List area is in the lower left portion of the Shell screen. As shown in figure 15.1, the Main Program area is the program group displayed when you first start the Shell. If, however, the Disk Utilities group is displayed, double-click on Main or highlight Main with the arrow keys and press Enter.

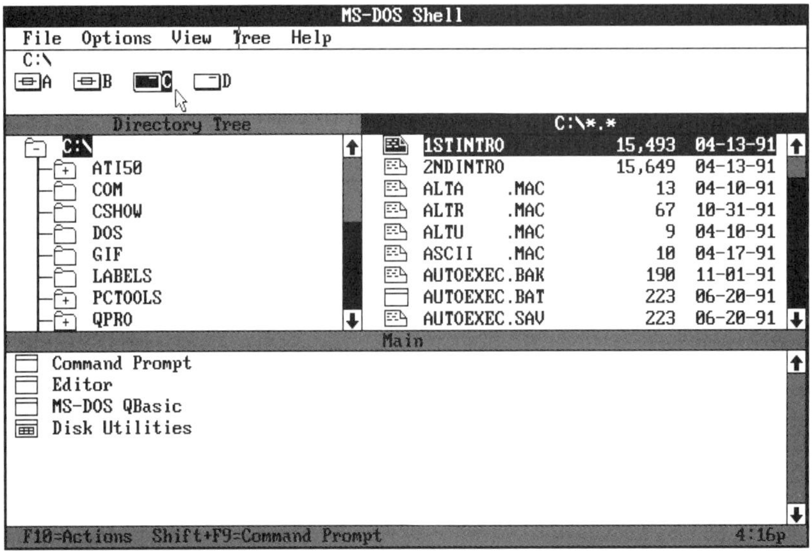

Fig. 15.1. The Main Program area is displayed when the Shell first starts.

The Main Program area contains the following choices: Command Prompt, Editor, MS-DOS QBasic, and Disk Utilities. The first three choices are *program items*. The fourth choice, Disk Utilities, is a *program group*. Notice that the icon beside a program group differs from the icon beside a program item. As the name indicates, a program group contains a group (or collection) of programs.

To view the items in a group, you first must open that group. If you haven't started the DOS Shell, do so now. You open the Disk Utilities group by following these simple steps:

1. Double-click the Disk Utilities group name or icon. Or, press Tab until the Main title bar is highlighted, press the up- or down-arrow key to highlight the Disk Utilities group, and press Enter.

   Your screen should look like figure 15.2.

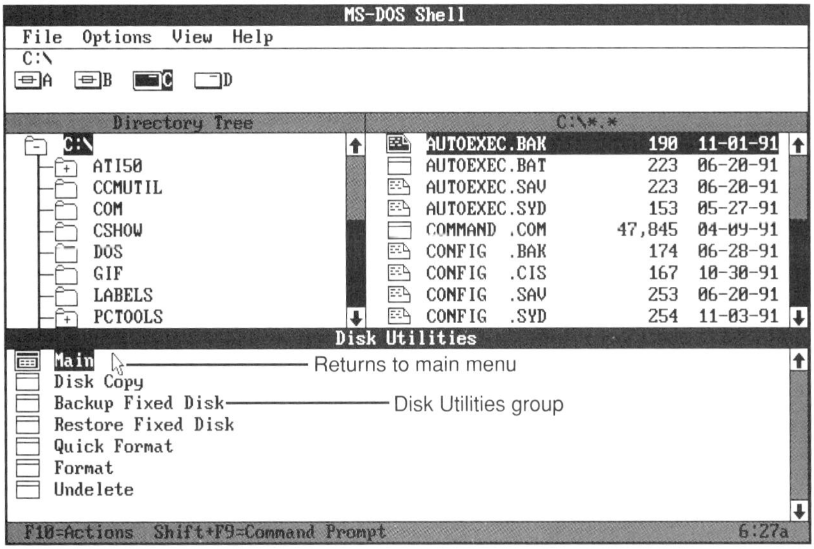

Fig. 15.2. The Disk Utilities group.

2. To close this group, double-click the Main group, or use the up- or down-arrow key to highlight the Main group and press Enter.

In other words, you close one group by simply opening another.

Starting a Program

There are three ways to start a program in the Shell: from a program group, from a file list, and by using the Run command. The following sections explain each of these methods.

Using the Program Group

If the program you want to start is listed in a group displayed in the program list, the easiest way to run the program is to choose it from the list.

A program you probably will use often is the Editor—a text editor that comes with DOS 5. A text editor is similar to a word processor. You learn more about the Editor in Lesson 17. To start this useful program, follow these steps:

1. If the Main group is not displayed in the Program List area, double-click the Main group. Or, press Tab until the title bar is highlighted, press the up- or down-arrow key to highlight the Main group, and press Enter.
2. Double-click Editor. Or, use the up- or down-arrow key to highlight Editor and press Enter.
3. A dialog box appears and asks for the name of the file you want to edit. Because this is just a demonstration of how to start a program, click OK or press Enter.

   You see the opening Editor screen (see fig. 15.3).

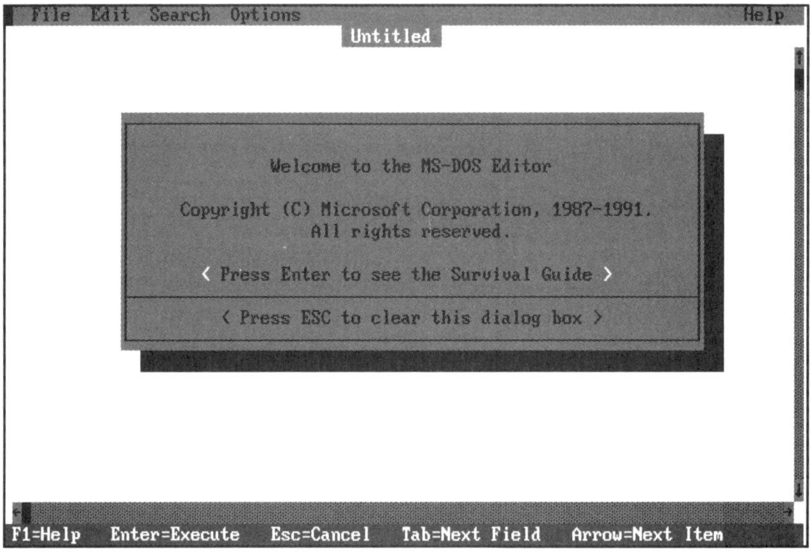

Fig. 15.3. The opening screen of the Editor.

4. Again, because this is only a demonstration, press Esc to bypass the Editor's Help system.
5. To exit Editor, click File and Exit. Or, press Alt, F, and X.

   You are returned to the Shell.

As you can see, starting programs from a group is the easiest way to use programs. In Lesson 16, you learn how to add program groups and items so that you can start all your programs easily and quickly.

Using the File List

Another way to start a program is by choosing the program file from the File List area. Program files have COM, EXE, or BAT *extensions* (the three letters to the right of the period).

To open the Editor using a file list, follow these steps:

1. In the Directory Tree area, double-click the DOS subdirectory. Or, press Tab to activate the Directory Tree title bar and then use the up- or down-arrow key to highlight the DOS subdirectory and press Enter.
2. In the File List area, use the scroll bar to scroll down to the EDIT.COM file; then double-click it. Or, press Tab to activate the File List title bar, use the up- or down-arrow key to highlight EDIT.COM, and press Enter.

   You see the opening Editor screen. Because you start the program directly instead of from the Program list, you are not asked for a file name to edit.
3. Press Esc.
4. To exit the Editor, click File and Exit. Or, press Alt, F, and X.

   You are returned to the Shell.

Notice that you are prompted to

```
Press any key to return to MS-DOS shell
```

This prompting can be controlled when starting programs from the Program List area, but this message is always displayed when you exit a program after starting it from the File List area.

Using the Run Command

Another way to start a program is by using the Run command from the File menu. To start the Editor using this method, follow these steps:

1. Click File and Run. Or, press Alt, F, and R.

   You see the Run dialog box (see fig. 15.4).

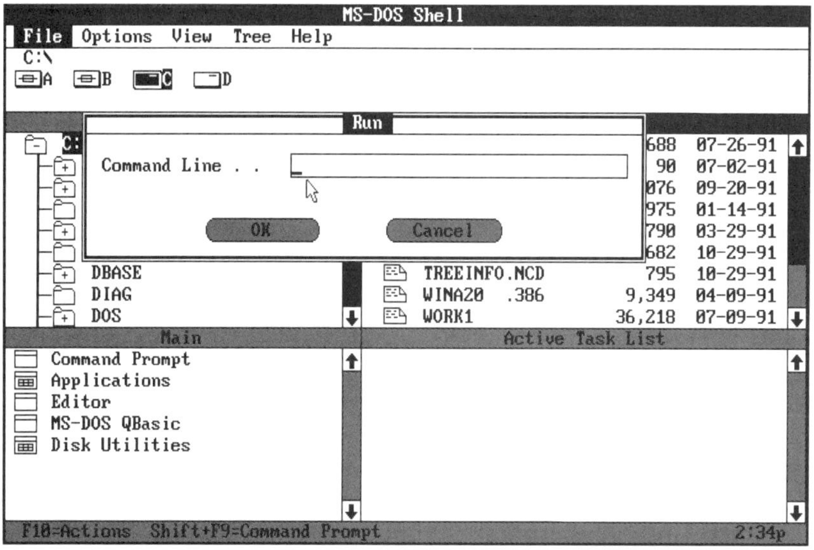

Fig. 15.4. The Run dialog box.

2. Type **EDIT** in the box and press Enter. (You can click OK after typing **EDIT**, but pressing Enter is faster.)

   If you change your mind and do not want to run the program, you can click Cancel or press Esc before pressing Enter.

3. Press Esc.

4. To exit the Editor, click File and Exit. Or, press Alt, F, and X.

   You are returned to the Shell.

> In this example, the program you want to run is in the current directory, so all you must do is type the program name, but this will not always be the case. Unless the file is in the current directory, you must know the drive and directory location of the file. Many PC users use the WordPerfect 5.1 word processing program, for example. If you want to run this program, which usually resides in a subdirectory called WP51, you must type **C:\WP51\WP** in the Run dialog box. This command tells DOS that the program you want to run resides in the WP51 subdirectory on drive C and is called WP.

Switching between Programs

One of the most outstanding features of DOS 5's Shell is its capability to run more than one program at a time, which enables you to switch back and forth between programs. This feature is called *task-swapping*. You no longer have to exit one program in order to start another, as in earlier versions of DOS.

Enabling the Task Swapper

To enable task swapping, click the Options menu and then click Enable Task Swapper. Or, you can press Alt, O, and E. A diamond appears beside the Enable Task Swapper command name and the Active Task list is displayed, as shown in figure 15.5.

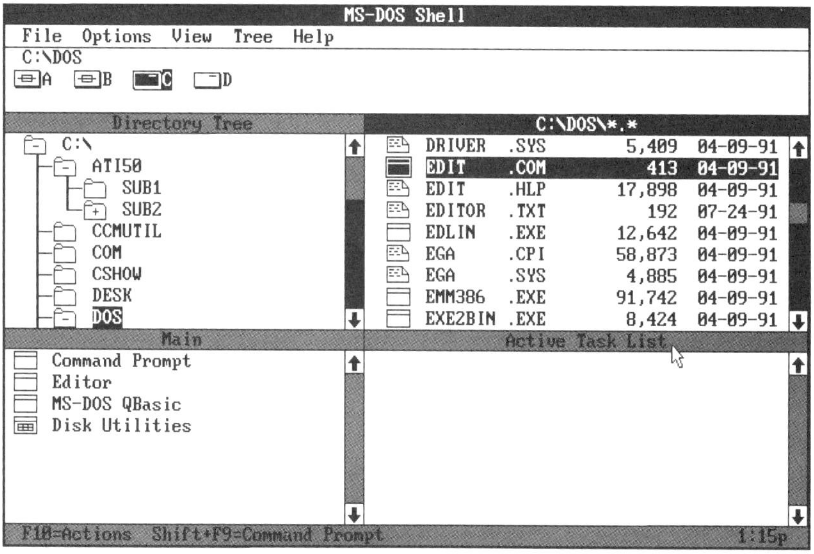

Fig. 15.5. The Active Task list after enabling task swapping.

The Active Task list displays the names of programs that you have started *after* enabling task swapping. Once you exit a program, its name is no longer listed. Currently, no programs are listed because task swapping has just been enabled. The following section explains how to load programs to use with the Task Swapper.

Loading Multiple Programs

Before continuing, make sure that you understand everything you have learned in this lesson about starting programs. If you need to do so, review that material.

In this section, you start three programs from the Shell and switch among them. The three programs used—Editor, Money Manager, and Nibbles!—come with DOS 5. Follow these steps:

1. Start the Editor from the Main Program list.
2. Once the Editor is on-screen, press Ctrl-Esc to return to the Shell.

   The Editor now appears in the Active Task list.
3. Now go to the DOS subdirectory by clicking on DOS or highlighting DOS with the arrow keys. Start the Money Manager program by selecting MONEY.BAS in the File List area and double-clicking the file name. Or, highlight the file name and press Enter.

   When the Money Manager title screen appears, press any key to display the main screen.

   Money Manager is a simple accounting program written in MS-DOS QBasic. Thorough instruction on this program is beyond the scope of *Hands-On MS-DOS 5*, so consult the documentation that came with your copy of DOS 5.

> An alternate method for adding a program to the Active Task list *without* starting that program is to highlight the program and then press Shift-Enter. The program is added to the Active Task list but the program does not start; it simply waits for you to switch to it like any other program on the list.

4. Once Money Manager is on-screen, press Ctrl-Esc again to return to the Shell.

   Notice that MONEY.BAS also appears in the Active Task list.
5. Go to the DOS subdirectory again and select the NIBBLES.BAS file in the File list. Start this program by double-clicking on it or by highlighting it and pressing Enter.

   You see the Nibbles! opening screen, as shown in figure 15.6.

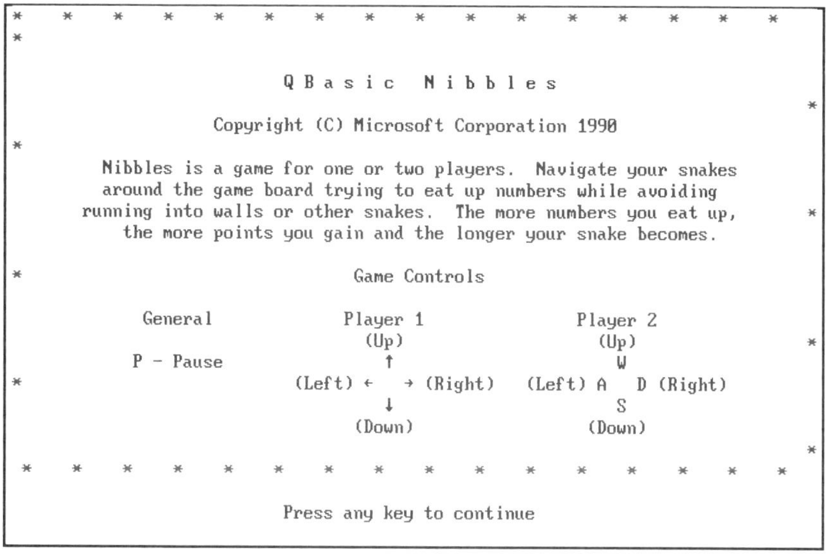

Fig. 15.6. The opening screen of the Nibbles! game.

When the Nibbles! title screen appears, read the directions to play this game. Press any key to continue. Choose Player 1 and press Enter, choose 1 for the skill level and press Enter, choose N to increase game speed during play and press Enter, and select M or C for monochrome or color and press Enter. Then press the space bar to start the game. Have fun!

Well, you had better get back to work—the boss could come in at any time. But there's no need to exit the game. Just stop the game wherever you are by pressing P, and go on to step 6.

6. Now, press and hold down the Alt key and press Tab once, but do not release Alt until step 7.

   The Nibbles! screen disappears and is replaced by the name of the next active program in the Active Task list. If you release the Alt key, you switch to the program shown.

7. Keep pressing Tab and watch the active program change. When you see `Editor` displayed, release the Alt key. The Editor reappears.

8. To go directly to the Shell from Editor (or any other program) press Ctrl-Esc.

9. Now, while you are in the Active Task list in the Shell, switch to Money Manager by double-clicking MONEY.BAS. Or, use the arrow keys to highlight MONEY.BAS and press Enter.

   Table 15.1 summarizes the keystrokes for task swapping.

Table 15.1. Keystrokes for Task Swapping

Key Combination	Effect
Alt-Tab	Changes to the next program in the Active Task list
Hold down Alt while pressing Tab several times	Cycles through the Active Task list
Ctrl-Esc	Switches directly to the Shell from any program
Shift-Enter	Adds a highlighted program to the Active Task list without starting the program

10. Exit Money Manager by using the arrow keys to highlight File and press Enter twice. Then press any other key to return to the QBasic Money Manager screen.
11. Exit the QBasic Money Manager by clicking File and Exit. Or, press Alt, F, and X, and then any other key to return to the Shell.
12. Switch to the Nibbles! game. At the end of the game, answer N to the question, `Play Again?`. Then press any key. Exit QBasic Nibbles by clicking File and Exit. Or, press Alt, F, and X, and then any other key to return to the Shell.

> If you want to quit Nibbles! in the middle of a game, press Ctrl-Break, and then exit QBasic Nibbles.

13. Switch to the Editor and exit it by clicking File and Exit. Or, press Alt, F, and X.
14. Disable task swapping by clicking the Options menu and choosing Enable Task Swapper. Or, you can press Alt, O, and E.

    The diamond disappears, and your screen returns to normal.

> Now that you have learned how to run more than one program at a time and switch among them, you probably will want task swapping enabled most, if not all, of the time.

Exiting a Program

It is best to exit a program in the usual manner when you want to remove it from the Active Task list. To exit correctly, simply switch to the program you want to exit, and then issue the program's normal exiting command.

You can use a different method to remove a program from the Active Task list, but you should use it *only* if a program fails or freezes. If this happens, switch to the Shell by pressing Ctrl-Esc, select the program you want to exit by highlighting it with the mouse or arrow keys, and press the Del key. The Shell displays a message warning you that data can be lost by continuing and that you should exit the application normally. Because the program failed or froze, however, you have no other choice. Choose OK to remove the program from the Active Task list.

> A program that fails can sometimes affect the stability of DOS and cause further problems later on. It is advisable, therefore, to exit the Shell and restart the computer after quitting a program in this manner.

Associating Files with a Program

If you have a set of files that you often use with a particular program, you can save time by *associating* the files with the program. This means that you can attach a particular file extension to a program. Then, when you open an associated file, the program starts with that file already loaded.

The Shell, for example, already is set up to associate all TXT files with the Editor. To illustrate this feature, follow these steps:

1. Click the DOS subdirectory in the Directory Tree of drive C. Or, press Tab to highlight the Directory Tree title bar and highlight the DOS subdirectory with the arrow keys.

2. Double-click the README.TXT file. Or, press Tab to highlight the File List title bar, use the arrow keys to highlight README.TXT, and press Enter. This procedure loads the Editor and the named text file because they now are associated.

   Your screen should look like the screen in figure 15.7.

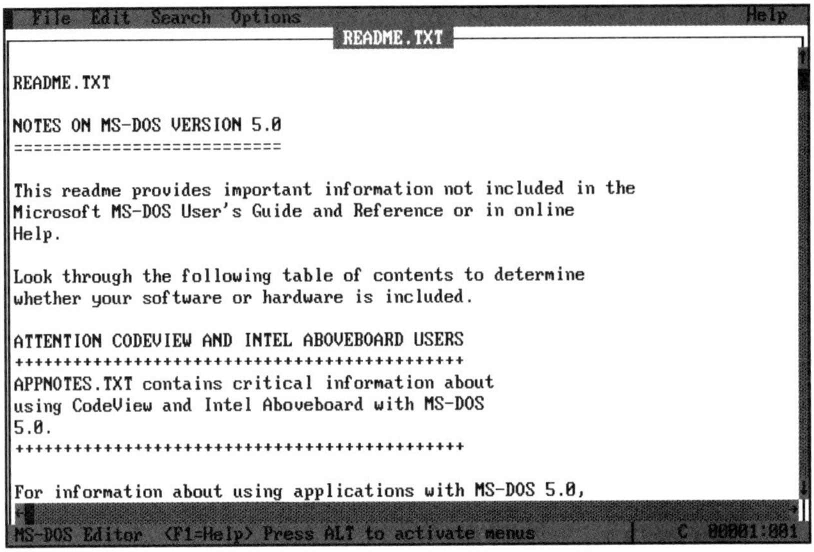

Fig. 15.7. A TXT file associated with the Editor.

In figure 15.7, you see a text file that provides additional information about DOS that was not included in the DOS manual.

3. To exit the Editor, click File and Exit. Or, press Alt, F, and X. Then press any key to return to the Shell.

Now, suppose that you want to associate other files, such as DOC files, with the Editor. DOC files commonly are used to indicate ASCII text files. You can associate DOC files with the Editor by following these steps:

1. While still in the DOS subdirectory, click (do *not* double-click) EDIT.COM in the File list or highlight the file name with the arrow keys.

2. Click Associate in the File Menu or press Alt, F, and A to display the Associate File dialog box shown in figure 15.8.

3. Type **DOC** in the dialog box, and then click OK or press Enter.

4. Click the ATI50\SUB1 subdirectory in the Directory Tree of drive C. Or, press Tab to highlight the Directory Tree title bar and highlight the subdirectory with the arrow keys.

> If the disk tutor was installed on a drive other than drive C, specify that drive instead of drive C.

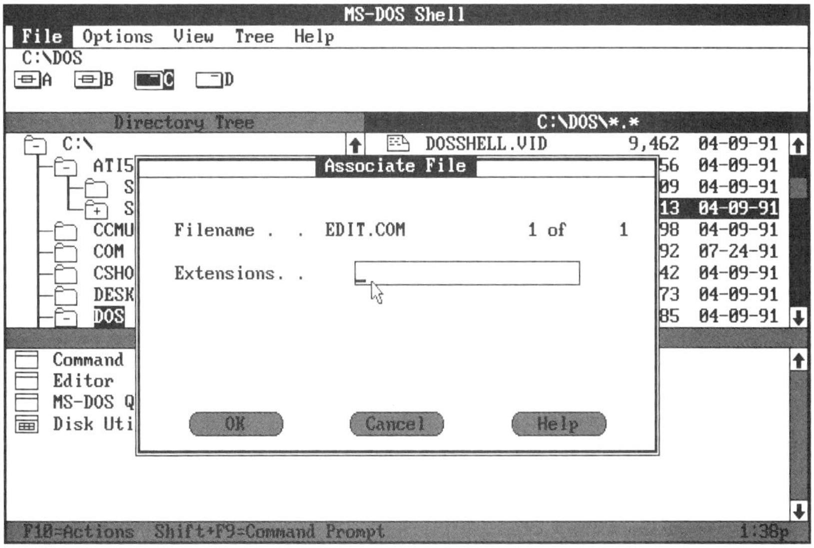

Fig. 15.8. The Associate File dialog box.

5. Double-click the LESSON15.DOC file. Or, press Tab to highlight the File List title bar, use the arrow keys to highlight LESSON15.DOC, and press Enter.

   You see the text file shown in figure 15.9.

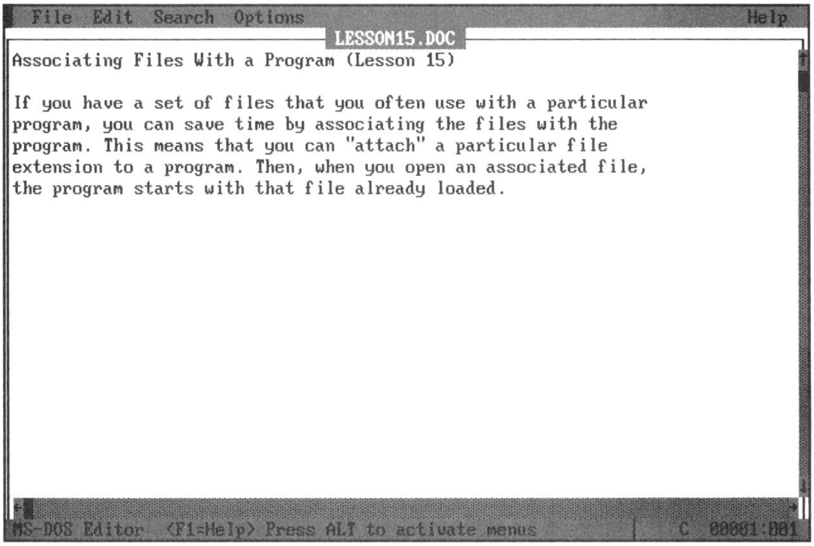

Fig. 15.9. A DOC file associated with the Editor.

6. To exit the Editor, click File and Exit. Or, press Alt, F, and X. Then press any key to return to the Shell.

> One limitation of the Associate command is that a particular extension can be associated with only *one* program. You cannot, for example, associate the DOC extension with both the Editor and your word processor. You can, however, associate more than one extension to a program. In fact, the Associate File dialog box accepts up to 79 characters, so you can associate many extensions with a program. The spreadsheet program Quattro Pro (Q.EXE), for example, uses the WQ1 extension for its spreadsheet files, but it also reads and writes the WK1 files of Lotus 1-2-3. You could, therefore, list both WQ1 and WK1 in the Associate File dialog box. This way, whenever you choose a worksheet file (WQ1 or WK1), you would start Quattro and load the chosen worksheet automatically.

Lesson Summary

- ☐ To open a program group, double-click the group name. Or, use the up- or down-arrow key to highlight the Disk Utilities group and press Enter.
- ☐ To start a program, double-click the program file name. Or, use the up- or down-arrow key to highlight the name of the file and press Enter.
- ☐ You also can start a program by choosing the Run command from the File menu and entering the path and program file name in the dialog box.
- ☐ With Task Swapper enabled, you can load multiple programs and easily switch among them by pressing Alt-Tab and Ctrl-Esc.
- ☐ Always exit a program normally to remove it from the Active Task list. If a program fails or freezes, you can remove it from the Task list with the Del key. A system reset is recommended.
- ☐ You can associate data files with program files, making it easy to load both at the same time.

Key Terms

Associate	To correlate or attach a particular file extension to a program
Launch	To start a program
Program group	Contains a group (or collection) of program items
Program item	An individual program listed in a group of programs
Task swapping	The capability to load more than one program and switch between them
Text Editor	A mini word processor that creates or changes text files

Exercises

Another practical use for task swapping is to run the disk tutor and then switch to the Shell.

You may, for example, want to go through the disk tutor again or repeat certain lessons. You can, therefore, start the disk tutor from the Shell. Then, when you learn a particular procedure in the disk tutor, you can switch to the Shell, immediately practice what you have learned, and then switch back to the disk tutor.

So that you know exactly how to switch to the disk tutor, follow these steps:

1. Enable task swapping (see "Enabling the Task Swapper").
2. Using a drive icon and the Directory Tree area, go to the drive and subdirectory where the disk tutor program is located. On most computers, the program will be in the ATI50 subdirectory on drive C (see "Viewing Program Groups").
3. Start the disk tutor by double-clicking ATI.EXE or by highlighting ATI.EXE and pressing Enter (see "Starting a Program").
4. At any time, press Ctrl-Esc to switch from the disk tutor to the Shell. Notice that ATI.EXE now is listed in the Active Task list if you are in the View Program/File List mode (see "Switching between Programs").

In the Shell, you can perform a task you learned about only moments before in the disk tutor. Using this technique, you can practice things immediately, without having to exit the disk tutor first.

5. Switch back to the disk tutor by double-clicking ATI.EXE or by highlighting ATI.EXE and pressing Enter.
6. When you are ready, exit the disk tutor as usual (see "Exiting a Program").

As you can see, the Shell's capability to run more than one program at a time and switch among them is a tremendous asset. This feature enables you to work faster and more efficiently.

Now that you have learned most of the features of the Shell, you are ready to learn how to customize the Shell, which is discussed in Lesson 16.

Lesson 16

Customizing the Shell

Until now, you have been using the Shell's default settings, for the most part. You can change a number of settings in the Shell, however, such as screen mode and colors. You also can add and delete program groups; add, change, or delete program items; and suppress various confirmation messages, which sometimes slow you down. Customizing the Shell makes your work more enjoyable.

In this lesson, you learn how to do the following:

- Change screen mode and colors
- Add and delete program groups
- Add, change, and delete program items
- Suppress confirmation messages

Estimated time to complete this lesson: 20-25 minutes

Changing Screen Colors

For color monitors, the Shell has several color schemes available, which you can change with a few mouse clicks or keystrokes. Follow these steps:

1. Click Options and then Colors. Or, press Alt, O, and O.

   The Color Scheme dialog box appears (see fig. 16.1).

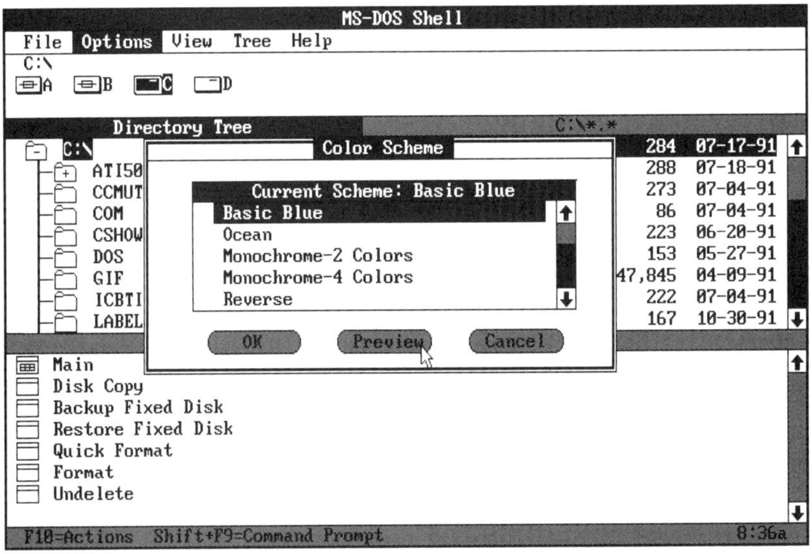

Fig. 16.1. The Color Scheme dialog box.

2. Use the arrow keys or the mouse and scroll arrows to highlight the color scheme you want.

3. If you want to see what the color scheme looks like without actually changing the screen, click Preview. Or, press Tab twice and then Enter.

4. Repeat the procedure as many times as you want to view other color schemes.

   You can cancel the procedure at any time by clicking Cancel or by pressing Esc.

5. When you find the color scheme you want, click OK (or double-click the color scheme choice) or press Enter.

Changing Screen Mode

As you learned in Lesson 4, if you do not have a graphics monitor, you can display the Shell only in text mode (see fig. 16.2).

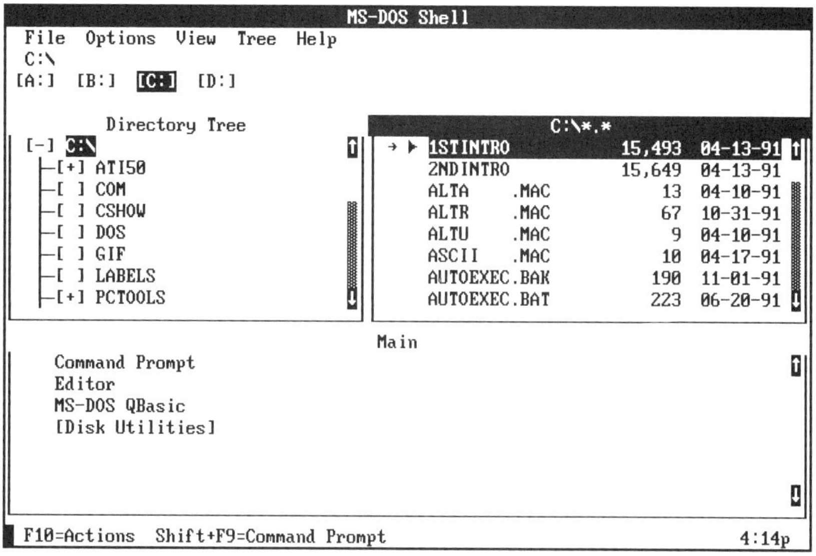

Fig. 16.2. The Shell displayed in text mode.

If you have a graphics monitor, however, you can display the Shell in graphics mode, as it has been throughout this book. You can control the appearance further by changing the screen mode, which controls the size and shape of the images on-screen. With a graphics monitor, you can choose how many lines to display.

To illustrate this idea and to show a practical use for displaying more than the default 25 lines, follow these steps (if you have a graphics monitor):

1. Make sure you are logged onto the root directory of drive C.
2. Click View and then Single File List. Or, press Alt, V, and S.

   The Single File list—valuable when doing heavy disk and file maintenance—is displayed.
3. Press Ctrl-* (asterisk) to expand the entire Directory Tree area.

The subdirectories on disk are displayed. Depending on how many directories you have, however, the tree may not display all of the subdirectories.

4. Click Options and then Display. Or, press Alt, O, and D.

   The Screen Display Mode dialog box appears (see fig. 16.3).

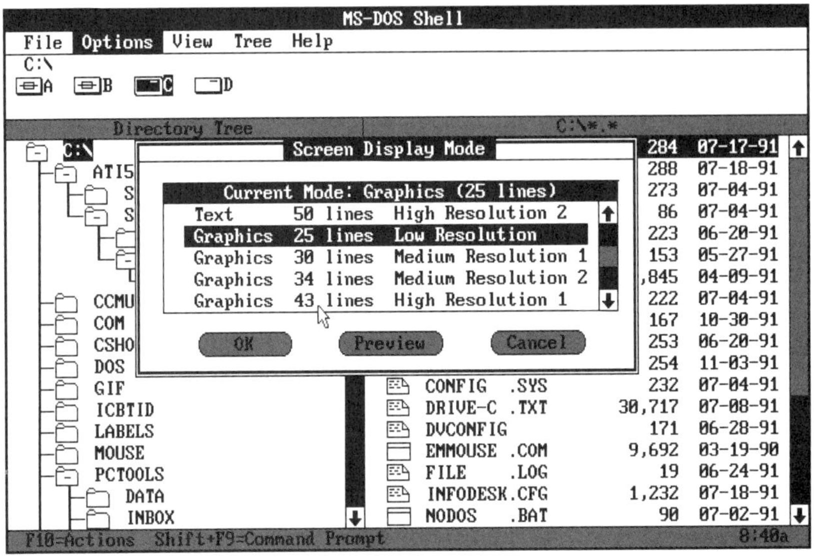

Fig. 16.3. The Screen Display Mode dialog box.

5. Use the mouse and scroll arrows and then click Graphics 43 Lines High Resolution 1, or highlight this choice with the arrow keys.

6. To preview this option, click Preview. Or, press Tab twice and then Enter.

   If you want to use this option, you can click OK instead, in which case your screen looks like figure 16.4.

   You may choose to use this display option because of how many more directories and files it displays, in contrast to the default 25-line display.

7. Repeat the procedure as often as you want to view other display modes. You can cancel the procedure at any time by clicking Cancel or by pressing Esc.

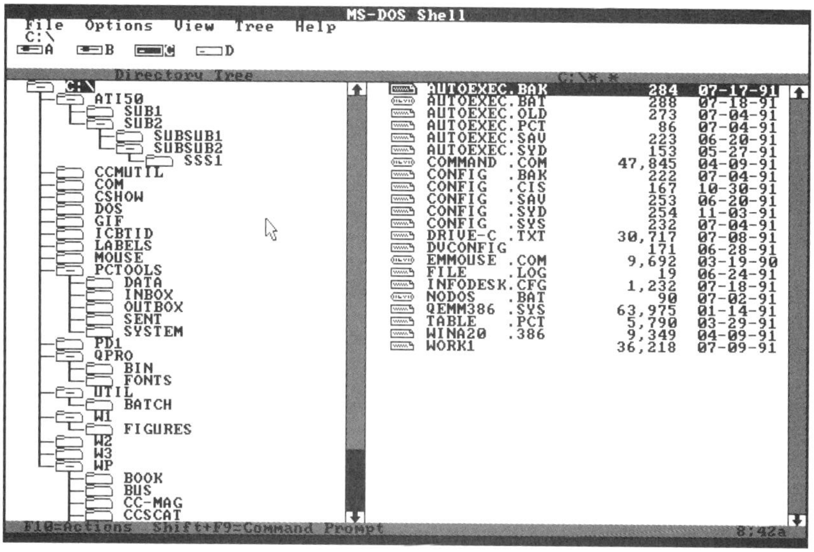

Fig. 16.4. A 43-line display.

8. When you find the display mode you want, click OK (or double-click the display mode choice) or press Enter.

To return to the Shell's default setting, choose 25 Line Low Resolution in Text or Graphics.

Working with Program Groups

As you already know, one advantage of the Shell is its capability to start your programs. The next section shows you how to add programs to the Shell's display.

Before learning to add programs, however, you must learn to use program groups, which organize your individual programs. You will probably want to organize your programs to fit your personal work habits. You could, for example, organize your programs into a business group, a personal group, and a pleasure group.

The following steps explain how to create a program group:

1. To ensure that the Program/File list is displayed, click View and then click Program/File List. Or, press Alt, V, and F.

Your screen may not change, but this step is necessary, because you will be working in the Program List area.

2. Activate the Program List area by clicking anywhere inside it or by pressing Tab until the title bar is highlighted.

3. Make sure the Main program group is displayed.

   If the Disk Utilities group is displayed, for example, double-click Main, or highlight Main with the arrow keys and press Enter.

4. Click File and then New. Or, press Alt, F, and N.

   The New Program Object dialog box appears (see fig. 16.5).

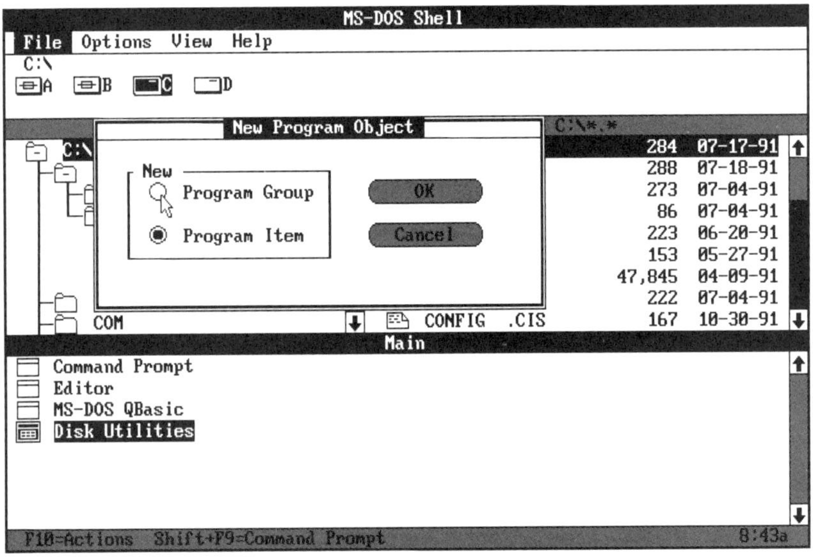

Fig. 16.5. The New Program Object dialog box.

5. Click Program Group and then OK. Or, press the up-arrow key once and then Enter.

   The Add Group dialog box now appears (see fig. 16.6).

6. Type **APPLICATIONS**.

7. Press Tab once to go to the Help Text Line.

   If you want to enter your own help text here, you may enter up to 255 characters, including spaces, in this text box. You can enter line breaks by typing **^M** (the caret symbol and the letter *m*).

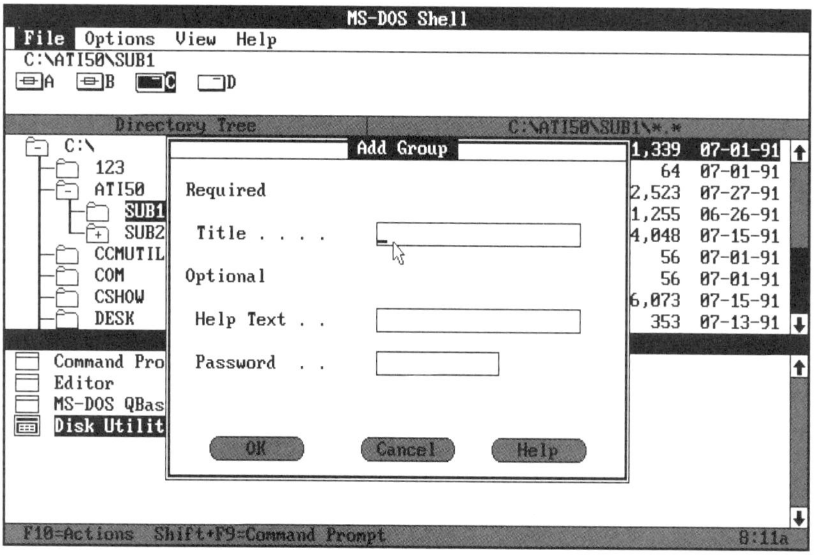

Fig. 16.6. The Add Group dialog box.

For practice, type the following on the help text line:

> This is the Main Applications group. It contains the major applications on this computer, such as word processing, spreadsheet, and database programs.

8. Press Tab once to go to the Password line.

   You can enter a 20-character password so that you alone can access this program group.

   For practice, type your name in upper- or lowercase letters. Make sure that you use one or the other. Remember the case you have used, because this feature is case-sensitive.

> This password feature offers security only in the DOS Shell. It does not prevent an unauthorized user from exiting the Shell and accessing your programs directly from the DOS prompt.

9. Press Enter.

   Notice that the Main Program list now should list the Applications group.

10. Click Applications, or highlight it with the arrow keys, and then press F1.

    Your help text is displayed (see fig. 16.7).

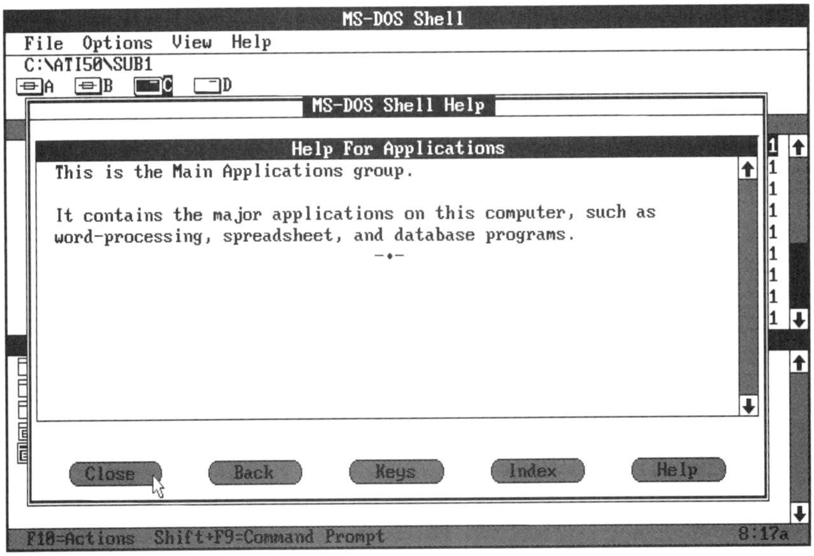

Fig. 16.7. Help text for newly created Applications group.

11. Exit the help window and then double-click Applications, or just press Enter. You now are prompted for the password.
12. Enter your password and press Enter. You now are in the Applications group, in which you have only one choice—the Main group—because you haven't added any programs to this group yet.
13. If you want to change any option in a group (other than the Main group, which cannot be changed), highlight the group as you did before, and then click File and Properties. Or, press Alt, F, and P.

    The Program Group Properties dialog box (identical to the Add Group dialog box except for the title) appears. You now can change any properties you want. You may want to remove the password, for example.
14. Return to the Main group by double-clicking or highlighting it and pressing Enter.

If you want to delete a program group, you can do so in three steps. Do not delete the group you just created, however, because you need it later. Refer to these steps when you must delete a group:

1. Make sure that the group has no programs in it. The Shell will not delete a group with programs listed.
2. Highlight the group and press Del.
3. Choose the OK button from the Delete Item dialog box.

Working with Program Items

Now that you know how to create program groups, you can add your programs to those groups. You also can reorder programs within a group or move programs to other groups.

Adding a Program Item

After you add the CHKDSK command to the Disk Utilities group in the following example, you should be able to add your own programs to groups.

To add a program to a group and configure it the way you want, follow these steps:

1. As before, be sure the Program/File list is displayed, because this is the area in which you will be working. If needed, click View and then Program/File List. Or, press Alt, V and F.
2. Activate the Program List area by clicking anywhere inside it or by pressing Tab until the title bar is highlighted.
3. Double-click the Disk Utilities group or highlight it with the arrow keys and press Enter.
4. Click File and then click New. Or, press Alt, F, and N.

   The New Program Object dialog box appears.
5. Because New Program Item already is selected, click OK or press Enter.

   The Add Program dialog box appears (see fig. 16.8).
6. In the Program Title box, type **CHECK DISK C:** to specify the title that appears in the Program group, and then press Tab to go to the next line.
7. Type **C:\DOS\CHKDSK C:** in the Commands box and then press Tab to go to the next line.

This line tells DOS what commands are needed to run your program. You may not need to include the entire path each time, but doing so is a good idea.

8. Type **C:\DOS** in the Startup Directory box and then press Tab to go to the next box.

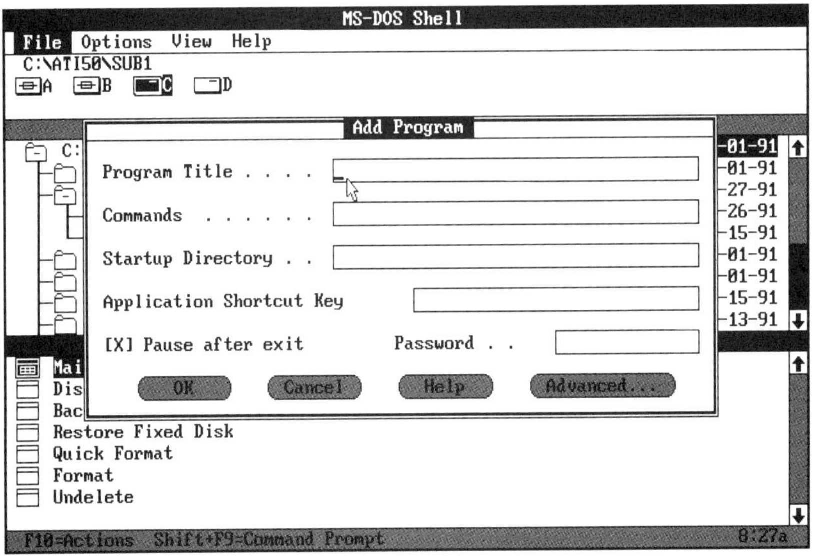

Fig. 16.8. The Add Program dialog box.

You really don't need to type **C:\DOS** in this case, but sometimes you may want DOS to change to a particular directory before starting a program. Lotus 1-2-3, for example, must be capable of finding a certain file when it starts, so you must be in the 1-2-3 directory when the program runs. Because specifying the start-up directory (such as C:\123) is necessary in cases such as this one, specifying a start-up directory is a good habit to form.

9. The Application Shortcut Key box enables you to assign the shortcut key combination you want to assign to this program.

Once your program is loaded, pressing this key combination enables you to switch directly to this program from another program or from the Shell itself. This builds on what you learned in the last lesson on task switching.

To assign a shortcut key, hold down the Ctrl, Shift, or Alt key and press a character. You can assign any key combination in this area, except for the following combinations:

Ctrl-M	Shift-Ctrl-M
Ctrl-I	Shift-Ctrl-I
Ctrl-H	Shift-Ctrl-H
Ctrl-C	Shift-Ctrl-C
Ctrl-[	Shift-Ctrl-[
Ctrl-5 (on keypad)	Shift-Ctrl-5 (on keypad)

Suppose that you assign Ctrl-L to Lotus 1-2-3. If, after starting 1-2-3, you switch back to the Shell and start another program, you then can switch directly to 1-2-3 from the second program by pressing Ctrl-L.

For this example, you do not need to assign a shortcut key, so just press Tab to go to the next line.

10. You now move to the Pause After Exit option.

    If, after exiting a program, you want the system to pause and display the message

    ```
    Press any key to return to MS-DOS Shell
    ```

    leave the X in the box. If you do not want the system to pause, press the space bar to erase the X.

    If you erase the X for this example, you are returned to the Shell before you can read the CHKDSK information. In this case, leave the X in the box. With most major applications, however, you want to erase the X so that you don't have to waste a keystroke to return to the Shell.

11. Press Tab to go to the Password box. As with a program group, you can enter a password, if you want. You probably don't want one here.

The Add Item dialog box and the Program Item Properties dialog box contain the Advanced button in the bottom right corner. Choosing this button displays another dialog box in which you can specify additional properties. The only option a beginner needs, however, is the Help option, which you can use to enter help messages in the same way as program groups. See *Using MS-DOS 5* for more information on advanced options.

12. After you finish, click OK or press Enter.

    The Disk Utilities group now should list the Check Disk C: program item.

13. If you want to change any program item options, highlight the item as before, and then click File and Properties. Or, press Alt, F, and P.

    The Program Item Properties dialog box—identical to the Add Program dialog box except for the title—appears.

To cancel anytime, click Cancel or press Esc. After making changes, click OK or press Enter.

You may want to erase the X in the Pause After Exit option of each of the program items in the Disk Utilities group. Doing so will save you a keystroke after a procedure is completed.

Deleting a program item is even easier than deleting a group. You probably do not want to delete any items now, so just refer to these steps when you must delete an item:

1. Highlight the program item you want to delete.
2. Press Del and choose OK from the Delete Item dialog box.

Reordering Items in a Group

You may not like the order in which programs are listed in a group. Suppose that you want to put your Applications group at the top of the list because you use it more than any of the others. Follow these steps:

1. Highlight the Applications group.
2. Click File and then Reorder. Or, press Alt, F, and E.

The following instructions appear at the bottom of the screen:

```
Select location to move to, then press ENTER.
Press ESC to cancel.
```

3. Double-click the new location (in this case, Command Prompt), or highlight Command Prompt with the arrow keys and press Enter.

The Applications group now should appear at the top of the list.

Copying an Item to Another Group

Sometimes you may want to copy or move a program item from one group to another. Suppose that you want to copy the Editor program item from the Main group to your newly created Applications group so that you have it handy. Follow these steps:

1. Highlight the program item you want to copy—in this case, Editor.
2. Click File and Copy. Or, press Alt, F, and C.

   The following instructions appear at the bottom of the screen:

   ```
   Display the group to copy to, then press F2.
   Press ESC to cancel.
   ```

3. Double-click the Applications group, or highlight it and press Enter.
4. Press F2.

   The Editor program item now should appear in the Applications list.

5. Return to the Main group by double-clicking it or by highlighting it and pressing Enter.

> If you want, you can delete the Editor from the Main group, thereby "moving" it from one group to another.

Suppressing Confirmation Messages

As you know, the Shell prompts you for confirmation at certain times, such as when you delete a file. After you gain some proficiency with the

Shell, however, you may want to suppress such prompts to speed up your work.

To suppress certain messages, follow these steps:

1. Click Options and then Confirmation. Or, press Alt, O, and C.

   The Confirmation dialog box appears (see fig. 16.9).

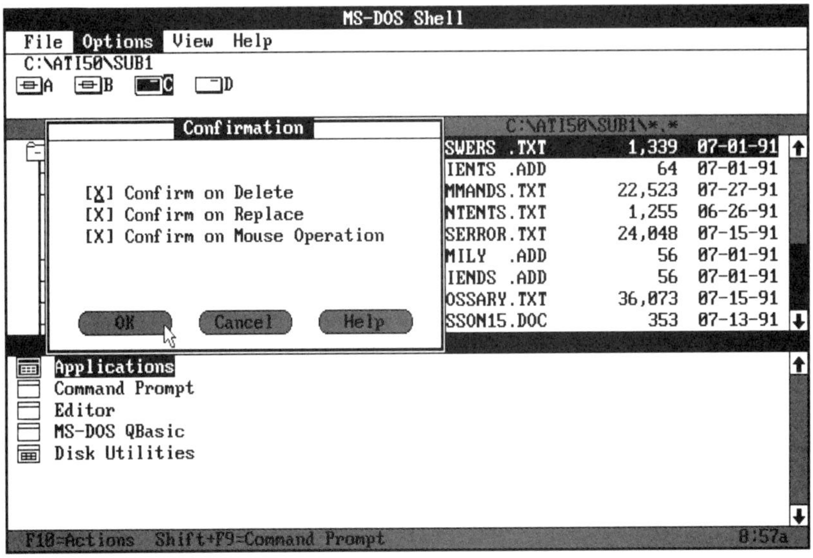

Fig. 16.9. The Confirmation dialog box.

The choices in the Confirmation dialog box follow:

Option	Warning Message Appears
Confirm on Delete	Before deleting files or directories
Confirm on Replace	Before replacing an existing file
Confirm on Mouse Operation	Before copying, dragging, or moving an item using the mouse

2. For each confirmation option you want to suppress, remove the X by clicking it or moving to it with the Tab key and then pressing the space bar.

You are certainly free to suppress whatever options you want, but you should be totally comfortable with the procedure involved. If you erase the X for confirming file deletion, for example, you should be proficient in tagging and deleting files. Otherwise, you may delete wanted files without ever realizing it.

3. If you choose to make changes, click OK or press Enter. Press Esc or click Cancel if you don't want to make changes.

Lesson Summary

- If you have a color monitor, you can choose from a number of color schemes in the Shell by using the Options Colors option.
- If you have a graphics monitor, you can display more than the default number of lines on-screen by using the Options Display option.
- To add a program group or program item, use the File New option.
- To delete a program group or program item, highlight it and press Del.
- To change the position of a program item in a group, use the File Reorder option.
- Use the File Copy option to copy a program item to another group.
- You can turn off confirmation messages, such as those for file deletion, by using the Options Confirmation option.

Key Terms

Confirmation message	Asks you to verify an action before final execution
Program group	Contains group (or collection) of program items
Program item	Individual program listed in a program group
Screen mode	Controls size and shape of images on-screen
Shortcut key	Key combination that switches you directly from one program to another

Exercises

You can organize programs in any way you want. You may want to put all your major programs in the Applications group you created earlier in the lesson. Otherwise, you may want to create a group called Word Processing, in which you list your word processor and DOS editor.

Perhaps you have more than one database program, all of which you want to put in a group called Databases. You may want to change the name of the Disk Utilities group to DOS Commands, and then create another group called Utilities, in which you list applications such as Norton Utilities.

However you would like to do it, go ahead and organize the Shell, if you want, and "make it your way." Follow this basic procedure:

1. Using the Shell's Directory Tree and File List areas, browse through the directories on your hard disk and jot down program names and path names on a piece of paper so that this information will be handy when you need it.
2. Create your program groups according to the procedure you learned in the "Working with Program Groups" section.
3. Add the desired program items to each program group according to the procedure you learned in the "Working with Program Items" section.

For More Information

For more beginner-level and some intermediate information concerning this lesson, see *MS-DOS 5 QuickStart* (Que Corporation). For a more in-depth handling of these subjects, refer to *Using MS-DOS 5* (Que Corporation, Chapter 14).

Now that you know how to customize the Shell, go to Lesson 17 to learn some ways to customize DOS itself.

Lesson 17

Customizing DOS

Hands-On MS-DOS 5 has been designed as a beginner-level book. It is for this reason that intermediate and advanced topics have been omitted. This lesson, however, presents just a few procedures that help prepare you for the more advanced topics that you encounter as you gain experience with DOS. While this lesson is *optional*, it is still *recommended*, but only after you are thoroughly comfortable with all the material in the previous lessons.

In Lesson 16, you learned how to customize the Shell. You can do many things in DOS itself to customize the way it operates. A thorough handling of this is beyond the scope of this book, but there are a few things that even the beginner can do to customize DOS. In this final lesson, you learn to do the following:

- Use DOS 5's text editor
- Work with the AUTOEXEC.BAT file
- Work with the CONFIG.SYS file
- Create an informative system prompt
- Use file-deletion tracking
- Install the PRINT command
- Use the DOSKEY program

Estimated time to complete this lesson: 30-45 minutes

Using the Editor

One of the most outstanding new features of DOS 5 is the Editor. Technically, the Editor is a *text editor*, a "mini word processor" that creates or changes text files. Unlike a word processor, a text editor does not have such capabilities as underlining and other sophisticated features found in full-featured word processors, such as WordPerfect or Microsoft Word. The Editor is still ideal, however, for writing short text files, such as memos, short letters, and batch files.

Although a full exploration of the Editor is beyond the scope of this book, the fundamentals are outlined in this lesson.

Starting the Editor

To start the Editor, follow these steps:

1. Start the DOS Shell, if it is not already running.
2. Double-click Editor. Or, press Tab to go to the main title bar, use the arrow keys to highlight Editor, and press Enter.

   A dialog box asks for the file name of the file you want to edit (see fig. 17.1).

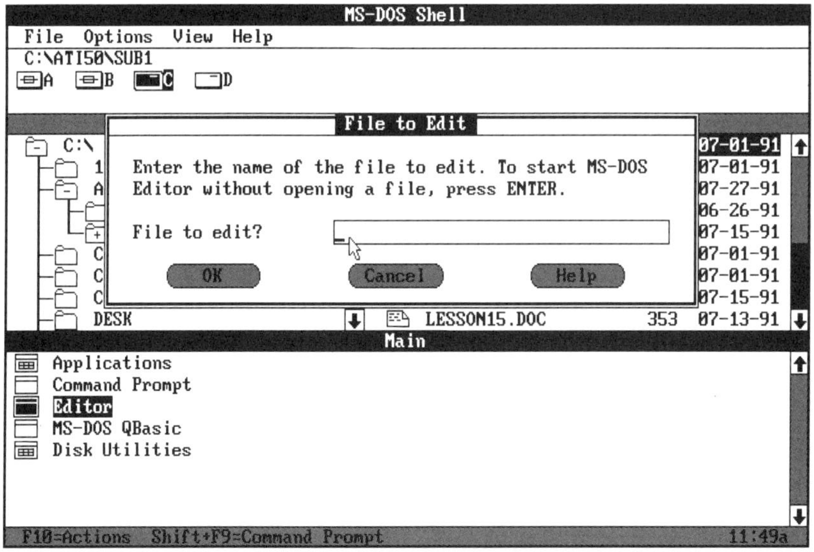

Fig. 17.1. The File To Edit dialog box.

3. Type **C:\DOS\EDITOR.TXT** and press Enter.

   Your file is placed in the DOS subdirectory and the main editor screen is displayed (see fig. 17.2).

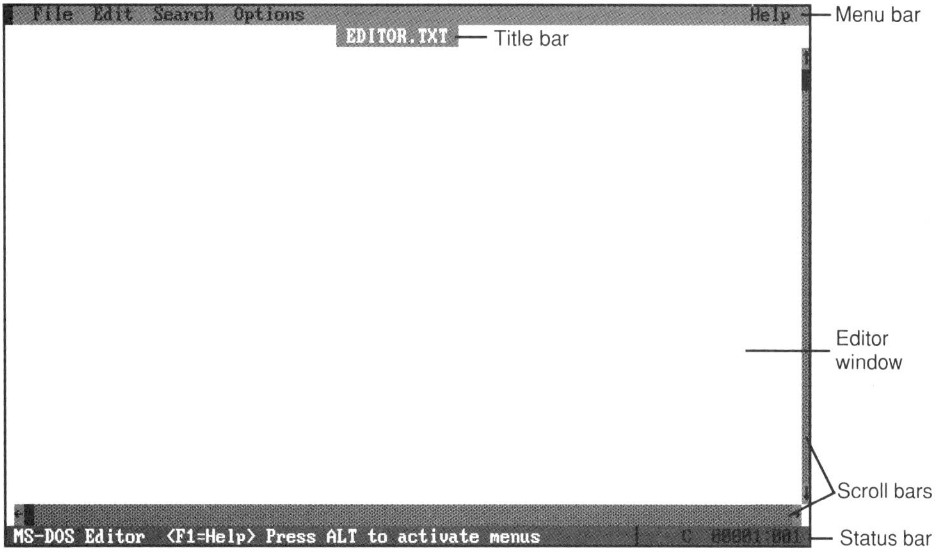

Fig. 17.2. The main Editor screen.

As you can see, the areas of the Editor screen are similar to those of the Shell:

Area	Function
Editor window	Displays text in file. A flashing cursor appears in the upper left corner of the Editor window; this indicates where typed text will be placed.
Menu bar	Lists the available menus. Menus are activated and options are chosen in the same way as in the Shell.
Scroll bars	Scrolls through the file (used with the mouse).
Status bar	Indicates the position of the cursor by line and column number, as well as certain shortcut key options.
Title bar	Contains the name of the file being edited; if no file is given when you start the Editor, the word `Untitled` appears in the title bar.

Creating a Text File with the Editor

Perform the following procedure to get some hands-on experience with the Editor:

1. Type **This is the line of my file EDITOR.TXT**.

   If you make a mistake, just press the Backspace key to correct it. You also can move through the line with the arrow keys, as the next step illustrates.

2. Press the left-arrow key to go back to the *l* in the word *line*. Type the word **FIRST** and press the space bar once.

   This illustrates that the Editor is by default in *insert mode*, which means that you will always insert text at the cursor location.

   If, on the other hand, you press the Ins key, this activates *overtype mode*, which means that any new character you type overwrites the character presently at the cursor location.

3. Now press the End key to move the cursor to the end of the line, and then press Enter.

   This causes the cursor to go to the end of the line and then to the next line.

4. Type the following lines, pressing Enter at the end of each one:

   This is the second line of my file EDITOR.TXT.
   This is the third line of my file EDITOR.TXT.

   Notice the number (00004:001) on the far right of the status bar; it shows that the cursor is now on the fourth line and first column. You can keep track of where you are with this number.

5. Now move the cursor to the beginning of line 2, press and hold down the Shift key, press the End key, and then release both keys.

   This action marks a block of text.

   You also can use the arrow keys (with the Shift key) to mark any block of text you want.

6. Click on Edit and then on Copy. Or, press Alt, E, and C.

7. Move back to the beginning of line 4 by pressing the down-arrow key twice and the Home key once.

8. Click on Edit and then on Paste. Or, press Alt, E, and P.

   This copies the marked text to line 4 of your file.

   This block of text stays in memory until you replace it with another block. You therefore can copy this block to other parts of the file.

9. Press the right-arrow key to place the cursor on the *s* in the word *second.*

10. Press the Ins key to turn on overwriting, type the word *fourth*, and press Ins again to turn off overtyping.

    The new word overwrites the old word.

11. To save your file, click on File and then on Save. Or, press Alt, F, and S.

12. You can print this file by clicking on File and then on Print. Or, you can press Alt, F, and P.

    Printing a text file from the Editor is an alternative to using the COPY or PRINT command.

13. Do not exit the Editor; you will learn more about it in the following section.

> Remember that TXT files are *associated* with the Editor and that you can associate other files with the Editor, as you learned in Lesson 15. If a file is associated with the Editor, the next time you need to edit it, you just select it and the Editor loads automatically. Review Lesson 15, if necessary.

Learning More About the Editor

As noted earlier, a full exploration of the Editor is beyond the scope of this book. To learn more about how to use the Editor, see the "For More Information" section at the end of this lesson.

Another good way of learning more about the Editor is to use its own online help system, just as you would in the Shell. To see the teaching power of the Editor's help system, follow these steps:

1. Press F1 to enter the help system; then press Tab and Enter.

   This displays the keyboard help menu in figure 17.3.

   Notice that your file EDITOR.TXT is displayed in a window at the bottom of the screen. You'll see why in a moment.

2. To display help on a listed topic, just press Tab to move the cursor to the topic and press Enter. To get help on the Editor's shortcut keys, for example, press Tab twice and then press Enter.

3. If you want to have the help screen visible while you work in your file, press F6. This key toggles between the two windows.

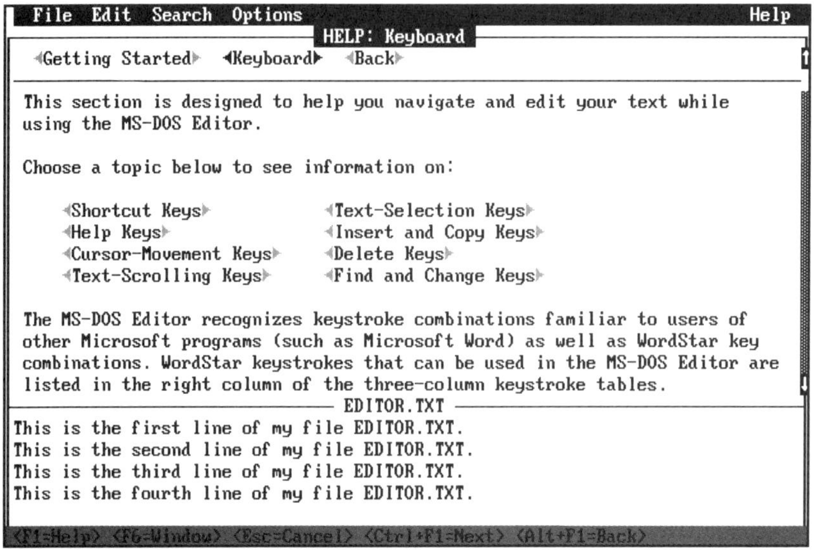

Fig. 17.3. The Editor's Keyboard Help Menu.

4. To exit the help system, press Esc.
5. Exit the Editor by clicking on File and then on Exit. Or, press Alt, F, and X.

> Even though you can use a mouse with the Editor, you may soon discover that the keyboard offers much more power and speed than does the mouse. This is not only because of the shortcut key commands, but also because your fingers simply spend more time on the keyboard than on the mouse.

Searching for Text in the Editor

One other capability of the Editor that you need to know about is how it searches for text. Follow these steps:

1. While in the Shell, go to the ATI50\SUB1 subdirectory and double-click on COMMANDS.TXT or highlight it and press Enter.

   The Editor is loaded and COMMANDS.TXT is displayed. This text file is Appendix A, DOS Command Summary.

2. Click on Search and then on Find. Or, press Alt, S, and F.
3. Type **FORMAT** (in uppercase letters) in the Find dialog box.
4. Press Tab to go to the Match Upper/Lowercase check box and then press the space bar to insert an X.

   Putting an X here forces a case-sensitive search; in this example, DOS looks for the word *FORMAT* in uppercase only.

   If you do not put an X in the check box, DOS does a *case-insensitive search*—it finds the first occurrence of the word, regardless of the case.
5. Press Enter.

   The Editor immediately finds the word *FORMAT*.
6. Press F3 to find the next occurrence of the word *FORMAT*.

   This simple example shows the power of the Editor's search capability. You can use this technique as a reference tool with Appendixes A, B, and C to find quick answers to questions on DOS commands, computer terms, and DOS error messages.
7. Exit the Editor.

The Editor has many more capabilities, such as searching for and replacing text automatically, putting a marker in one location of the text so you can go to another location and instantly return to the original location, and so on. Explore the Editor on your own or refer to the "For More Information" section at the end of this lesson.

Working with the AUTOEXEC.BAT File

Another topic that this book can only touch on is the AUTOEXEC.BAT file. This odd-sounding file is called a *batch file*. The word *batch* means just what you think it does—a bunch, or a group. A batch file contains a bunch of commands that execute automatically when the batch file runs; the batch file itself runs when you type its name, just as you type the name of an executable program (a file with an EXE or COM extension).

You can create batch files with the DOS Editor or another text editor, by putting the commands you want in a file and giving the file the BAT extension. As your experience with computers grows, you may want to learn more about batch files because they help you speed up your work. Again, see the "For More Information" section at the end of this lesson.

What is an AUTOEXEC.BAT File?

The AUTOEXEC.BAT file is a very special batch file, as well as a very important file in general. Each time DOS starts (when you turn on the computer or reboot with Ctrl-Alt-Del), DOS looks for an AUTOEXEC.BAT in the root directory of the boot disk (usually drive C). If DOS does not find an AUTOEXEC.BAT file, it simply prompts you for the current date and time (if your computer automatically keeps track of the date and time, DOS will not even do this). If, however, DOS does find an AUTOEXEC.BAT, it carries out all the commands in it before turning the system over to you.

As you can see, an AUTOEXEC.BAT file does even more of the work for you than does a regular batch file. In addition to executing the commands for you, AUTOEXEC.BAT runs automatically when you start your computer.

Why You Need an AUTOEXEC.BAT File

There are at least three reasons why it is highly recommended that you have an AUTOEXEC.BAT file.

First, you will want to put the PATH command in your AUTOEXEC.BAT. The PATH command is very important. It may look like this:

```
PATH=C:\;C:\DOS;C:\UTILITY
```

This tells DOS that when a command is issued at the DOS prompt, DOS should look in the subdirectories listed in the PATH command. In the above example, DOS looks in the root directory, the DOS directory, and a directory called UTILITY for whatever command or program you type. This way, you can be in any subdirectory and still have access to any command or program. Without the PATH command, however, you must be in the correct subdirectory before you can run the command you want.

Second, you also want an AUTOEXEC.BAT so that you can set the system prompt the way you like it. The most popular system prompt, for example, occurs with this command:

```
PROMPT $P$G
```

This command always tells you which subdirectory you are in. If you are in the root directory, your prompt will be: C:\>; if you are in the DOS directory, your prompt will be: C:\DOS>; and so on. You will learn about other uses for the PROMPT command in “Customizing the System Prompt,” later in this lesson.

Third, you also want an AUTOEXEC.BAT so that you can automatically run certain programs at start-up. Many users, for example, load a desktop organizing program like Sidekick into memory each time they start their computer. Your AUTOEXEC.BAT can run any programs you want on bootup.

Editing the AUTOEXEC.BAT File

Fortunately, when it is installed, DOS 5 creates an AUTOEXEC.BAT file for you, if one does not already exist. If one does exist, DOS adds certain lines to it. DOS 5's generic AUTOEXEC.BAT looks something like this:

```
@ECHO OFF
PROMPT $P$G
PATH=C:\DOS;
SET TEMP=C:\DOS
```

There will be times, however, when you will need or want to change your AUTOEXEC.BAT file. The Editor is ideal for this task. Follow these steps:

1. Double-click on Editor or highlight it and press Enter.
2. Type **C:\AUTOEXEC.BAT** in the File To Edit dialog box and press Enter.

> Do not associate BAT files with the Editor, as you would other text files. BAT files are executable programs (like EXE and COM files). Double-clicking on one or highlighting it and pressing Enter will launch it instead of load it into the Editor.

3. You now may edit AUTOEXEC.BAT as you want and then resave it.

   You may want to add other subdirectories to your PATH, for example. You will learn about a few additions you may want to make to AUTOEXEC.BAT later in the lesson.

4. Exit the Editor by clicking File and Exit or by pressing Alt, F, and X.

> **Guidelines for an AUTOEXEC.BAT File**
>
> - You must name the file AUTOEXEC.BAT and place it in the root directory of the boot disk (usually C:\).
> - You must place the DATE and TIME commands in the AUTOEXEC.BAT file (unless the computer keeps track of the date and time).

- You should include a PATH command and a PROMPT command in your AUTOEXEC.BAT file.
- Place commands in the AUTOEXEC.BAT file in the order in which you want them to be executed.

Working with the CONFIG.SYS File

There is another file that DOS automatically looks for when you boot your computer—the CONFIG.SYS file. This file provides a means for altering your system, and although it is not compulsory, it is strongly recommended. The CONFIG.SYS file has a tremendous influence on how your computer performs. You can add configuration commands that attach new hardware devices, create RAM disks, set the number of buffers and files that can be accessed by DOS, change the keyboard and video display for an international character set, and much more. And, like the AUTOEXEC.BAT file, the CONFIG.SYS file is so important that DOS 5 automatically creates a generic one if one does not already exist:

```
DEVICE=C:\DOS\SETVER.EXE
DEVICE=C:\DOS\HIMEM.SYS
DOS=HIGH
FILES=10
SHELL=C:\DOS\COMMAND.COM C:\DOS\  /P
STACKS=0,0
```

The first command ensures that older programs running under earlier versions of DOS now will run under DOS 5. The second and third commands control how your computer uses memory; these commands are used only with 286, 386, and 486 computers. The fourth line is the subject of the next section, and the last two lines are beyond the scope of this book.

As a beginning user, you need only be concerned about two CONFIG.SYS settings. You will learn about these briefly and then learn how to edit the CONFIG.SYS file.

The FILES Setting

Application programs, such as word processors and spreadsheets, usually enable DOS to do the work of opening and closing files. After all, that's what an operating system is for—to do the menial tasks. To do this, however, DOS must set aside a little of the computer's memory; it sets up *file handles*, which are used to store information about each file with which you are working.

The default CONFIG.SYS file listed in the preceding section includes the command FILES=10, which establishes 10 file handles. This number seldom is enough, however, in light of the large application programs used today. In fact, some applications will not run at all if the files setting is not large enough. The general guideline for the files setting is 20. The RAM cost is only about 48 bytes per handle, so 20 will cost only 1K. You will edit this number in a moment.

The ANSI.SYS Device Driver

A *device driver* is a software program that controls or enhances a device, such as your display. The easiest of the six device drivers in DOS to understand and use is ANSI.SYS. You can use ANSI.SYS to give you more control over the keyboard and display. It's very important for you to understand ANSI.SYS, because some software packages require that it be installed.

Because ANSI.SYS is a separate program (like an external command), you must tell DOS where it is before DOS can execute it. DOS 5 installs ANSI.SYS in the \DOS subdirectory on drive C. The following line, therefore, is needed in CONFIG.SYS:

```
DEVICE=C:\DOS\ANSI.SYS
```

In the following section, you install ANSI.SYS in the CONFIG.SYS file.

Editing the CONFIG.SYS File

To edit the CONFIG.SYS file, follow these steps:

1. Double-click Editor or highlight it and press Enter.
2. Type **C:\CONFIG.SYS** in the File To Edit dialog box and press Enter.
3. Increase the FILES setting to 20.

   If, after trying to run one of your application programs, you receive an error message about *file handles*, you should increase this number again. Increase it by 5 until the program runs.
4. Add the command **DEVICE=C:\DOS\ANSI.SYS** to the end of the file (if it is not already present somewhere in the file).

   If you started with the default CONFIG.SYS file, it now will resemble the following:

```
DEVICE=C:\DOS\SETVER.EXE
DEVICE=C:\DOS\HIMEM.SYS
DOS=HIGH
FILES=20
SHELL=C:\DOS\COMMAND.COM C:\DOS\  /P
STACKS=0,0
DEVICE=C:\DOS\ANSI.SYS
```

5. Resave the file and exit the Editor.
6. From the DOS prompt (exit the Shell with F3 if needed), reboot your computer by pressing Ctrl-Alt-Del.

   You must reboot, because changes in AUTOEXEC.BAT and CONFIG.SYS do not take effect until the next time you start DOS.
7. To prepare for the next section, you should be at the DOS prompt (exit the Shell, if necessary).

Customizing the System Prompt

As you know, the command PROMPT PG enables you to tell at a glance which subdirectory you are in. The PROMPT command can be even more informative than this, however. It can display the date, time, DOS version, or any message you want. PROMPT does all this by using $parameters, which are called *meta strings*. Table 17.1 lists the meta strings used with PROMPT. Note that the meta strings are not case-sensitive.

Table 17.1. Meta Strings Used with the PROMPT Command

Meta String	Displayed Information or Result
$_	Carriage return, line-feed (moves cursor to first position of next line)
$B	Vertical bar character (|)
$D	Current date
$E	Escape character (ASCII character 27)
$G	Greater than sign (>)
$H	Backspace character (moves cursor one space to the left and erases the preceding character)
$L	Less than sign (<)
$N	Current disk drive name

Meta String	Displayed Information or Result
$P	Current disk drive, path (directory)
$Q	Equal sign (=)
$T	Current time
$V	DOS version number

PROMPT is very versatile, and because it is an internal command, you can execute it anytime. Moreover, PROMPT is the most harmless DOS command there is. You can "play" with it all day and not hurt a thing.

Here are some examples of what you can do with PROMPT. To return the prompt to normal, just type **PROMPT PG** and press Enter.

The command

PROMPT The current directory is PG

produces this prompt (if you are in the DOS subdirectory):

The current directory is C:\DOS>.

You may want something helpful, such as

PROMPT May I help you? (followed by a space)

Perhaps you want to combine these two on separate lines:

PROMPT The current directory is P_May I help you?<space>

If you'd like something cute, try

PROMPT ^A$G or PROMPT ^B$G

Enter the ^A and ^B by holding down the Control key and typing the letter.

Here's another cute prompt:

PROMPT ($P)$_What's Up, Doc? $G

If you need to be more serious, try this prompt:

PROMPT V_$D THHH$_Current Directory $Q P_Your Command:

This produces an impressive result similar to this:

```
MS-DOS Version 5.0
Thu  07-25-1991  16:40:10
Current Directory = C:\DOS
Your Command:
```

Note the three $H characters; these erase the hundredths of a second that the $T prints; put in three more if you want to erase the seconds altogether. Also notice the two spaces between $D and $T.

> The last three examples are possible only if you installed ANSI.SYS, as outlined earlier.

You can display an elaborate system prompt with this line:

PROMPT $E[S$E[1;67HDE[2;67HTHHH$E[U$_PG

This displays the date and time in the upper right corner of your screen, jumps to the next line, and lists the current drive and directory.

A variation of the above, which adds some reverse video, is

PROMPT$E[S$E[1;67HDE[2;67HTHHH$E[U$_$E[7M$PGE[M<space>

For those who have a color monitor, the command

PROMPT PG$E[44;37m
CLS

displays the familiar current drive and directory prompt but also changes your display to white letters (foreground) on a blue background. Make sure that you separate the color codes (44 and 37 above) with a semicolon and that the letter *m* is in lowercase. If you want the foreground in high intensity white, use **PROMPT PG$E[44;37;1m**.

By placing this command in your AUTOEXEC.BAT file, your screen takes on a new configuration on bootup. Other combinations are possible by using the ANSI color codes and attribute codes in tables 17.2 and 17.3.

> As in the preceding examples, the $E[characters precede color commands; the commands then are entered, separated by semicolons, and the small *m* ends the command. Remember, the *m* is case-sensitive; it *must* be a small m.

Your screen still may be white on black when you first boot up, and some programs reset the screen colors to the standard white on black after they end, but a CLS command usually sets things right.

Table 17.2. Screen Color Codes for Use with ANSI.SYS

Color	Foreground	Background
Black	30	40
Red	31	41
Green	32	42
Yellow	33	43
Blue	34	44
Magenta	35	45
Cyan	36	46
White	37	47

Table 17.3. Display Attributes for Use with ANSI.SYS

Display	Code
Normal display	0
High intensity	1
Underline	4
Blink	5
Reverse video	7

Here's one more prompt that will really impress your friends. As you type this long command, allow the cursor to wrap to the second line by itself; the & character is used to denote where you should type a space:

```
PROMPT
$E[44;37;1m$E[6C/$B$_&&&\'o.o'$_&&&$Q(___)$Q$_&&&&&&
U$_MEOW!&$P$G
```

Notice that the 44;37;1m portion of the command defines the color and intensity of the characters. You easily can change this to suit your own taste.

If all goes well, your prompt now should look like the following (if you are in the DOS subdirectory):

```
          / ¦
        \ 'o.o'
        =(___)=
           U

MEOW! C:\DOS>_
```

As you can see, PROMPT enables you to personalize DOS. In addition to being informative, it also can be a lot of fun.

Installing File-Deletion Tracking

In Lesson 11, you learned how to undelete files, but as you recall, you must undelete a file immediately. DOS 5, however, also provides a small utility that keeps track of files on a deleted disk. If you delete a file while the MIRROR program is installed, MIRROR records the information that UNDELETE needs to restore the file in a file named PCTRACKR.DEL, which resides in the root directory of the specified drive. This way, if you forget to undelete a file immediately, you have a much better chance of recovering it later.

The default number of files that MIRROR stores in the PCTRACKR.DEL file depends on the size of the disk that MIRROR is tracking. Table 17.4 lists the default number of files tracked for each disk size and the size of PCTRACKR.DEL.

Table 17.4. Default Number of Files Tracked by MIRROR and Size of PCTRACKR.DEL

Disk Size Tracked	Number of Entries	Size of PCTRACKR.DEL
360K	25	5K
720K	50	9K
1.2M	75	14K
1.44M	75	14K
20M	101	18K
32M	202	36K
More than 32M	303	55K

To install MIRROR to track deleted files on drives C and A, for example, type the following at the system prompt:

MIRROR /TA /TC

If drive A is a 1.2M drive and drive C is a 32M hard disk, this command tracks a maximum number of 75 files deleted from drive A and a maximum of 202 files deleted from drive C.

> Be warned that after you delete the default number of files, MIRROR begins to drop files off the bottom of the list as it adds new ones to the top of the list.

As you may have guessed, if you want to install MIRROR on your computer, you can place it in your AUTOEXEC.BAT file, as outlined in "Editing the AUTOEXEC.BAT File," earlier in this lesson.

> MIRROR has a low memory consumption (only 6.4K), so it is a wise addition to your computer system, even though it will slow down your system a little if you delete a large number of files.

To briefly illustrate MIRROR, suppose that you deleted DISKCOPY.COM from your DOS subdirectory by mistake, but didn't notice it for a few days. With MIRROR installed, you still have a good chance of recovering the file. In Lesson 11, you saw the message the UNDELETE command displays when MIRROR is not installed. In contrast, here is what UNDELETE displays when MIRROR is installed:

```
C:\DOS>UNDELETE

Directory:  C:\DOS
File Specifications:  *.*

    Deletion-tracking file contains  1 deleted files.
    Of those,     1 files have all clusters available,
                  0 files have some clusters available,
                  0 files have no clusters available.

    MS-DOS directory contains  1 deleted files.
    Of those,     1 files may be recovered.

Using the deletion-tracking file.

    DISKCOPY.COM 11793  4-09-91     5:00a  ...A Deleted:
    7-26-91      8:28a
All of the clusters for these files are available. Undelete
(Y/N)?
```

At this point, you simply press Y, and the following message is displayed:

```
File successfully undeleted
```

Loading the DOS Shell Automatically

If the DOS Shell does not appear automatically when you turn on your computer, but you would like it to, you can add the DOSSHELL command as the *last line* of your AUTOEXEC.BAT file. The next time you start or reboot your computer, the DOS Shell appears automatically.

Installing the PRINT Command

In Lesson 13, you learned how to use your printer and the PRINT command. You may recall that using PRINT enables you to do other things while files are being printed. If you want to have the PRINT command ready to use at anytime, you can put the command in your AUTOEXEC.BAT file, as outlined earlier in "Editing the AUTOEXEC.BAT File."

> If you choose to add the PRINT command to your AUTOEXEC.BAT file, it is not crucial where the command is placed; a rule of thumb is to place it near the end of the file. If, however, you want the DOSSHELL (or other program) to load automatically from AUTOEXEC.BAT, then make sure DOSSHELL (or the other program's command name) is the last line.

Using the DOSKEY Program

This section will be of interest to you only if you plan on working from the DOS prompt often. If you plan to use the DOS Shell most of the time, you may want to skip this section.

The DOSKEY program enables you recall a history of the DOS commands that have been entered at the prompt and to enter them again without retyping. The DOSKEY program also enables you to enter more than one command at a time on the command line, as well as other things that are beyond the scope of this book.

If you want to give DOSKEY a try, follow these steps:

1. If you are in the Shell, exit it permanently by pressing F3.

> Do not continue if you exited the Shell temporarily with Shift-F9. If you install DOSKEY while exited temporarily, your computer will lock up and you will have to reboot.

2. Type **DOSKEY** and press Enter.

   The following message should appear on your screen:

   ```
   DOSKey installed
   ```

   This message means that DOSKEY has been installed into your computer's memory and will remain there until you reboot the computer. Your computer will continue to run normally.

3. Make sure of your starting place by typing **CD\DOS** and pressing Enter.

   You now should be at the following DOS prompt:

   ```
   C:\DOS>
   ```

4. Type the following commands, pressing Enter after each one:

   CHKDSK
   DIR/W
   VER

5. Now press the up arrow once to recall the last command you entered (VER). Keep pressing the up arrow to go through the stack of commands.

   At any point, you can reissue one of these commands by simply pressing Enter.

   Sometimes the quickest way to reissue a command is to press F7 to list all the commands in memory, press F9 (at which time the `Line Number:` prompt appears), and then type the number you want.

6. Press Esc to erase the command line, type **CD\ATI50**, press the space bar, press Ctrl-T, press the space bar again, type **DIR**, and press Enter.

   Your command should look like the following:

```
C:\DOS>CD\ATI50 ¶ DIR
```

With this action, you issued two commands at once instead of issuing each one separately. Using this technique, you can type as many commands as you want on one line, as long as the total length of the line does not exceed 128 characters.

7. Press the up arrow to recall the last command, and then use the left arrow to move the cursor back through the line until it is between the first command and the ¶ symbol.

   Your command line should look like this:

   ```
   C:\DOS>CD\ATI50_¶ DIR
   ```

8. Now press the Ins key (notice how the cursor changes shape), type **\SUB1**, and press Enter.

As you can see, you can use the left- and right-arrow keys to move the cursor through the command line and change parts of the command. To overwrite existing characters, just start typing; to insert characters, press the Ins key first.

If you like working from the DOS command line, you will want to use DOSKEY, and you probably will want to add the command to your AUTOEXEC.BAT file so that it will load automatically each time you boot up. Refer to the "For More Information" section, later in this chapter, to learn more about these and other features of DOSKEY.

> If you choose to add the DOSKEY command to your AUTOEXEC.BAT file, it is not crucial where the command is placed; a rule of thumb is to place it near the end of the file. If, however, you want the DOSSHELL (or other program) to load automatically from AUTOEXEC.BAT, then make sure DOSSHELL (or the other program's command name) is the last line.

Remember: Changes to the AUTOEXEC.BAT file and the CONFIG.SYS file will *not* take effect until you reboot your computer.

Lesson Summary

- ☐ The Editor is ideal for writing short text files, such as memos, short letters, and batch files.
- ☐ The AUTOEXEC.BAT file is extremely valuable for running the commands and programs of your choice on bootup. It greatly aids in the configuring of your computer.

- The CONFIG.SYS file is indispensable for attaching hardware devices, creating RAM disks, setting the number of buffers and files that can be accessed by DOS, changing the keyboard and video display for an international character set, and much more.
- You can install the ANSI.SYS device driver to give you greater control over your keyboard and display.
- You can use the PROMPT command to design an informative and elaborate system prompt.
- The MIRROR program keeps track of deleted files and is a wise addition to your computer system.
- You can install the PRINT command program so that you can use background printing of files at anytime.
- The DOSKEY program is extremely useful if you do a lot of your work from the DOS prompt.

Key Terms

ANSI.SYS	A device driver that provides more control over the keyboard and display.
AUTOEXEC.BAT file	A special batch file that automatically executes when the computer starts up.
Batch file	A file that contains a group of commands that execute automatically when the batch file runs.
CONFIG.SYS file	A special text file that contains configuration commands.
Device driver	A software program that controls or enhances a device, such as your display.
DOSKEY program	A small utility that enables you to recall previously entered commands.
File handle	A value that DOS uses to store information about each file with which it is working.
Insert mode	Any new character you type is inserted at the cursor location, and old characters are pushed to the right as you type.
MIRROR program	A small utility that keeps track of files on a deleted disk, making file-undeleting more reliable.
Overtype mode	Any new character you type will overwrite the character at the cursor location.

PATH command	Tells DOS in which directories to look for a command or program entered at the DOS prompt.
PROMPT command	Customizes the DOS system prompt (C>).
Text editor	A "mini word processor" that creates or changes text files.

Exercises

Instead of doing a separate exercise for each subject covered in this lesson, the best thing you can do here is to repeat the procedures in the sections of this lesson that were of interest to you.

One subject, however, should be reemphasized in an exercise—the Editor. For further experience with the Editor, follow these steps:

1. If you are in the Shell, exit it permanently by pressing F3.

> Do not do Step 2 if you have exited the Shell temporarily; doing so could lock up your computer, which will require a system reboot.

2. At the DOS prompt, type **PRINT** and press Enter. DOS displays the following message:

   ```
   Name of the list device [PRN]:
   ```

   Press Enter to accept the default printer port PRN (also called LPT1). DOS now displays

   ```
   Resident part of PRINT installed
   ```

   which means the print utility has been loaded into memory.

3. Type **DOSSHELL** and press Enter.
4. Double-click on Editor in the Main Program Group or use Tab and the arrow keys to highlight Editor and press Enter.
5. Type **C:\ATI50\SUB1\PRN_TEST.TXT** in the File To Edit dialog box and press Enter.

   This means that the text file you are about to create will be stored in the ATI50\SUB1 directory on drive C.

6. Type in the first paragraph of the "Using the Editor" section, earlier in this lesson.

Because the Editor does not have word-wrap, as do most word processors, you will need to press Enter at the end of each line. The first number at the far right of the status bar displays the current line number, and the second number displays the current row number. Press Enter after typing 65-70 characters.

7. Move the cursor to the beginning of the paragraph and mark and copy this entire block of text, as outlined in steps 5 and 6 of "Creating a Text File with the Editor," earlier in the lesson.
8. Move the cursor a couple of lines below the paragraph and paste the marked text into the document, as outlined in step 8 of "Creating a Text File with the Editor," earlier in this lesson.
9. Repeat step 8 seven or eight more times. This gives you about two pages of text.
10. Save your file by clicking File and Save or by pressing Alt, F, and S.
11. Exit the Shell, or if you have task switching enabled, just switch to the Shell by pressing Ctrl-Esc.
12. Select the ATI50\SUB1 directory in the Directory Tree area, and then select the PRN_TEST.TXT file in the File List area.

    If the file is not displayed, press F5 to refresh (update) the screen display (as mentioned in Lesson 5).
13. Make sure that you have paper properly loaded in your printer. Then, click File and Print or press Alt, F, and P.

You could print the file directly from the Editor, but the Editor does not work with the PRINT command as does the Shell. As your file is printing from the Shell, you can start other programs and continue to work.

For More Information

For a more in-depth handling of the subjects covered in this lesson, refer to the following sections of *Using MS-DOS 5* (Que Corporation):

If you want more on	*Then see*
The Editor	Chapter 12
AUTOEXEC.BAT file	Pages 407-416
CONFIG.SYS and its contents	Chapter 15
MIRROR	Pages 511-516
DOSKEY	Pages 442-451

Now that you've completed the 17 lessons in this book, where do you go from here? To your computer, of course. You now are equipped to handle all the major functions of a DOS-based personal computer. What's more, you now are equipped to use a PC more efficiently and more productively.

The following appendixes contain additional material that will further your knowledge and understanding of DOS and computers in general. Study them at your leisure. This book, and the TXT files of Appendixes A, B, and C will serve you well as indispensable desktop and computer-based references.

The author and all the people at Que Corporation who brought this book to you wish you great success as you use DOS for business and pleasure.

Appendix A

DOS Command Summary

This appendix provides a summary of the DOS 5 commands that the novice may use. This summary is not an exhaustive listing of all the commands for DOS 5—only the most common commands. For a complete reference, see *Using MS-DOS 5*.

A summary of commands also is contained in the COMMANDS.TXT file, which you can display with the View command in the Shell, the DOS Editor, or the TYPE command. To activate the TYPE command, enter the following:

```
TYPE C:\ATI50\SUB1\COMMANDS.TXT | MORE
```

One of the most confusing aspects of DOS is its complicated syntax; therefore, the syntax has been simplified here. For example, *file(s)* represents not only a file or set of files, but also a complete pathname including drive, subdirectory, and file name.

DOS Commands

This section contains the most often used DOS 5 commands. It does not contain configuration commands (such as FILES), because these are listed separately in the "Configuration Commands" section.

APPEND *paths*

This command sets a search path for data files. In other words, this command specifies one or more directories that DOS searches for a data file not found in the current directory.

To tell DOS to search for data files in the subdirectories 123\MKT and WP\LETTERS, enter the following:

```
APPEND \123\MKT;\WP\LETTERS
```

To limit the search for data files to the current directory, enter the following:

```
APPEND ;
```

ATTRIB *setting(s) file(s) /S*

This command displays, sets, or resets the read-only attribute of a file. A read-only file cannot be changed or deleted. Generally, read-only is used for security purposes. This command also is used to control the archive attribute of a file. The command tells DOS (or other programs that check the archive attribute) whether a file has been changed since its last backup.

The settings for the ATTRIB command follow:

Setting	Effect
+A	Sets the archive attribute
-A	Removes the archive attribute
+R	Makes a file read-only
-R	Removes the read-only attribute
/S	Applies the command to all subdirectories contained in the file(s)

The following command displays an R to the left of the file name if the file is read-only:

ATTRIB *filename*

DOS also displays an A if the file has changed since its last backup.

The following command makes the file REPORT.JAN read-only:

ATTRIB +R REPORT.JAN

To reset the archive bit of every file on a disk so that all files are copied by XCOPY or BACKUP (both of which turn off the archive bit), type the following command:

ATTRIB +A C:*.* /S

BACKUP *file(s) d: switches*

This command makes backup copies of one or more files from a fixed disk to floppy disk, floppy disk to floppy disk, floppy disk to hard disk, or hard disk to hard disk.

The backup files cannot be read because they are stored in a special DOS BACKUP format; you can retrieve them with the RESTORE command only.

File(s) refers to the file(s) to be backed up. Wild cards (* and ?) are accepted. *d:* is the name of the hard or floppy disk which receives the backup files.

The switches available for the BACKUP command follow:

Switch	Effect
/A	Adds the backup files to the backup disk; otherwise, the files on disk are erased.
/D:*mm-dd-yy*	Backs up only those files that have been modified since the specified date.
/M	Backs up files which have been created or changed since the last BACKUP only.
/S	Causes files in all subdirectories below the specified directory to be backed up.

To back up all files on fixed disk drive C to the disk in drive A, type the following:

BACKUP C:\ A: /S

To back up all files on fixed disk drive C that were created or modified since the last backup to the disk in drive A, type the following command:

BACKUP C:\ A: /S /M

To back up all files on fixed disk drive C that have been created or modified since the last backup to the disk in drive A and to add to the files already on the drive A disk, type the following:

BACKUP C:\ A: /S /M /A

To back up all files on fixed disk drive C that have been created or modified since March 25, 1991 to the disk in drive A, type the following:

BACKUP C:\ A: /S /D:03-25-91

BREAK ON or OFF

This command determines how often DOS checks for a Ctrl-Break or a Ctrl-C to stop a program. ON tells DOS to extend its checks to include the times DOS reads from or writes to a disk. For more information on the BREAK configuration command, see "Configuration Commands," later in this chapter.

CD or CHDIR *path*

This command changes the current directory or displays the current directory path.

To change the current directory on the default drive to the root directory, enter the following:

CD\

To change the current directory on the default drive to the DATA directory, which is a subdirectory of the LOTUS directory, which in turn is a subdirectory of the root directory, type the following command:

CD\LOTUS\DATA

If the current directory is C:\WP\LETTERS\PERSONAL, the command CD.. takes you up one level in the path (C:\WP\LETTERS). Entering the command again takes you up one more level, and so on.

CHKDSK *files switches*

This command reports the distribution of disk storage, the total amount of disk space, how much disk space is used by directories and files, how much space is available, and how much free RAM exists. This command also checks the FAT (file allocation table) for errors. *Files* specifies the specific file(s) to be checked for noncontiguous (nonconsecutive) sectors.

The switches available for the CHKDSK command follow:

Switch	Effect
/F	Fixes errors found in the directory or FAT
/V	Displays the full path name of each directory and the file name of every file on the disk being checked

To analyze the current drive, type the following:

CHKDSK

To check a disk in drive A when the current drive is drive C, type the following:

CHKDSK A:

To analyze the current drive and to check the FAT for any errors, type the following:

CHKDSK /F

If you want to save the CHKDSK report for future reference, you can redirect the report to a disk file you name or to your printer.

To redirect the report to a disk file for future reference, type the following:

CHKDSK C:>*filename* (*.ext optional*)

To redirect the report to the printer, type the following:

CHKDSK C:>PRN

To check all the files on a disk to see if each is stored in contiguous (consecutive) sectors, type the following:

CHKDSK *.*

CLS

This command clears the screen display and places the cursor in the upper left corner of the screen.

COPY *file(s)1 switches1 file(s)2 switches2*

This command copies one or more files between disks or other devices. *File(s)1* is the source file(s). *File(s)2* is the destination.

The available switches for COPY follow:

Switch	Effect
/A (for ASCII)	Treats the file as a text file
/B (for Binary)	Treats the file as a program file (binary)
/V	Verifies that the copy is recorded correctly

You also can use COPY to copy files between system devices (to the printer or display, for example). You can use the + sign to *concatenate* (combine) two or more files as they are copied, resulting in the target file being a combination of the source files. You can use COPY CON to copy (create) a file from the keyboard.

To copy the file PERSONAL.LTR from the current directory on drive C to the current directory on drive A, enter the following command:

```
COPY PERSONAL.LTR A:
```

The copied file has the same name as the original file.

To copy all files in the BUSINESS directory on drive C that have a file name extension of DAT to the current directory on drive A, enter the following:

```
COPY C:\BUSINESS\*.DAT A:
```

The copies have the same names as the originals. The BUSINESS directory is a subdirectory of the root directory.

To copy all files in the current directory of drive A to the current directory of drive C, enter the following:

```
A:\>COPY *.* C: (often you will have a path after C:)
```

DATE *mm-dd-yy* or *mm/dd/yy*

This command displays and sets the date known to the system. DOS prompts you for the date and time when you start the system unless it finds an AUTOEXEC.BAT file. If you use an AUTOEXEC.BAT file, you probably want to include DATE and TIME. Many systems these days have a clock calendar card which does all this for you.

To set the date to November 22, 1992, enter the following:

```
DATE 11-22-92
```

To display the date and let DOS prompt you for a new date, enter the following:

DATE

The following prompt is displayed:

```
Current date is Tue 1-01-1980
Enter new date (mm-dd-yy):
```

Type **11-22-92** and press Enter.

DEL *file(s)*

This command removes files from a disk. The DEL and ERASE commands perform identically.

File(s) is the file name of the file(s) to be erased. You can specify a drive and path, as well as wild cards (? and *). If you do not specify a drive or directory, DOS assumes the current drive or directory. If you do not specify a file, DOS assumes *.* (all files).

To erase the file REPORT.OLD in the current directory on the default drive, enter the following:

DEL REPORT.OLD

To erase the file REPORT.OLD in the current directory on the default drive and ask for confirmation before deleting the file, enter the following:

DEL REPORT.OLD /P

The /P switch pauses for confirmation before deleting a file. /P is the only switch used with DEL.

To erase REPORT.OLD from the BUDGET subdirectory on the default drive, enter the following:

DEL \BUDGET\REPORT.OLD

To erase all files in the current directory on the default drive, type **DEL *.***.

DIR *file(s) switches*

File(s) is the file name of the file or files whose directory information is displayed. You can specify a drive and path; if you do not specify these, DOS assumes the defaults (that is, the current drive and directory). You can use the wild cards * and ? with DIR.

You can use the following switches with the DIR command:

Switch	Effect
/P	Pauses the display when the screen is full
/W	Gives a wide display, listing only the file names/extensions

To display directory information for all files in the current directory of the default drive, enter the following:

DIR

To display directory information for all files in the current directory of drive A and pause the display when the screen is full, enter the following:

DIR A:/P

To see if a file called BUDGET.DAT is on the current directory and to display it, enter the following:

DIR BUDGET.DAT

DISKCOMP *d1: d2:*

This command compares the entire contents of two disks sector by sector and reports the side and track of any sectors that differ. This command is most useful after a crucial DISKCOPY operation to ensure that the diskettes are identical. *D1:* is the drive letter of the first diskette, and *d2:* is the drive letter of the second diskette.

DISKCOPY *d1: d2:*

This command makes an exact, sector-by-sector copy of one diskette (source) to another diskette (target). If the target diskette is not formatted, DISKCOPY formats the target disk as it executes.

D1: is the drive letter of the diskette to be copied, and *d2:* is the drive letter of the diskette to which you are copying.

> Any data that exists on the diskette before the DISKCOPY is wiped away. In addition, because DISKCOPY makes an identical copy, it copies fragmented files, which can cause problems. You should format a disk before using it as a target disk to ensure that no bad sectors are on the disk.

DOSSHELL

This command starts the DOS Shell.

ERASE *file(s)*

This command removes files from a disk and is identical to the DEL command.

FORMAT *d: switches*

This command prepares a disk to accept DOS information and files. It also checks for and marks bad sectors so that DOS does not try to store data in the bad areas. *d:* is the drive of the disk to be formatted. DOS prompts you for a volume label.

The switches for the FORMAT command follow:

Switch	Effect
/F:*size*	Formats a disk to less than maximum size, where *size* equals the capacity of the drive in kilobytes (K).
/S	Copies the operating system files to the new disk to make it bootable.
/V:*label*	Enables you to assign a volume label to the disk when you execute the command.

> FORMAT destroys any data that may be present on a disk.

To format a diskette in drive A, enter the following:

    FORMAT A:

To format a diskette in drive A and give it the volume label *1992DATA*, enter the following:

    FORMAT A: /V:1992DATA

To format a diskette in drive A and add the operating system files so that the disk can start DOS, enter the following:

    FORMAT A: /S

HELP *commandname*

Typing **HELP** at the DOS prompt displays a complete list of all DOS commands and a one-line explanation. Typing **HELP** followed by a command (or the command followed by the /? switch) displays a screen of help information on that command.

LABEL *d: name*

This command enables you to create, change, or delete a disk volume label (a disk name, for example). *d:* is the drive letter. *Name* is the label (name) to be placed on the disk. A label can contain up to 11 characters. Typing **LABEL** and pressing Enter again erases the current label.

MD or MKDIR *path*

This command creates a new subdirectory. *Path* is the drive and/or directory path of the new subdirectory. If *path* begins with a backslash (\), DOS makes the new directory a subdirectory of the root. If *path* does not begin with a backslash, DOS makes the new directory a subdirectory of the current directory.

To create a subdirectory named LOTUS in the root directory of the default drive, enter the following:

```
MD\LOTUS
```

To create a subdirectory named DATA in the directory LOTUS of the default drive, enter the following:

```
MD\LOTUS\DATA
```

MODE

This command enables DOS to work with various parts of your computer's hardware. You can use MODE to set the operation mode on a printer and a display.

To set the operation mode on a printer to 1 to 132 characters per line and 8 lines per inch, enter the following:

```
MODE LPT1:132,8
```

To switch to or reset the color/graphics display, enable color, and set the width to 80 characters, enter the following:

MODE CO80

MORE

This command pauses the display when the screen is full to prevent data from scrolling off screen. The message `—More—` appears on the bottom line when the screen is full, and the system is halted until you press any key.

To display the contents of the text file MYFILE.TXT in the current directory on the current drive one full screen at a time, enter the following:

TYPE MYFILE.TXT | MORE

PATH *directories*

This command tells DOS which directories to search for commands, programs, or batch files that are not in the current directory. *Directories* is the drive/path you want to use in the search. If you type **PATH** by itself, DOS displays the present path. You may specify multiple drives and path names, separated by semicolons. DOS performs any path search in the order that each directory appears. It's a good idea to put a PATH statement in your AUTOEXEC.BAT file so that the path is set each time DOS is started. A PATH statement saves a great deal of time and effort because you don't have to be in the directory in which a command or program resides in order to run that program.

The following path command tells DOS to look in the root directory, the DOS directory, a UTIL (utilities) directory, and a directory called BATCH (batch files) each time you enter a command:

PATH C:\;C:\DOS;C:\UTIL;C:\BATCH

After DOS finds the command, it executes it.

PROMPT *string*

This command defines the system prompt, which DOS usually displays as the current drive letter followed by a greater than (>) symbol (for example, C>). *String* specifies the characters that define the new prompt. Typing **PROMPT** alone resets the system prompt to the DOS default. The recommended prompt command is **PROMPT PG**, which displays the default drive, the current directory, and a > at the end of the prompt.

RD or RMDIR *path*

This command removes a subdirectory. *Path* is the drive and/or directory path of the subdirectory to remove. You first must delete all files in the subdirectory before you can remove the subdirectory.

To remove a subdirectory named LOTUS in the root directory of the default drive, enter the following:

RD\LOTUS (or) RD LOTUS

To remove a subdirectory named DATA in the directory LOTUS of the default drive, enter the following:

RD\LOTUS\DATA

REN (RENAME) *file(s)1 file(s)2*

This command changes the name of a file or a set of files. DOS changes only the directory name for the file. The file remains in the same directory on the same disk after DOS changes the name.

To rename the file REPORT.DOC to FINALRPT.DOC, enter the following command:

REN REPORT.DOC FINALRPT.DOC

To rename all files that have the file name extension OLD in the current directory on the default drive to the new extension NEW, enter the following command:

REN *.OLD *.NEW

RESTORE *d: file(s) switches*

This command restores files that you backed up with the BACKUP command. DOS restores these files from the backup disk(s) to the original disk. *d:* indicates the drive that will contain the backup files. *File(s)* indicates the name of the file(s) to be restored.

The available switches for the RESTORE command follow:

Switch	Effect
/P	Asks if a file changed since the last backup or designated as read-only should be restored
/S	Indicates that subdirectories are to be restored

To restore all files in all subdirectories from the diskette in drive A to fixed disk drive C, enter the following:

RESTORE A: C:\ /S

TIME *hh:mm:ss:xx*

This command displays and sets the time of day known to the system. DOS prompts you for the date and time when you start the system unless it finds an AUTOEXEC.BAT file. If you use an AUTOEXEC.BAT file, you probably want to include DATE and TIME. Many systems these days have a clock calendar card which sets the date and time for you.

DOS 3.3 and earlier versions display time in 24-hour format. DOS 4.0 and 5.0 display time in a 12-hour format. Entering partial time information (only the hour and minutes, for example) sets the remaining fields to zero. Entering TIME with no parameters displays the current time setting and prompts you for a new time. Pressing Enter accepts the time that is displayed. Specifying hours and minutes only is sufficient for most applications.

To set the time to 4:30 p.m., enter the following:

TIME 4:30p or TIME 16:30

To display the time and tell DOS to prompt you for a new time, enter the following:

TIME

The following message appears on-screen:

```
Current Time is 4:30:11.33p

Enter new time:
```

Type the time and press Enter.

TREE *path switch*

This command displays a graphic representation of the current directory and any directories beneath the current directory. This command also optionally displays all files. *Path* is the drive letter and directory to be displayed. If omitted, the default drive is assumed. You can use the /F switch to display the names of all files in each subdirectory.

To display a graphic representation of all directories on drive C, enter the following:

TREE C:

To display a graphic representation of all directories on drive C, to list all files in each directory, and to pause the display when the screen is full, enter the following:

TREE C:/F | MORE

To redirect the output of the preceding example to your printer, enter the following:

TREE C:/F > PRN

TYPE *file*

This command displays the contents of a text file on the standard output device—usually the display screen. You cannot use wild cards (* and ?) in the file name or extension with the TYPE command.

To display the contents of REPORT.DOC, which is in the current directory on the default drive, enter the following:

TYPE REPORT.DOC

To add the MORE filter to pause with each full screen, enter the following:

TYPE REPORT.DOC | MORE

VER

This command displays the DOS version number currently in use.
A number to the left of a decimal point shows the major version, and any number(s) to the right shows a minor version. Using this command is a quick way to check which version of DOS you are using, especially on an unfamiliar machine.

VERIFY ON or OFF

This command turns on or off the verify feature that confirms that data is written correctly to disk. Using this command is the same as using the /V switch in the COPY command.

VOL *d:*

This command displays the volume label (name) of a disk so the disk can be identified. *d:* is the letter of the drive containing the disk whose volume label is to be displayed. If you do not specify a drive, DOS assumes the default drive.

Configuration Commands

The following four configuration commands are the most important commands the beginning DOS user will encounter; they are the most crucial commands in providing smooth and efficient performance.

BREAK=ON or OFF

This command determines how often DOS checks for a Ctrl-Break or a Ctrl-C to stop a program. If BREAK is set to OFF, DOS checks for a Ctrl-Break only when it is working with the video display, keyboard, printer, and serial ports. If BREAK is set to ON, DOS checks to see if you have pressed Ctrl-Break whenever a program requests some activity from DOS, making it easier to break out of programs. Typing **BREAK** alone reports the status of BREAK control. OFF is the default when DOS starts. Your system runs a little faster when BREAK is off, but you have fewer opportunities to stop a program.

BUFFERS=*number*

This command sets the number of disk buffers DOS allocates in memory. *Buffers* are blocks of memory used to hold data that was read from disk or will be written to disk. This command decreases the number of times DOS has to read data from disk. Each buffer increases the resident size of DOS by 512 bytes—that is, each consumes 512 bytes of additional RAM.

Significant improvements in disk read/write time may be realized by using buffers. If your computer has enough memory so that your applications are not adversely affected by a small reduction in available memory, try running with 12 or more buffers and see if performance improves. Finding the right number of buffers for your system may take some experimenting. A word processor or database program would benefit from setting BUFFERS to somewhere between 15 and 20. Setting BUFFERS to over 30, however, may actually slow down your system.

DEVICE=*device name*

A *device driver* is a software program that controls or enhances a device, such as your display. The easiest of the six device drivers to understand and use in DOS is ANSI.SYS. You can use this device driver to give you more control over the keyboard and display. You should understand ANSI.SYS because some software packages require that it be installed.

Because ANSI.SYS is a separate program (like an external command), you must tell DOS where ANSI.SYS is before it can be executed by DOS. DOS 5 installs ANSI.SYS in the \DOS subdirectory on drive C. You need to include the following line, therefore, in your CONFIG.SYS file:

```
DEVICE=C:\DOS\ANSI.SYS
```

You may encounter other device drivers when you purchase software packages; you can install these drivers by using the DEVICE= command. Consult the documentation that comes with the software for more details.

FILES=*number*

This command sets the number of files that you can have open at the same time. The *number* can be between 8 (the default) and 255. For every file over 8, DOS requires another 39 bytesof memory. DOS 5 allocates 10 *file handles* (a value DOS uses to store information about each file with which it is working) in its default CONFIG.SYS file, but this number is seldom enough with the large application programs used today. The general guideline for the FILES setting is 20. If, after trying to run one of your application programs, you receive an error message about file handles, you should increase this number again. Increase the number in increments of 5 until the program runs.

Appendix B

Glossary of Computer Terms

Every new computer user is flooded with new terms, most of which sound like a foreign language (which really isn't far from the truth). This appendix is not only a master glossary of the terms used in this book, but also a small dictionary of the most common computer terms. Each term is defined in simple-to-understand English. The listing is, of course, alphabetical for easy reference.

This summary is also contained in the GLOSSARY.TXT file, which you can display with the View command in the Shell, the DOS Editor, or the TYPE command (**TYPE C:\ATI50\SUB1\GLOSSARY.TXT | MORE**).

A

Application Program A computer program (like a word processor, spreadsheet, database, and so on) that performs a specific task.

Archive To duplicate files on a separate disk for the purpose of safekeeping in case data is lost on the original disk.

ASCII Short for *American Standard Code for Information Interchange*. Standard format used by computers to store and transfer data. Standard code for representing characters as binary numbers. Many text editors, such as DOS 5's Editor, create pure ASCII text files. See *Binary*.

Associate a File To correlate, or "attach" a particular file extension to a program. Doing this allows a program to automatically start when an associated file is chosen.

Asynchronous Communications Adapter A hardware device, usually a port on the back of a PC, that provides serial communications capabilities to communicate with other computers or devices supporting the RS-232 communications standard. See *Modem*.

AUTOEXEC.BAT A batch file that executes when the computer starts up; it usually contains programs and commands that configure the system the way the user wants.

AUX Abbreviation of *auxiliary*. This is the communications port DOS uses unless told otherwise. It can be COM1 or COM2 in DOS 3.2 and earlier versions, or COM1 through COM4 in DOS 3.3 and later versions. See *COM1, COM2, COM3, COM4*.

B

Back Up To make copies of files for storage, in case the originals get damaged or lost.

BAK An extension given by EDLIN (the DOS text editor), as well as many word processors and text editors, to the most recent copy of a file. This is done in case the current version is damaged. See *Extension*.

BASIC Acronym for *Beginner's All-Purpose Symbolic Instruction Code*. An easy-to-learn computer programming language. New with DOS 5 is QBasic, a much more sophisticated language than earlier BASIC languages (such as GWBASIC).

BAT See *Batch File*.

Batch File A file of commands and batch subcommands to be executed when the name of the batch file is entered. The commands are executed as though they were entered through the keyboard. Batch files must have BAT as the file name extension.

Baud The rate at which information is transmitted through a communications line. Baud rates are expressed in bits per second. As a rule of thumb, a baud rate divided by 10 equals characters per second. A baud rate of 300 is equivalent to 30 characters per second, for example. Modems are rated according to baud rate; 1200 and 2400 baud are typical. See *Modem*.

BBS See *Bulletin Board Service*.

Binary A numeric system based on the powers of 2. The numbering system of computers. Uses only the numbers 0 and 1. See *Bit.*

BIOS Acronym for *basic input/output system.* A set of routines in ROM necessary for booting the computer. These routines handle all input/output functions, including graphics. In contrast, routines in the operating system (*DOS calls*) do not support graphics. Thus, most software must call routines in the BIOS as well as DOS.

Bit Short for *binary digit.* The smallest unit of storage on a computer. A bit can have a value of 0 or 1. You can think of a bit like a light switch; it is on or off. A bit is a 0 or 1, signifying the OFF or ON position of an electronic circuit. The 0 and 1 values of 8 bits (2 to the 8th power) result in 256 unique states, accounting for the 256 ASCII codes of the computer.

Boot To clear the computer's memory and to load and start DOS. Derived from the expression *Pull yourself up by the bootstraps.* See *Cold Boot* and *Warm Boot.*

Bootable Disk A disk (hard or floppy) that contains the DOS system files and which can be used to boot (start) the computer. You can create a bootable floppy disk with this command: FORMAT A: /S. Remember, however, that issuing this command will destroy the contents of the target disk.

Break To terminate the current operation. Most DOS commands and programs can be "broken" by holding down the Ctrl key and pressing the Break key or C. This also is called a Ctrl-Break.

Bulletin Board Service A private telecommunications utility, usually set up by a PC hobbyist for the enjoyment of other hobbyists. Used to communicate with other users and to upload (send) and download (receive) public domain and shareware software. With the emergence of computer viruses, however, the BBS has suffered. For this reason, if you use a BBS, use virus-protection software (such as FluShot+) on any programs you download before using them on your computer. See *Virus.*

Bus A computer's main avenue of communication; consists of a set of parallel wires to which the CPU (central processing unit, or microprocessor), the memory, and all input/output devices are connected. The 8088 microprocessor (original IBM PC) has an 8-bit bus; the AT (or 286) microprocessor has a 16-bit bus, and the 386 and 486 have a 32-bit bus. The larger the bus, the faster the CPU can communicate with devices.

Byte A collection of bits—usually 8. Depending on the value of each bit (or whether each switch is on or off), a byte can have a value of 0 through 255. A byte is basically equivalent to one character or letter. The English alphabet is 26 bytes, for example; therefore, a double-spaced, typewritten page is about 1,500 bytes.

C

Character String A group of characters (letters, numbers, and so on) that you tell DOS to treat as such, instead of as a command. You tell the FIND command which characters to search for in a text file, for example.

Child Directory A directory immediately under another directory (the parent); another name for a subdirectory. See *Parent Directory*.

Chip A small, thin, silicon wafer on which thousands of transistors are deposited. These are the building blocks of computers.

Clock A circuit that generates a series of evenly spaced pulses; all the switching activity in the computer occurs while the clock is sending out a pulse. Clock speed is measured in megahertz (MHz), where 1 MHz = 1,000,000 cycles per second. Higher clock speeds result in faster computing. It is very misleading to compare clock speeds of microprocessors, however. Because of the larger bus, for example, a 286 machine running at 8 MHz will run much faster than an 8088 running at 8 MHz.

Cluster One or more consecutive sectors of disk storage. DOS keeps track of files on disk by storing the locations of *file clusters* (the sectors where file contents are stored) in a table called the file allocation table (or FAT). When DOS reads a file's information from disk, it searches the FAT, finds the addresses of the clusters that contain that file's information, and then reads the information from the appropriate clusters. See *Sector* and *Track*.

Cold Boot To start the computer from a power-off condition. See *Warm Boot*.

Color Graphics Adapter (CGA) A printed circuit board in the computer system that controls the display by showing graphics and text in a low resolution in up to four colors.

COM1, COM2, COM3, COM4 Short for *communications*. The names for serial communications ports. COM1 and COM2 are recognized by DOS Version 3.2 and earlier, and COM1 through COM4 are recognized by Version 3.3 and later.

Command An instruction you give to the computer that executes a DOS function or a program.

Command Line The place on-screen where you enter a command. The command line begins with the *DOS prompt* such as A> or C> and contains three elements, as in the following example:

```
C> FORMAT A: /S
```

Where FORMAT is the command, A: is the parameter, and /S is the switch. See *Command Name*, *Parameter*, and *Switch*.

Command Name Refers to the command you want to execute. Tells DOS *what* you want to do. Compare with *Parameter* and *Switch*. Also, see *Command Line*.

Command Processor See *COMMAND.COM*.

COMMAND.COM A special file that contains the instructions needed to activate DOS and make it usable. It also contains the internal DOS commands and the batch subcommand processor, which are loaded into memory when DOS is started.

Communications Also called *telecommunications*. The transferring of data between computers. See *Modem*.

CON Short for *console*. The name DOS uses to refer to the keyboard (input) and the screen (output).

CONFIG.SYS A special text file that contains configuration commands that attach new hardware devices, create RAM disks, set the number of buffers and files that can be accessed by DOS, change the keyboard and video display for an international character set, and more. DOS 5 also has CONFIG.SYS commands that manage extended and expanded memory.

Confirmation Message A message used in the DOS Shell that asks you to verify an action before final execution. The Shell enables you to turn off such messages in order to speed up your work.

Control-Alt-Del Pressing this key combination reboots the computer; this is a *warm boot*, which does not do a memory check as does a *cold boot*.

Control-Break See *Break*.

CPU Acronym for *central processing unit*. The main part of a computer that performs calculations and processes information; also called a *microprocessor*. Examples of CPUs are the 8088, 80286, 80386, and 80486 microprocessors, on which thousands of transistors reside, as in the following chart:

Processor	Approximate Number of Transistors
8086/8088	29,000
286	134,000
386	375,000
486	1,200,000

Current Directory The directory of a disk that DOS uses by default—that is, if no other directory is referred to. Because DOS enables you to create multiple directories, you must indicate with which directory you want to work. If you do not specify a file's directory in a DOS command, DOS uses the current directory by default.

Current Drive The drive containing the disk on which DOS looks for a file by default—that is, if no other drive is referred to.

D

Database A collection of interrelated files, arranged in a highly organized fashion, which is created and managed by a database management system (DBMS). There are two general types of database programs: the *flat file* type (also called single file or file manager type) and the *relational* type (also called multifile). Flat file databases operate on one set of information at a time, and relational databases work with many interrelated sets of data at once. An example of a flat file type is cards in a recipe box; the cards can be sorted, searched and checked—one at a time. In contrast, the relational database can interrelate a set of recipe cards to a set of cooks and a set of diners and a set of dates available for dinner—all at the same time. An excellent flat file database is the shareware program File Express. Relational databases include dBASE, R:BASE, and Paradox. Relational databases also have their own program language which can be used to design custom database applications for your own use or even distribution to others. A flat file database, however, will meet the needs of most PC users.

DBMS Database management system. See *Database*.

Default Directory See *Current Directory*.

Default Drive See *Current Drive*.

Device A piece of computer equipment (hardware), such as a printer or disk drive, that performs a specific task.

Device Driver A computer program that controls or enhances a device, such as a printer or a display.

Device Names The special name by which DOS refers to a device, such as

Name	Specifies
CON	Console (keyboard/screen)
COM1 (or AUX)	First asynchronous communications port
COM2	Second asynchronous communications port
LPT1 (or PRN)	First parallel printer
LPT2	Second parallel printer

Name	Specifies
LPT3	Third parallel printer
NUL	Nonexistent device for application testing

DIP Switch Acronym for *dual in-line package*. A series or block of tiny switches built into circuit boards. Controls various configurations of the computer hardware.

Directory A special file used by DOS to keep track of files and subdirectories that contains the names of files, their sizes (in bytes), the times and dates they were last written to or updated, and the names of any subdirectories. The DIR command displays directory information. *Directory* and *subdirectory* often are used interchangeably. See *Subdirectory*.

Disk A magnetically coated device used to store electronic data. A generic term when no distinction is needed between a diskette and fixed disk (hard disk). See *Diskette* and *Hard Disk*.

Disk Drive See *Floppy Disk Drive* and *Hard Disk*.

Diskette A flexible, magnetically coated plastic device used to store electronic data.

Display The screen on which the computer displays information.

DOS Acronym for *disk operating system*. An operating system controls the hardware of the computer and manages files and other things which would otherwise demand additional software. See *Software* and *Hardware*.

DOS Prompt The characters DOS displays to inform you that you can enter a command. For example, C:\> is a DOS prompt.

Dot Pitch In a display or printer system that uses dots, this is the distance from the center of one dot to the center of an adjacent dot. If a laser printer has a resolution of 300 dpi, for example, the dot pitch is 1/300th inch. See *Pixel*.

DPI Acronym for *dots per inch*. See *Dot Pitch*.

Drive Letter The letter which identifies a disk drive to DOS—for example, A for a diskette drive or C for a fixed disk. A drive letter usually is followed by a colon (:), which to DOS always signifies a disk drive.

E

End-Of-File Marker A special ASCII code used by DOS to denote the end of a file. This character is Ctrl-Z.

Enhanced Graphics Adapter (EGA) Printed circuit board in the system unit that controls the display. Shows text and graphics in medium resolution in up to 16 colors.

Extension An optional suffix of one to three characters that helps to identify a file more precisely. See *File*.

External Command A DOS command that resides in a disk file. DOS has *internal commands* and *external commands*. Internal commands are stored in memory and can be executed even if a disk containing DOS is not in use. However, to execute an external command (which is a separate program), a disk containing the command file must be in use. See *Internal Command*.

F

FAT Acronym for *file allocation table*. This table keeps track of all the sectors on a disk and tells whether a sector is free or in use by a file. As you may guess, the FAT is extremely important, so DOS keeps two copies of it in case one becomes damaged.

File A named collection of information stored on disk. Usually contains data or a computer program. Identified by its file name and an optional extension.

File Handle A value DOS uses to store information about each file with which it is working.

File Name A one- to eight-character string which identifies a file. A file must have a file name and may have a one- to three- character file name extension. See *Extension*.

Filespec Short for *file specification*. A filespec completely identifies a file to DOS; it can include a drive letter, path name, file name, and extension.

Filter A program or command that receives data from a standard input device, changes the data, and writes the results to a standard output device. DOS filters include SORT, FIND, and MORE.

First-Level Directories The directories immediately down from the root directory.

Floppy Disk Drive A device into which you insert flexible storage disks used to store data. Common sizes for floppy disk drives are 360K, 1.2M (which use 5 1/4-inch diskettes); 720K, 1.44M; and 2.88M (which use 3 1/2-inch diskettes). Unlike a hard disk (on which the read/write heads float on a cushion of air), the read/write heads in a floppy drive actually contact the surface of the disk. A hard disk is preferable over a floppy disk because the floppy disk drive is much slower. Additionally, a hard disk is much more convenient.

Format To prepare a disk for use by DOS. Physical formatting divides the disk into *tracks* and *sectors*. Logical formatting divides the disk into four areas: the boot record, file allocation table (FAT), root directory, and data area. See Appendix D, "More about DOS," for further information.

Fragmented File A file that has many nonsequential or fragmented sectors. DOS tries to allocate a file's data in contiguous (consecutive) areas, but cannot always do so if many files have been erased and added to the disk. Fragmented files take longer to access, because DOS cannot read them sequentially.

G

Gigabyte (G) Some businesses need very large storage capacity. Another unit of measuring *bytes* is the gigabyte (G), which is equal to 1,000M or about 1 billion bytes. In the example under *Byte*, this is roughly equal to 666,666 double-spaced, typewritten pages.

Graphical User Interface A GUI is a user interface that uses pictures and objects to communicate with the user, instead of the commands and menus that are used in traditional text-based interfaces. Microsoft Windows is a popular GUI.

GUI (pronounced *gooey*) See *Graphical User Interface*.

H

Hard Copy A printout on paper of computer data, in contrast to data stored on disk or in memory.

Hard Disk Several firm disk platters sealed inside a case, which is never opened. The read/write heads float over the platters on a small cushion of air and never touch the surface. This enables the disk to spin much faster (about 3500 RPM) than a floppy disk, and thereby store and retrieve much more information faster. Hard disks are very sensitive and must be handled with care so that the heads never come in contact with the disk. The heads should be parked before moving the computer and even before turning it off; most newer hard disks, however, park themselves when the computer is powered down. IDE (integrated development environment) hard drives are the most desirable nowadays. See *IDE*.

Hardware The physical pieces of a computer, such as the keyboard, printer, disk drives, and system unit.

Hexadecimal The base-16 numbering system whose digits are 0 through F (A through F represent 10 through 15). Often used in computer programming because it's easily converted to and from the *binary system* (the base-2 numbering system) used in a computer.

Hidden File A file, usually used by DOS only, that is not listed when the directory is displayed. A hidden file cannot be copied, erased, or otherwise affected by DOS.

Hierarchical Directory An organized, multilevel structure of directories.

I

IDE Acronym for *intelligent drive electronics*. The IDE hard disk is a hard disk for 286, 386, and 486 PCs that contains most of the controller circuitry within the drive itself. This type of drive is the most desirable for most users. See *Hard Disk*.

Initialize To prepare a disk for use; another term for formatting. See *Format*.

Input The data that a program reads. See *Input/Output*.

Input/Output (I/O) Refers to the devices and processes involved in reading (input) and writing (output) data.

Insert Mode A program mode used in word processing programs that inserts text and pushes existing text to the right. See *Overwrite*.

Integrated Circuit An electronic circuit that contains more than one transistor and other electronic components. See *Chip*.

Internal Command A DOS command stored in memory that may be executed without requiring a diskette containing DOS to be in use. The most commonly used commands, such as DIR, ERASE, CHDIR, DATE, RENAME, and others are internal commands. See *External Command*.

K

Keyboard The device (piece of hardware) consisting of alphabetic and other keys used to give instructions to a computer.

Kilobyte (K) The most common unit of measuring computer storage space, which is 1,024 bytes; a common practice is to round off a K to 1,000 bytes. In the example under *Byte*, a double-spaced, typewritten page is about 1.5K. See *Byte*.

L

LAN Acronym for *local area network*. A network (also called a LAN) connects two or more machines that are confined to the same area, such as an office or building, by using printed circuit boards, cables, and special software, and enables all of them to share resources, such as printers and drives. Another plus for the LAN is that it enables several people to enter data into a single database; some database programs, such as Paradox and dBASE, have network versions specifically for this purpose.

Launch To start a program.

LPT1, LPT2, LPT3 Short for *line printer*, these are the names DOS uses to refer to three ports to which parallel printers are attached.

M

Megabyte (M) Equal to 1,000K or about 1 million bytes. In the example under *Byte*, this equals roughly 666 double-spaced, typewritten pages. Large hard disks are very common these days. A 40M hard disk, for example, holds roughly 26,640 double-spaced, typewritten pages. Even larger hard disks, such as 200M, are getting more common all the time.

Megahertz (Mhz) Equal to 1,000,000 cycles per second. All computers have an internal clock that determines how fast the computer operates. See *Clock*.

Memory The temporary, electronic storage in a computer, which is in contrast to the permanent, magnetic storage of a disk. See *Disk*, *RAM*, and *ROM*.

Memory Chip A small silicon chip that uses electrical charges to store information. Usually located on memory boards or system boards (also called *motherboards*). These should not be confused with the CPU chip. See *CPU* and *Chip*.

Microcomputer A small computer usually used by one person.

Microprocessor See *CPU*.

Milliseconds (ms) Equal to 1/1,000 of a second. Most frequently used to measure the speed of a hard disk. The smaller the number, the faster the drive. 40ms drives are considered slow. You should purchase 28ms or even 18ms drives.

Modem Short for *modulator-demodulator*, this device enables data to be transferred over telephone lines. See *Baud*.

Monitor See *Display*.

Monochrome A computer display screen that only displays one color—usually amber, white, or green.

Monochrome Display Adapter (MDA) Printed circuit board in the system unit that controls the display. Shows text in medium resolution in only one color.

Monthly Backup Strategy A systematic way of backing up the entire hard disk once a month and modified files once a day.

Multicolor Graphics Array (MCGA) Printed circuit board in the system unit that controls the display. Shows text and graphics in low to medium resolution in up to 256 colors; used in IBM PS/2 computers.

Multitasking The running of two or more programs at the same time. Do not confuse this with *task-swapping*, which is simply the loading of two or more programs and switching between them. In task-swapping, two or more programs are present in memory, but only one at a time is running. In multitasking, multiple programs are actually running. Both Microsoft Windows and DESQView support multitasking.

N

Nanoseconds (ns) Equal to 1/1,000,000,000 of a second. Most frequently used to measure the speed of memory chips. The lower the number, the faster the chips. Chips over 100ns are slow and not desirable. The best PCs have 80ns or faster chips.

Network See *LAN*.

O

Off-Line See *On-Line*.

On-Line Used to describe whether a device that is connected to the computer is in communication with the computer. When your printer is on-line, for example, it is ready to print; if it is off-line, it will not print when the computer sends it information.

Operating System See *DOS*.

Overtype Mode See *Overwrite*.

Overwrite To type information on top of previously recorded information, thereby eliminating the existing information. Most text editors and word processors have an overwrite (or overtype) mode, which is the opposite of *insert mode*—the mode which simply inserts characters onscreen by pushing other characters to the right.

P

Parallel A common means of transferring data over parallel (several) separate wires simultaneously. Faster than serial transfer. See *Serial*.

Parallel Port The port in the back of the computer to which a printer is attached.

Parameter A value passed to a command which gives the command specific instructions. Most DOS commands have one or more parameters. Tells DOS *where* you want to carry out a command. See *Command Line*, *Command Name*, and *Switch*.

Parent Directory A directory contains a listing of files and other directories. Parent directory is merely another name for a subdirectory that contains other subdirectories; subdirectories under it also are called child directories.

Path In DOS, the list of directory names, separated by a backslash (\), that defines the location of a specific directory or file.

Piping A DOS feature which enables you to use screen output of one command or program as input to another command or program.

Pixel A single dot on a graphics display. Also called a *pel* (for *picture element*). The resolutions of display screens are compared by their pixel specifications. The more pixels, the better the resolution.

Port The electrical connection, usually located in the back of the computer unit, through which the computer sends and receives data to and from specific devices.

Power Down To physically turn off the computer.

Power Up To physically turn on the computer.

Print Queue A list of files to be printed that is stored in memory. You created this list by a special command (the PRINT command in DOS).

Printer A device that produces images of text and graphics on paper.

PRN Short for *printer*, this is the printer DOS uses unless told otherwise.

Program A set of computer instructions.

Program Group Contains a group (or collection) of program items in the DOS Shell.

Program Item An individual program listed in a group of programs in the DOS Shell.

Prompt **1**. A character or message that appears on-screen informing you that the computer is ready to receive input. Typically, this is an on-screen question or instruction that tells you to do something. **2**. A way to refer to the DOS prompt. See *DOS Prompt*.

Q

QBasic See *BASIC*.

Queue See *Print Queue*.

R

RAM Short for *random-access memory*, this is the electronic memory DOS uses for programs and data. RAM changes constantly as you use programs and is lost when the machine is turned off or reset.

RAM Disk A portion of memory (RAM) used to simulate a disk drive. This treats a portion of the machine's memory as though it were a diskette. You can put programs on a RAM disk and run them from that disk, and you can read and write data to that disk. Information is read and written extremely fast, because no physical diskette has to be spun and accessed. The drawbacks of RAM disks are obvious; the amount of memory they occupy (the amount of memory allocated to a RAM disk reduces your available memory by an equal amount), and the fact that their contents are lost when DOS is restarted or the power supply is interrupted.

Read/Write Head A small, electromagnetic device that retrieves (reads) and stores (writes) information from or to a magnetic disk or tape.

Reboot To restart the operating system. Done by pressing Ctrl, Alt, and Del (Ctrl-Alt-Del). This also is called a *system reset*. Many computers also have reset buttons, which are very useful when keyboards freeze.

Redirection A DOS feature enabling a command to direct its output to a device other than the screen or to receive its input from a device other than the keyboard.

Replaceable Parameters The parameter variables of a batch file which may be assigned values at the time the batch file is started. There are 10 replaceable parameters available to a DOS batch file: %0 through %9.

ROM Short for *read-only memory*, this type of memory contains non-erasable computer instructions embedded in hardware chips.

Root Directory The main directory in a hierarchy of directories that DOS creates on every disk. The \ is the symbol for the root directory. The root directory of a double-sided diskette can hold 112 files. The root directory of a fixed disk is limited only by the available space on the disk.

S

Screen Mode Controls the size and shape of the images on-screen in the DOS Shell.

Scrolling refers to the movement of information on a computer screen. In DOS, for example, the DIR (directory) command may scroll information so fast that it can't be read; the /P switch will pause screen scrolling. Some keyboards also have a Pause key.

Sector A section of a track that serves as a disk's smallest storage unit. In DOS Version 2 and later, there are nine 512-byte sectors per track. See *Track* and *Cluster*.

Seek Time Time required to move a disk's read/write head to the desired track. Commonly used to compare the speed of hard disks in milliseconds. The smaller the number, the faster the drive. 40ms drives are considered slow. You should purchase 28ms or even 18ms drives.

Serial Communication Transferring data one bit at a time over a single wire. See *Parallel*.

Serial Port The communications port (COM1, COM2, COM3, or COM4) to which devices like a modem or serial printer are attached.

Serial Printer An interface to a printer wherein the eight bits representing a character are sent one at a time. This is distinguished from a *parallel* printer interface, which sends all eight bits of a character at one time.

Shareware Software that is distributed free of charge or for a nominal copying fee ($2 to $5) from a distributor. This is the try-before-you-buy concept. You are encouraged to try the software and see if you like it. If you continue to use the software, you are bound morally and often legally to send the author the registration price he or she asks. Registering your software often entitles you to a printed manual, support, and program updates. Shareware is quite often of high quality.

Shortcut Key A key combination that switches you directly from one program to another in the DOS Shell. You could, for example, define the Ctrl-W key combination to switch you immediately from whatever you are doing to your word processor.

Software The programs used with a computer.

Source Disk The disk you want to make a copy of. See *Target Disk*.

Spin life The lifespan of a disk. The spin life of a floppy disk is about 1,000 hours, and the spin life of a hard disk is about 50,000 hours. This number can sometimes be arbitrary, however, because disks sometimes fail long before their life should be over.

Spreadsheet An application program similar to an accountant's lined worksheet, organized in an array of rows and columns used for entering calculations and simple database needs. Lotus 1-2-3 and Quattro Pro are two leading spreadsheet programs.

Stop Bit A signal used in serial communications that marks the end of a character.

Subdirectory A special file that contains directory entries. A directory that lies within another directory. DOS enables you to create directories in a hierarchical (tree) manner. The highest level directory is called the *root directory*, which is created by DOS when a disk is formatted. You may create directories within the root directory, directories within those directories, and so on. *Subdirectory* and *directory* often are used interchangeably. See *directory* and *root directory*.

Surge Protector An electronic device that protects computer equipment from electrical current fluctuations and spikes.

Switch A value that gives a command even more specific information about the command, over and above the parameter. Tells DOS *how* you want a command carried out. Compare with *Command Line*, *Command Name*, and *Parameter*.

System Program See *DOS*.

System Prompt See *DOS Prompt*.

System Reset See *Reboot*.

T

Target Disk The disk that you copy the *source disk to*. See *Source Disk*.

Task-Swapping The ability to load more than one program and switch between them. See *Multitasking*.

Telecommunications See *Communications*.

Terabyte (T) 1000 Gigabytes, or about 1 trillion bytes. In view of the example under *Byte*, this is roughly 666,666,666 double-spaced, typewritten pages.

Text Editor A program used to create or change text files. DOS 5 supplies its own high-quality editor, called Editor.

Text File A file containing normal, readable letters, numbers, and punctuation.

Track An invisible, electronically produced circle on a disk where data is stored. A 360K disk, for example, has 40 tracks (concentric circles) on each side of the diskette. Each track is divided into nine areas, called *sectors*. Each sector contains 512 bytes (characters) of information. See *Cluster* and *Sector*.

Tree Structure An analogy of an inverted tree that shows how directories are related to each other in the same way that branches of a tree are related.

U

Update To change a file, to make a new version.

Upgrade To install the newer version of a program or DOS. For example, "I upgraded from DOS Version 3.3 to Version 5.0."

V

Video Graphics Array (VGA) Circuit board in the system unit that controls the display. Shows text and graphics in medium to high resolution in up to 256 colors. Has become the standard in today's PCs.

Virtual Disk Another name for a RAM disk. See *RAM Disk*.

Virus A small piece of computer code that replicates itself and copies itself to other programs and disks. Often designed to damage other programs, alter data, and then self-destruct, leaving no trace of itself or the person who wrote it. A *Trojan horse*, named for the wooden horse that smuggled Greek soldiers into the city of Troy, is a delivery vehicle for putting destructive codes into a computer. A Trojan appears to be a useful program, but carries destruction, either by carrying a virus or *logic bomb*, or just doing the damage on its own. Trojans are sometimes disguised as new versions of shareware programs, for example. A Logic Bomb, like a real bomb, lies dormant until a specific date or event, at which time it is triggered. Likewise, a *worm* is a destructive program, but it is not time-activated. Many anti-virus programs are available today that will protect you from viruses, including Norton Anti-Virus and FluShot+.

Volume Label A name given electronically to a disk for grouping or identifying purposes.

W

Wait State Pauses built into many chips to ensure that all other components are ready to receive data. This is a dormant state during which the computer simply marks time, waiting for an operation to occur. Wait states often are used for synchronization purposes—for example, when a fast CPU must wait for information from a memory area that cannot operate as quickly. The best machines have zero wait states and 80-nanosecond memory chips. See *Nanoseconds*.

Warm Boot Restarting a PC while the power is on. This is performed by pressing Ctrl, Alt, and Del simultaneously. The physical difference between a cold boot and a warm boot is that a warm boot does not go through the memory-checking process and is, therefore, faster. A warm boot is preferred over a cold boot because powering up your computer puts more strain on the electronics. The better computers sold nowadays, however, have a reset button on them that does a cold boot without shutting off the computer. This is a great benefit when the computer and keyboard lock up, making a warm boot impossible.

Wild Card A symbol used in file names and extensions to represent one or multiple characters. In DOS the * is used to represent all characters in a file name or extension, and the ? is used to represent one character. The specification *.DOC, for example, includes all files with the DOC extension, and ?AC.DOC includes all files with any letter followed by AC and the DOC extension.

Window A portion of the screen, usually a box, dedicated to a specific activity. Some software enables you to divide the screen into multiple windows, thereby turning the screen into a desktop, where various files can be open at once.

Windows Environment An operating environment, such as Microsoft Windows and DESQview, that enables you to have multiple windows on the display screen. Such environments enable you to exchange data between windows and run multiple programs simultaneously. Many experts feel that window-type environments are the future of PC computing.

Word processor An application program that enables you to enter, manipulate, format, and print textual information. A word processor is a highly advanced text editor. About 80 percent of PCs today have word processing as the number one use. There are many word processors available today, WordPerfect being the most popular.

Write Protect To cover the small notch or opening on a diskette so that no data can be written to the disk, thereby protecting the data already on the disk.

For More Information

For a more thorough dictionary of computer terms, consult *Que's Computer User's Dictionary*, 2nd Edition.

Appendix C

Common DOS Error Messages

This appendix presents error messages that the beginning or DOS Version 5 user is likely to encounter. Obviously, this list is not exhaustive, but it does cover many of the messages you are most likely to see.

The actual wording of common error messages varies for different implementations and versions of DOS. Sometimes the differences may be as slight as punctuation and capitalization. At other times, the entire content of the message may differ. If you see a message that you cannot locate in this guide, refer to *Using MS-DOS 5* or your computer's DOS manual.

The messages in this appendix may appear when you are starting DOS or when you are using your computer. Most start-up errors indicate that DOS did not start and that you must reboot the system. Most of the other error messages indicate that DOS terminated (*aborted*) the program and returned to the system prompt. This summary also is contained in DOSERROR.TXT, which you can display with the View command in the Shell, the DOS Editor, or the TYPE command. For example, enter the following command:

TYPE C:\ATI50\SUB1\DOSERROR.TXT | MORE

The following messages are listed in alphabetical order for easy reference.

Access denied

You or a program tried to change or erase a file that is marked as read-only or that is not in use. You can use the ATTRIB command to change the read-only status of a file.

Attempted write-protect violation

The floppy disk you are trying to format is write-protected. If you want to format this disk, remove the write-protect tab on 5 1/4-inch disks, or close the write-protect shutter on 3 1/2-inch disks. If the disk in the drive is the wrong disk, insert another disk and try the command again.

Bad command or filename

The command you entered is not valid for invoking a command, program, or batch file. The most frequent causes follow:

- You misspelled a name.
- You omitted a needed disk drive or path name.
- You gave the parameters without the command name.

Check the spelling on the command line. Make sure that the command, program, or batch file is in the location specified (disk drive and directory path). Then try the command again.

Bad or missing command interpreter

DOS cannot find the command interpreter, COMMAND.COM, and cannot start. If you are starting DOS, this message means that COMMAND.COM is not on the boot disk or that a version of COMMAND.COM from a previous version of DOS is on the disk. Insert into the floppy disk drive another disk that contains the operating system and the reboot the system. After DOS starts, copy COMMAND.COM to the original startup disk so that you can boot from that disk.

If this message appears while you are running DOS, COMMAND.COM may have been erased from the disk and directory you used when starting DOS. This message may also indicate that a version of COMMAND.COM from a previous version of DOS has overwritten the good version. You must restart DOS by resetting the system.

If resetting the system does not solve your problem, use a copy of the DOS master disk to restart the computer. Copy COMMAND.COM from this floppy disk to the bad disk.

Bad or missing filename

DOS was directed to load a device driver that could not be located, an error occurred when the device driver was loaded, or a break address for the device driver was out of bounds for the size of RAM memory being used in the computer. DOS continues its boot but does not use the device driver file name.

If DOS loads, check your CONFIG.SYS file for the line `DEVICE=filename`. Make sure that the line is spelled correctly and that the device driver is where you specified. If this line is correct, reboot the system. If the message appears again, copy the file from its original disk to the boot disk and try booting DOS again. If the error continues, contact the dealer who sold you the driver because the device driver is bad.

Batch file missing

DOS could not find the batch file it was processing. The batch file may have been erased or renamed. For DOS 3.0 only, the disk containing the batch file may have been changed. DOS aborts the processing of the batch file.

If you are using DOS 3.0 and you changed the floppy disk that contains the batch file, restart the batch file and do not change the disk. You may need to edit the batch file so that you do not need to change disks.

If you renamed the batch file, rename it again, using the original name. If required, edit the batch file to ensure that the file name does not get changed again.

If the file was erased, re-create the batch file from its backup file, if possible. Edit the file to ensure that the batch file does not erase itself.

Cannot load COMMAND.COM, system halted

DOS attempted to reload COMMAND.COM, but the area where DOS keeps track of available and used memory was destroyed, or the command processor was not found. The system halts.

This message may indicate that COMMAND.COM has been erased from the disk and directory you used when starting DOS. Restart DOS. If DOS does not start, the copy of COMMAND.COM has been erased. Restart DOS from the original master disks and copy COMMAND.COM to your working disk.

Another possible cause for this message is that an erroneous program corrupted the memory allocation table where DOS tracks available memory. Reboot and then try running the same program that was in the computer when the system halted. If the problem occurs again, the program is defective. Contact the dealer who sold you the program.

Cannot read file allocation table

The file allocation table (FAT) resides in a bad sector of the disk. Recovering the data may be impossible, but utilities such as Norton Disk Doctor may be able to recover it.

Cannot start COMMAND.COM, exiting

DOS was directed to load an additional copy of COMMAND.COM, but could not. Either your CONFIG.SYS FILES= command is set too low, or you do not have enough free memory for another copy of COMMAND.COM.

If your system has 256K or more and FILES is less than 10, edit the CONFIG.SYS file on your start-up disk and use FILES=15 or FILES=20; then reboot.

If the problem occurs again, you do not have enough memory in your computer or you have too many programs competing for memory space. Restart DOS again and do not load any resident or background programs you do not need. If necessary, eliminate unneeded device drivers or RAM-disk software. Another alternative is to increase the amount of random-access memory in your system.

Cannot use PRINT - use NET PRINT

You tried to use the PRINT command over a network. Use NET PRINT or consult your system administrator for the correct procedure for printing files over the network.

Configuration too large

DOS could not load itself because you specified too many files or buffers in your CONFIG.SYS file. Restart DOS with a different disk and edit the CONFIG.SYS file on your boot disk, lowering the number of files and/or buffers. Restart DOS with the edited disk. Another alternative is to increase the RAM memory in your system.

Copy process ended

The DISKCOPY process ended before completion. Try the process again, or copy the remaining files onto the target disk with the COPY command.

Current drive is no longer valid

You have set the system prompt to PROMPT $P. At the system level, DOS attempted to read the current directory for the disk drive and found the drive no longer valid.

If the current disk drive is set for a floppy disk, this warning appears when you do not have a disk in the disk drive. DOS reports a `Drive not ready` error. You press F for Fail (which is the same as A for Abort) or I to ignore the error. Then insert a floppy disk into the disk drive.

The `invalid drive` error message also may appear if you have a networked disk drive that has been deleted or disconnected. Simply change the current disk to a valid disk drive.

Disk boot failure

An error occurred when DOS tried to load itself into memory. The disk contained IO.SYS and MSDOS.SYS, but one of the two files could not be loaded. DOS did not boot.

Try starting DOS from the disk again. If the error recurs, try booting DOS from a disk you know is good, such as a copy of your DOS master disk. If the action fails, you have a hardware disk drive problem. Contact your local dealer.

Divide overflow

DOS aborted a program that attempted to divide by zero; the program was incorrectly entered or has a logical flaw. Report the problem to the dealer or publisher of the program.

Drive not ready

An error occurred while DOS tried to read or write to the disk drive. For floppy disk drives, the drive door may be open, the disk may not be inserted, or the disk may not be formatted. For hard disk drives, the drive may not be properly prepared or you may have a hardware problem.

Drive or diskette types not compatible

This message is displayed when you use DISKCOPY or DISKCOMP and indicates that you specified two drives of different capacities. You see this error message, for example, if you try to use DISKCOPY from a 1.2M drive to a 360K drive. Retype the command using compatible drives.

Duplicate filename or file not found

This message appears when you try to rename a file to a file name that already exists, or when the file you specified could not be found.

Check the directory to make sure the file name exists and that you have spelled it correctly. Then try again.

Error in EXE file

DOS detected an error while attempting to load a program stored in an EXE file. The problem is in the relocation information DOS needs to load the program. This problem can occur if the EXE file has been altered in any way.

Restart DOS and try the program again, this time using a backup copy of the program. If the message reappears, the program is flawed. If you are using a purchased program, contact the dealer or publisher.

Error loading operating system

A disk error occurred while DOS was loading itself from the hard disk. DOS does not boot.

Restart the computer. If the error occurs after several tries, restart DOS from the floppy disk drive.

If the hard disk does not respond (that is, if you cannot run DIR or CHKDSK without getting an error message), you have a problem with the hard disk. Contact your local dealer.

If the hard disk does respond, use the SYS command to put another copy of DOS onto your hard disk. You may need to copy COMMAND.COM to the hard disk also.

Error reading directory

During a FORMAT procedure, DOS was unable to read the directory; bad sectors may have developed on the part of the disk in which the file allocation table (FAT) resides. If the message occurs while you are using a floppy disk, the disk is unusable and should be thrown away. If the message occurs with a hard disk, however, you have a serious problem. You must reformat the disk or replace it. Be sure to keep regular backups to prevent major data loss.

Fatal: internal stack failure, system halted

A *stack* is an area of memory that DOS uses as a "holding tank" for the CPU (central processing unit, or microprocessor). High-speed computer instructions continuously put items into the stack and take items out of the stack. Sometimes, the stack becomes overloaded and the computer comes to an abrupt stop and displays this message.

A line such as `STACKS=12,128` needs to be added to the CONFIG.SYS file. This means that DOS should establish 12 stacks of 128 bytes each. This is considered to be a generic stacks directive and should work in most situations.

File allocation table bad, drive *x* abort, retry, fail?

DOS encountered a problem in the file allocation table (FAT) of the disk indicated by *x*. Press R several times to retry; if the message persists, press A to abort or F to abort and change to another drive.

Run CHKDSK /F to attempt to check and repair the FAT. If this message is displayed again, you must reformat the disk. If you are using a floppy, try to copy all the files to another disk, and reformat the original disk. If you are using a hard disk, back up as many files as possible, and then reformat it. You cannot use the disk until it is reformatted.

File creation error

A program or DOS attempted to add a new file to the directory or replace an existing file, but failed.

If the file already exists, it may be a read-only file. If it is not a read-only file, run CHKDSK without the /F switch to determine whether the directory is full, the disk is full, or some other problem exists with the disk. (You use the /F switch to fix problems in the FAT; see Appendix D for more information.)

File not found

DOS could not find the file you specified. The file is not on the disk or directory you specified or you misspelled the disk drive name, path name, or file name. Check these possibilities and try the command again.

General failure

This is a catchall error message. The error usually occurs when you use an unformatted floppy disk or hard disk, or when you leave the disk drive door open. This message can indicate a serious problem, however. If, for example, you see this message while booting the computer from a hard disk, it may indicate that the hard disk is unusable.

Incorrect DOS version

The copy of the file holding the command you just entered is from a different version of DOS. If this message appears, chances are good that you booted one version of DOS but then ran an external command from another version.

Use the VER command to verify the version that was used to boot the computer. Then get a copy of the command from the correct version of DOS (from a bootable floppy disk, for example) and try the command again. If the floppy disk or hard disk you are using has been updated to hold new versions of the DOS programs, copy those versions over the old ones.

Due to slight differences between DOS versions, never mix versions on one computer. One potential danger in mixing versions of DOS is that the backups made with the BACKUP command from one version may not restore with the RESTORE command in another version.

Insert disk with \COMMAND.COM in drive *x* and strike any key when ready

DOS needs to reload COMMAND.COM but cannot find it on the start-up disk. If you are using floppy disks, the disk in drive A probably has been changed.

Insert a disk holding a good copy of COMMAND.COM into drive A and press any key.

Insert disk with batch file and strike any key when ready

DOS is attempting to execute the next command from a batch file, but the disk holding the batch file was removed from the disk drive. This message occurs for MS-DOS 3.1 and later versions. MS-DOS 3.0 displays an error message when the disk is changed.

Insert the disk holding the batch file into the disk drive and press any key to continue.

Insufficient disk space

The disk does not have enough free space to hold the file being written. All DOS programs terminate when this problem occurs, but some non-DOS programs continue.

If you think that the disk has enough room to hold this file, run CHKDSK to see whether the floppy disk or hard disk has a problem. Sometimes when you terminate programs early by pressing Ctrl-Break, DOS cannot do the necessary clean-up work. When this happens, disk space is temporarily trapped. CHKDSK can "free" these areas.

If you simply have run out of disk space, free some disk space by deleting unneeded files or moving needed files to a floppy disk or the hard disk. Try the command again.

Insufficient memory

The computer does not have enough free RAM to execute the program or command.

If you loaded a RAM-resident program like SideKick or ProKey, restart DOS and try the command before loading any resident programs. If this method fails, remove any unneeded device driver or RAM-disk software from the CONFIG.SYS file and restart DOS again. If this action fails, your computer does not have enough memory for this command. You must increase your random-access memory to run the command.

Invalid COMMAND.COM in drive *x*

DOS tried to reload COMMAND.COM from the disk in drive *x* and found that it contained a different version of DOS. You see a message instructing you to insert a disk with the correct version and press any key. Follow the directions for that message.

If you frequently use the disk that was originally in the disk drive, copy the correct version of COMMAND.COM to that disk.

Invalid COMMAND.COM, system halted

DOS could not find COMMAND.COM on the hard disk. DOS halts and must be restarted.

COMMAND.COM may have been erased. Restart the computer from the hard disk. If you see a message indicating that COMMAND.COM is missing, that file was erased. Restart DOS from a floppy disk and recopy COMMAND.COM to the root directory of the hard disk.

If you restart DOS and this message appears later, a program or batch file may be erasing COMMAND.COM. If a batch file is erasing COMMAND.COM, edit the batch file. If a program is erasing COMMAND.COM, contact the dealer who sold you the program.

Invalid directory

One of the following errors occurred:

- You specified a directory name that does not exist.
- You misspelled the directory name.
- The directory path is on a different disk
- You forgot to give the path character (\) at the beginning of the name.
- You did not separate the directory names with the path character.

Check your directory names, ensure that the directories do exist, and try the command again.

Invalid drive in search path

One specification you gave to the PATH command has an invalid disk drive name, or a named disk drive is nonexistent. Use PATH to check the paths you instructed DOS to search. If you gave a nonexistent disk drive name, use the PATH command again and enter the correct search paths. Or, you can just ignore the warning message.

Invalid drive specification

This message is given when one of the following errors occurs:

- You have entered the name of an invalid or nonexistent disk drive as a parameter to a command.
- You have given the same disk drive for the source and destination, which is not permitted for the command.

- By not giving a parameter, you have defaulted to the same source and destination disk drive.

Certain DOS commands temporarily hide disk drive names while the command is in effect. Check the disk drive names. If the command is objecting to a missing parameter and defaulting to the wrong disk drive, explicitly name the correct disk drive.

Invalid drive specification Specified drive does not exist or is non-removable

One of the following errors occurred:

- You gave the name of a nonexistent disk drive.
- You named the hard disk drive when using commands for floppy disks only.
- You did not give a disk drive name and defaulted to the hard disk when using commands for floppy disks only.
- You named or defaulted to a RAM-disk drive when using commands for a "real" floppy disk only.

Remember that certain DOS commands temporarily hide disk drive names while the command is in effect. Check the disk drive name you gave and try the command again.

Invalid number of parameters

You have given too few or too many parameters to a command. One of the following errors occurred:

- You omitted required information.
- You forgot a colon immediately after the disk drive name.
- You put a space in the wrong place or omitted a needed space.
- You forgot to place a slash (/) in front of a switch.

Invalid parameter

Incorrect parameter

At least one parameter you entered for the command is not valid. One of the following occurred:

- You omitted required information.
- You forgot a colon immediately after the disk drive name.
- You put a space in the wrong place or omitted a needed space.
- You forgot to place a slash (/) in front of a switch.
- You used a switch the command does not recognize.

Invalid path

One of the following errors has occurred in a path name you entered:

- The path name contains illegal characters.
- The name has more than 63 characters.
- One of the directory names within the path is misspelled or does not exist.

Check the spelling of the path name. If needed, use the DIR or TREE command to ensure that the directory you specified does exist and that you have the correct path name. Be sure that the path name contains 63 characters or fewer. If necessary, change the current directory to a directory "closer" to the file and shorten the path name.

Invalid path, not directory, or directory not empty

This message appears when you are unable to remove a directory because the path does not exist (often due to a typing error) or because the directory is not empty.

Memory allocation error

Cannot load COMMAND, system halted

A program destroyed the area where DOS keeps track of in-use and available memory. You must restart MS-DOS.

If this error occurs again with the same program, the program has a flaw. Use a backup copy of the program. If the problem persists, contact the dealer or program publisher.

MIRROR cannot operate with a network

MIRROR cannot save file reconstruction information when your computer's hard disk is redirected to a network.

Missing operating system

The DOS hard disk partition does not have a copy of DOS on it. DOS does not boot. Start DOS from a floppy disk. If you have existing files on the hard disk, back up the files. Issue FORMAT /S to put a copy of the operating system on the hard disk. If necessary, restore the files that you backed up.

No paper

The printer is out of paper or is not turned on.

Non-DOS disk

The disk is unusable. You can abort and run CHKDSK on the disk to see whether any corrective action is possible. If CHKDSK fails, your alternative is to reformat the disk. Reformatting, however, destroys any remaining information on the disk. If you use more than one operating system, the disk was probably formatted under the operating system you're using and should not be reformatted.

Non-System disk or disk error Replace and strike any key when ready

Your floppy disk or hard disk does not contain DOS, or a read error occurred when you started the system. DOS does not boot.

If you are using a floppy disk system, insert a bootable disk into drive A and press any key. The most frequent cause of this message on hard disk systems is that you left a nonbootable floppy disk in drive A with the door closed. Open the door to drive A and press any key. DOS boots from the hard disk.

Not enough memory Insufficient memory

The computer does not have enough free random-access memory to execute the program or command.

If you loaded a RAM-resident program like SideKick or ProKey, restart DOS and try the command again before loading any resident program. If this method fails, remove any unneeded device driver or RAM-disk software from the CONFIG.SYS file and restart DOS again. If this option fails also, your computer does not have enough memory for this command. You must increase your RAM to run the command.

Not ready

A device is not ready and cannot receive or transmit data. Check the connections, make sure that the power is on, and check to see whether the device is ready.

Out of memory

This error occurs in the DOS 5 Editor. The amount of memory is insufficient to perform the operation you requested.

Packed File Corrupt

This error may occur when a packed executable (EXE) file is loaded into memory and indicates that the program could not load into the first 64K of memory.

Use the LOADFIX command to load the offending program above 64K. If the SAMPLE.EXE program gave you this error message, for example, load it with this command:

```
LOADFIX SAMPLE.EXE
```

Path not found

A file or directory path you named does not exist. You may have misspelled the file name or directory name, or you omitted a path character (\) between directory names or between the final directory name and file name. Another possibility is that the file or directory does not exist where you specified. Check these possibilities and try again.

Path too long

You have given a path name that exceeds the 63-character limit of DOS. The name is too long or you omitted a space between file names. Check the command line. If the phrasing is correct, change to a directory that is closer to the file you want and try the command again.

Program too big to fit in memory

If you have resident programs loaded (such as SideKick), restart DOS and try the command again without loading the resident programs. If this message appears again, reduce the number of buffers (BUFFERS=) in the CONFIG.SYS file, eliminate unneeded device drivers or RAM-disk software, and restart DOS. If these actions do not solve the problem, your computer does not have enough memory for the program or command. You must increase the amount of RAM in your computer to run this command.

Read fault

DOS was unable to read the data, usually from a hard disk or floppy disk. Check the disk drive doors and be sure that the disk is properly inserted.

Sector not found

The disk drive was unable to locate the sector on the floppy disk or hard disk platter. This error is usually the result of a defective spot on the disk or of defective drive electronics. Some copy-protection schemes also use this method to prevent unauthorized duplication of disks.

Seek

The disk drive could not locate the proper track on the floppy disk or hard disk platter. This error is usually the result of a defective spot on the floppy disk or hard disk platter, an unformatted disk, or drive electronics problems.

SOURCE diskette bad or incompatible

The disk you attempted to read during a copy process was damaged or in the wrong format (a high-density disk in a double-density disk drive, for example). DOS cannot read the disk.

Syntax error

You phrased a command improperly by doing one of the following:

- Omitting needed information
- Giving extraneous information
- Putting an extra space in a file name or path name
- Using an incorrect switch

Check the command line for these possibilities and try the command again.

TARGET diskette bad or incompatible

Target diskette may be unusable

Target diskette unusable

A problem exists with the target disk. DOS does not recognize the format of the target disk or the disk is defective.

Make sure that the target disk is the same density as the source disk, run CHKDSK on the target disk to determine the problem, or try to reformat the disk before continuing the copying process.

Unable to create directory

Either you or a program has attempted to create a directory, and one of the following has occurred:

- A directory by the same name already exists.
- A file by the same name already exists.
- You are adding a directory to the root directory and the root directory is full.
- The directory name has illegal characters or is a device name.

Use the DIR command to make sure that no file or directory already exists with the same name. If you are adding the directory to the root directory, remove or move (copy and then erase) any unneeded files or directives. Check the spelling of the directory and ensure that the command is properly phrased.

Unrecognized command in CONFIG.SYS

DOS detected an improperly phrased directive in CONFIG.SYS. The directive is ignored, and MS-DOS continues to start; DOS does not indicate the incorrect line, however. Examine the CONFIG.SYS file, looking for improperly phrased or incorrect directives. Edit the line, save the file, and restart DOS.

Write fault error writing drive *x*

DOS could not write the data to the specified device (represented by *x*). Perhaps you inserted the floppy disk improperly or you left the disk door open. Another possibility is that an electronics failure could have occurred in the floppy or hard disk drive. The most frequent cause is a bad spot on the disk.

Write protect error writing drive *x*

You tried to write data on a write-protected disk (represented by *x*).

If the disk has a write-protect tab on it (or the write-protect window on a 3 1/2-inch disk is open), you must remove the tab (or close the window) before you can write to the disk. If there is no write-protect tab on the disk (or the window is already closed), the disk is probably physically bad and cannot be written to. Try reformatting the disk and writing to it again or simply use a different disk.

Wrong DOS

The version of DOS is incompatible with the UNFORMAT command.

Appendix D

More About DOS

A Brief History of DOS

To better introduce DOS to you, here is a brief history of DOS. Don't worry if you don't understand every term now. As you progress through this book, these terms will become clearer. Some terms, in fact, include a reference to another part of the book.

Early Versions of DOS

PC DOS Version 1.0 was released in August 1982 along with the original IBM PC. DOS 1.0 was tiny and full of little *bugs* (errors). What's more, it could handle only one side of a floppy disk (160K in those days). Version 1.1 fixed a number of bugs and could handle both sides of a floppy (320K). MS-DOS Version 1.25 was the first Microsoft release of DOS. Version 2.0 came along in March 1983 when a 10M hard disk was added to the IBM PC. This version was a quantum leap; in fact, some users still use a 2.x version today. With Version 2.0 came CLS, DEBUG, PRINT (the DOS print spooler), BACKUP, FIND, PATH, ANSI.SYS, and batch commands such as ECHO, GOTO, and others. MS-DOS 2.0 was full of bugs, however, so MS-DOS 2.1 was introduced in March 1984. Versions 2.11, 2.2, and 2.25 followed. Some people still use 2.1 today, but they really shouldn't. Version 2.1 gives slow disk access, and Version 3.x simply adds so much more power and capability that continuing to use 2.x is really counterproductive.

This brings us to MS-DOS 3.0. This version was needed to handle the 286 microprocessor, which came with IBM's PC-AT, as well as the 1.2M floppy disk storage format. Although 3.0 added a few nice features, such as enabling you to make files read-only and making it harder to format your hard disk, it really wasn't that much of an improvement over 2.x. Then came Version 3.1 in November 1984. This version added networking capabilities, two new commands (JOIN and SUBST), and a few subtle improvements. The same was true of MS-DOS 3.2, which added 3 1/2-inch disk support and the fantastic XCOPY command. But it was Version 3.3 which finally made DOS usable.

MS-DOS 3.3

MS-DOS 3.3 has for quite some time been the version of choice—and with good reason. It has 14 new commands and files and nine others that have been enhanced. The BACKUP command is finally usable; it's faster, it creates a log file that tells which files it put on what disks, and it formats floppies as it runs (although no parameters can be stated, unfortunately). A great addition is the batch file command CALL, which enables you to call one batch file from anywhere inside another, execute it, and return to the original batch file. Such *nesting* of batch files was possible in prior versions, but CALL is much cleaner and faster. Also, you can use the @ symbol to suppress the words ECHO OFF in batch files, just as ECHO OFF prevents screen clutter when you make it the first statement in the batch file.

The BUFFERS command (DOS's disk cache utility) also was enhanced. Before Version 3.3, BUFFERS assumed two buffers for a PC or XT and three for an AT; of course, you could (and should) manually change the number. Version 3.3, however, automatically looks at how much RAM you have and allocates from two to 15 buffers. FASTOPEN also was added—an external command which serves as a file name cache utility. While BUFFERS speeds up the reading and writing information to several files, FASTOPEN speeds up performance when dealing with the key portions of a single file. Basically, FASTOPEN caches directory information, keeping in memory the disk location of frequently used files and directories.

One of the greatest additions to MS-DOS 3.3 is the APPEND command. The PATH command sets the directory search path. When you type a command, DOS looks in all the directories listed in the PATH and executes the command. However, this works only with COM, EXE, and BAT files, respectively. The APPEND command now gives this capability to nonexecutable files, such as data files. Another great enhancement is found in the ATTRIB command. This command was introduced in 3.0, and 3.3 added the /S switch, which enables you to change file attributes and archive bits in a directory and its related subdirectories.

MS-DOS 4.0

MS-DOS 4.0 was a major upgrade from Version 3.3 and provides some significant enhancements to earlier versions of DOS. Most significantly, it includes a DOS Shell program that enables you, via the keyboard or a mouse, to *point and shoot* DOS commands offered on a menu. You start a command by highlighting (pointing to) a command and selecting (shooting) it by pressing a button on the mouse or a key on the keyboard. This menu-style interface enables you to access the most common commands without learning a large number of commands. Other enhancements to DOS 4.0 include an automatic installation program and device drivers that can provide expanded memory conforming with the Lotus Intel Microsoft (LIM) 4.0 Expanded Memory Specification (EMS) on your suitably configured computer.

DOS 4.0 has some other advantages. A major advantage is that it supports larger DOS partitions on a hard disk. A hard disk *partition* is a division on a hard disk; you could, for example, divide a 40M hard disk into two 20M partitions. DOS 3.3 supports only 32M partitions, but Version 4.0 supports as much as 2 gigabytes in a primary partition. Some users need larger partitions than 32M—people who have extremely large data files in a database, for example. Others need large partitions for desktop publishing and graphics; Ventura Publisher and PageMaker files, for example, can get incredibly large. Various changes and enhancements of specific commands also have been made in Version 4.0. The /P switch, for example, has been added to the DEL command; it enables you to verify each file name before DOS deletes it.

Version 4.0 also has some disadvantages, however. For one thing, many users simply don't need partitions larger than 32M; in fact, larger partitions can make disk organization and maintenance more difficult. Another disadvantage is that Version 4.0 takes up 128K of RAM. This is twice as much as Version 3.3. This can be a serious problem if you don't have extended or expanded memory and you have to rely only on the conventional 640K limit. If you then have any memory-resident programs, you very easily can run into memory problems. Finally, even though Version 4.0's DOS Shell is adequate, there are more powerful shells available. Because of some of these shortcomings, Version 4.0 was not greatly successful.

MS-DOS 5

MS-DOS 5 is, in the opinions of many, the very best operating system for the IBM PC or compatible. It is what DOS should be—an easy-to-use interface that enables users to get their work done with the least amount of effort. For years, users have struggled with the operating system, but those years are over.

The DOS Shell in Version 5 has been completely redesigned (see Lessons 4 and 5 for more information). It is faster, smaller, and easier to use. In addition, the Shell has been redone so that it is similar in layout to Microsoft Windows 3.0. This is a great advantage to users with older computers who are planning to upgrade in the future; they can use DOS 5 now and get used to the Windows environment. Also similar to Windows is Version 5's task-switching capability (see Lesson 15), which enables you to switch quickly between programs with a few keystrokes. Version 5 also uses substantially less memory than Version 4.0, even on older machines. In addition, if you have a 286 machine with as little as 64K of extended memory (memory above the standard 640K), then Version 5 will load most of DOS in this extended memory, leaving over 600K in conventional memory.

A full-screen, full-featured text editor (see Lesson 17) also has been added to replace the old and awkward line editor (EDLIN). Also replaced was the outdated GW-BASIC; DOS now comes with Microsoft QuickBASIC Interpreter (QBASIC), a powerful programming language, with which you can write your own programs as your computer skills improve. Version 5 even has an undelete utility that enables you to recover a file that you accidentally erased (see Lesson 11). Still another great addition is the /? switch on every DOS command. Typing **DIR /?**, for example, displays a brief help text for that command (see Lesson 6). DOS now has on-line help!

These are just a few of the new features in DOS 5. Some users hesitate to upgrade their DOS for fear that some of their programs will not run with the new version. This fear now is unwarranted with Version 5's SETVER command; with it you can "fool" your programs into thinking that Version 5 is an older version. This is necessary with some older programs that will not run under DOS 5.

How DOS Is Organized

DOS is organized into three parts:

- The input/output system
- The command processor
- The utilities

Figure D.1 shows the various layers of DOS. The foundation layer is the computer hardware itself, and each layer is built on this base. As a user, you are outside these layers and interact with the outermost layer when you issue DOS commands from the DOS prompt (C>). DOS, in turn, interprets the commands and passes the necessary information to the next layer closer to the foundation and back out again until your command is completed. Figure D.1 is more fully explained in the sections that follow.

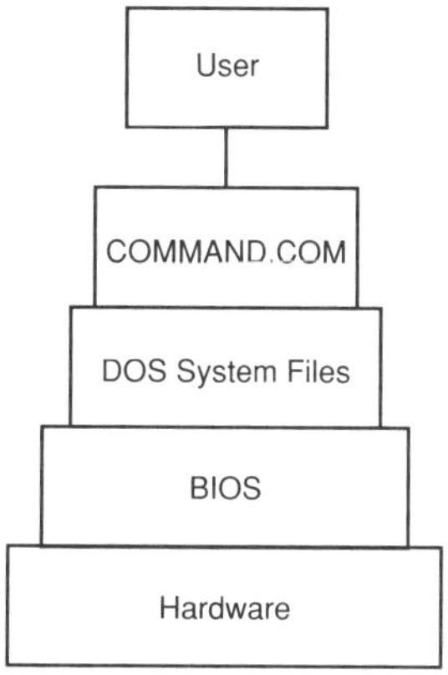

Fig. D.1. The layers of DOS.

MS-DOS 5, however, adds an additional layer of software between you and the fundamental parts of the computer. Figure D.2 shows how the DOS Shell makes using DOS easier (it also is more fully explained in the sections that follow).

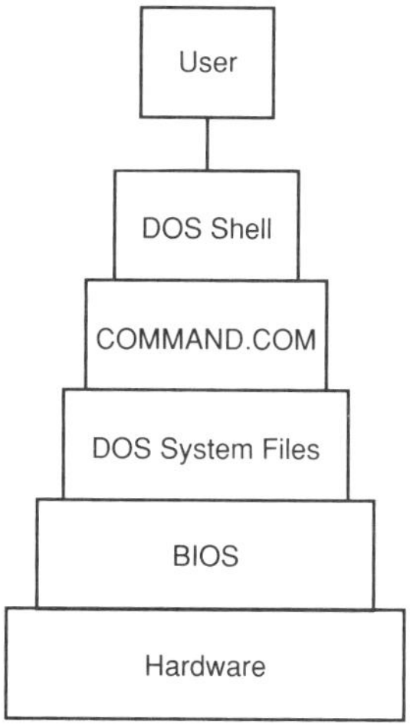

Fig. D.2. The layers of MS-DOS Version 5.

If you are running an application program such as a word processor or a spreadsheet, the program will communicate with DOS for you. When you instruct DOS to do something for you—to copy a file, for example—you are actually interacting with the command processor (COMMAND.COM). The command processor in turn uses the input/output system to control the disk drive and perform the copy command.

Input/Output System

As its name implies, the input/output (I/O) system handles everything that comes into and goes out of your computer. More specifically, the I/O system handles every character that is typed, displayed, printed, and received or sent through communications adapters. The system has *disk file handlers*, which store and retrieve programs and information from the disk drives, and contains the *nondisk peripheral handler*—the software that controls the keyboard, video display, communications, printer, and similar devices.

Two disk files are responsible for the work of the input/output system of the IBM personal computer systems running under MS-DOS: IO.SYS and MSDOS.SYS. Together, these system files provide a unified set of routines for controlling and directing the computer's resources. Among other things, these files are responsible for

- Creating files
- Writing information to files
- Reading information from files
- Changing names of files
- Listing names of files
- Listing sizes of files
- Removing files
- Loading and running programs
- Handling the hierarchical directory system

These files work with special read-only memory (ROM) situated in the computer. This ROM contains programs called the *BIOS*—short for basic input/output system.

The I/O system of MS-DOS does the hard work for you. All you have to do is learn how to tell DOS what you want done. The lessons in this book have been specifically designed to teach you to do just that.

Command Processor

The *command processor*, or command interpreter, is the program with which you communicate. This program, in turn, tells DOS what function to perform. The disk file COMMAND.COM is responsible for these activities.

COMMAND.COM displays the system prompt (C>) on-screen when you begin DOS. When you type a command after the C>, you are communicating with COMMAND.COM, which then interprets what you have typed and takes appropriate action.

Utilities

The utility programs perform housekeeping tasks for DOS. These utilities format diskettes and hard disks (FORMAT), give statistics on the disk size and available memory (CHKDSK), compare diskettes (DISKCOMP) and files (COMP), and much more. The utility programs reside on the disk and are loaded into memory for use.

Disk Formatting

As you learned in Lesson 6, *physical formatting* simply divides the disk into tracks and sectors. *Logical formatting*, however, does much more. Logical formatting organizes the disk into four main areas. The first area is called the *boot record*. This area always occupies the first sector of the first track of the first side of a disk. The boot record is a tiny program (the boot code) that reads in the rest of the operating system on bootable disks; this process is what actually starts your computer.

The second area of the disk is called the *file allocation table*, commonly called the FAT. This table keeps track of all the sectors on a disk and tells you whether a sector is free or in use by a file. As you may guess, the FAT is extremely important; it is so important, that DOS keeps two copies of it in case one of them becomes damaged.

The third area of a disk is the *root directory*, which lists all files (including subdirectories) on the disk, where each one starts, its name, size, date, and type. The root directory forms an index of what is on your disk. On a 360K floppy disk, for example, FORMAT creates a root directory (index) with room for 112 entries (files and subdirectories). Naturally, as disk capacity increases, so does the size of the root directory.

The fourth area of a disk is the *data area*. This area takes up all the remaining space on the disk and is for the information you want to save.

CHKDSK

Two switches are used with CHKDSK (see Lesson 8), the most important of which is the /F (fix) switch. The /F switch fixes errors that CHKDSK finds in the file allocation table (FAT). DOS uses the FAT to keep track of all sectors on a disk; it tells whether a sector is in use by a file. Sometimes this table gets garbled and a file becomes unusable. The /F switch may help recover some or even all of the lost data.

If you encounter the following message when running CHKDSK, you need to run CHKDSK again with the /F switch added:

```
Errors found, F parameter not specified
Corrections will not be written to disk
```

For practice, try this command by following these steps:

1. Exit the Shell permanently by pressing F3.

> You cannot run CHKDSK /F from the Shell or even from the DOS command line if you exited the Shell temporarily. If you try to do either, this message appears:
>
> ```
> CHKDSK /F cannot be done in a Windows/DosShell
> Command Prompt
> ```

2. Type **CHKDSK /F** and press Enter.
3. Look for a message similar to this:

   ```
   xxxx lost allocation units found in xxx chains
   Convert lost chains to files (Y/N)?_
   ```

   If this message appears, press Y for Yes and press Enter.

   CHKDSK then converts these lost chains to files and places them in the root directory of the disk using the name(s) FILE*xxxx*.CHK, in which *xxxx* is a consecutive number between 0000 and 9999.

   You then can use the TYPE command to examine these files to see if they contain anything useful. If they don't, you can delete them.

> It's a good idea to run CHKDSK (without /F) on your hard disk at least once a week, and daily if there is extreme file activity. If CHKDSK encounters any problems, it will tell you if you didn't use /F. You then can issue the command again with /F to fix the problems.

4. To return to the Shell, type **DOSSHELL** and press Enter.

Another switch used with CHKDSK is the /V switch. The V is short for *verbose*. You can use this switch to display a complete list of the directories, subdirectories, and files on a disk. Try this switch on your drives. Enter this command:

```
CHKDSK C: /V
```

A practical use for the /V switch is making a list of all the files on your disk and storing it as a disk file or printing it. To make a list of all the files on drive C and store it in a disk file, for example, enter this command:

```
CHKDSK C: /V > DRIVE-C.TXT
```

Instead of displaying the file list on-screen, this command *redirects* the list to the file DRIVE-C.TXT and places it in the root directory. You can view this file with the TYPE command or print it with the COPY command.

You also can print the list directly from the CHKDSK command. Instead of redirecting the list to a file, you can print it by entering this command:

```
CHKDSK C: /V > PRN
```

These techniques are useful anytime you need a listing of all the files on your disk(s).

BACKUP: Special Cases

Lesson 14 explains how to back up an entire hard disk or individual files on the disk and how to restore files to the hard disk. In addition to routine backup, you may want to use the backup and restore procedures in two other special instances:

- When you reorganize your hard disk
- When you have heavy fragmentation of the hard disk

Reorganizing a hard disk involves copying many files to different directories. The task also may involve creating new directories, deleting unused directories, and deleting old copies of files. After you reorganize the hard disk, be sure to back it up. Additionally, you should back up the disk before reorganizing it, just in case you make some major errors.

Fragmentation means that a file is not stored contiguously on the surface of the hard disk. After you have deleted and added information to a file several times, a file can be scattered across the entire hard disk. One result of fragmentation is that DOS must work harder to retrieve a file because the recording heads must move across the disk several times to read the file. As a result, the hard disk performs slower and less efficiently. As time goes on, in fact, disk performance greatly deteriorates. Another result of fragmentation is that portions of an accidentally deleted file are sometimes harder to undelete, and sometimes even impossible.

To solve the fragmentation problem, you can do one of two things:

- Purchase a special program that will defragment your disk, as well reorganize the directory structure any way you want.
- Back up the entire hard disk, reformat it, and then restore the files.

If you can afford the purchase, the first option is *highly* recommended. Many utilities available today can defragment your hard disk, such as PC Tools, Norton Utilities, Disk Optimizer, and DOG (Disk OrGanizer). These utilities will work in a matter of minutes, in contrast to the second option, which takes anywhere from two to several hours. Perhaps DOS will provide such a utility in a future release.

If, however, finances do not allow the purchase of such a utility, you can cure fragmentation by using BACKUP, FORMAT /S, and RESTORE. Formatting erases all files and directories from the hard disk. As you restore each file and subdirectory, the information is stored on consecutive sectors. This arrangement improves the performance of the hard disk, although it takes quite some time.

> One of the greatest failures of PC users is lack of hard disk management. Learning basic hard disk management skills will save you a lot of grief, as well as data.

> Do not try the reformatting technique if you are a beginning DOS user without supervision. If you follow the procedure incorrectly, you could lose all your data.

If you are forced to use the DOS method for defragmenting your hard disk, follow these steps:

1. Format a floppy disk with the operating system (/S). Label this disk *Hard Disk Defragmenting Disk*.

2. Copy the following programs from the DOS subdirectory of your hard disk to the new floppy:

   FORMAT.COM
   RESTORE.COM

3. Prepare a sufficient number of disks to hold the information from the hard disk (see Lesson 14).
4. Enter the command **VERIFY ON**.
5. Back up the entire hard disk, as outlined in Chapter 14.

> Before reformatting, be sure that you have a good backup copy of all the files on the hard disk; if you don't have good backup, you will lose data.

6. With the *Hard Disk Defragmenting Disk* in drive A, reboot the computer by pressing Ctrl-Alt-Del.
7. Reformat the hard disk by typing **FORMAT C: /S/V** and pressing Enter.
8. Restore the hard disk, as outlined in Lesson 14.
9. Remove the floppy disk from drive A and reboot the computer.

> How often should you defragment your hard disk? With moderate file editing, you will need to defragment the hard disk about once a month—more often if you do heavy file editing. To help you remember, just make it part of your monthly backup routine.

Appendix E

Additional Reading

What follows is a short list of other Que books that will be helpful to you as you learn about DOS and microcomputers in general.

- ***MS-DOS 5 QuickStart***

  Que Development Group

  The next step up from *Hands-On MS-DOS 5*, this is Que's easy-to-use graphic approach to learning DOS 5. Combines step-by-step instructions, examples, and graphics; explores all the new DOS 5 features, functions, and commands. Its award-winning illustrated format is ideal for all DOS beginners.

  Order #1293 $19.95 USA

- ***MS-DOS 5 Que Cards***

  Que Development Group

  The perfect flip-card reference to DOS. Speedy, efficient, and convenient guide for beginning users. Spiral-bound with built-in easel. Covers all essential DOS commands and operations.

  Order #1210 $19.95 USA

- ***Using MS-DOS 5*, 2nd Edition**

  Que Development Group

  The most helpful book on DOS available. Easy-to-use guide for the beginning to intermediate user. Packed with examples, hints, productivity tips, warnings, error messages, and a complete command reference. Also includes management techniques for disks, files, hardware devices, and batch files. This reference is a must for all DOS users.

Order #1278 $24.95 USA

- ***Upgrading to MS-DOS 5***

Que Development Group

The perfect book for those upgrading to DOS 5 from a previous version of DOS. Introduces all the new features and enhancements so that you can add power and sophistication to your computer system.

Order #1285 $14.95 USA

- ***Que's MS-DOS User's Guide,* Special Edition**

Que Development Group

The most in-depth coverage of DOS available anywhere. This is the comprehensive, easy-to-use guide for the intermediate-to-advanced DOS user. Includes Shell-customizing techniques, powerful batch file techniques, numerous power-boosting tips, and instructions on how to program in QBasic. This is the book you want in order to get the most out of DOS.

Order #1281 $29.95 USA

- ***MS-DOS 5 Quick Reference***

Que Development Group

The pocket-size instant reference for all DOS commands, including those new to DOS 5. Easy-to-use alphabetical format makes finding a command almost instantaneous.

Order #1256 $9.95 USA

- ***Que's Computer User's Dictionary*, 2nd Edition**

Bryan Pfaffenberger

An A-to-Z glossary of over 1,800 computer terms—for anyone who uses a personal computer. Also includes tips, cautions, illustrations, and cross references. Practical for business, school, and home use.

Order #1309 $10.95 USA

- ***Introduction to Business Software***

  Que Development Group

  Presents the essential concepts of the four leading IBM-compatible software programs: DOS 4, Lotus 1-2-3 Release 2.01, WordPerfect 5, and dBASE III Plus and IV. This is a comprehensive introduction to your personal computer and its primary business applications.

  Order #1034 $14.95 USA

Que also has titles on virtually every major subject and software title on the market. If you have a computer need, chances are Que has a book for you. Look in your local bookstore, or call 1-800-428-5331 for more information.

Index

C

D

E

F

G

H

I

K

L

M

N

O

P

Q

R

S

T

U

V

W

Count On Que For The Latest In DOS Information!

Using MS-DOS 5
Que Development Group
Versions 3.X, 4.X, & 5.0
Beginning/Intermediate
$24.95 USA
0-88022-668-4, 650 pp., 7 3/8 x 9 1/4

Que's MS-DOS 5 User's Guide, Special Edition
Que Development Group
Versions 3.X, 4.X, & 5.0
Beginning/Intermediate/Advanced
$29.95 USA
0-88022-671-4, 875 pp., 7 3/8 x 9 1/4

More DOS Titles from Que

MS-DOS 5 PC Tutor
Que Development Group
DOS 5
Beginning
$29.95 USA
0-88022-683-8, 400 pp., 7 3/8 x 9 1/4

MS-DOS 5 QueCards
Que Development Group
Versions 3.X, 4.X, & 5.0
Beginning/Intermediate
$19.95 USA
0-88022-615-3, 522 pp., 6 1/2 x 9

MS-DOS 5 Quick Reference
Que Development Group
Version 5.0
Beginning/Intermediate/Advanced
$9.95 USA
0-88022-646-3, 160 pp., 4 3/4 x 8

MS-DOS 5 QuickStart
Que Development Group
DOS 5
Beginning
$19.95 USA
0-88022-681-1, 400 pp., 7 3/8 x 9 1/4

Turbocharging MS-DOS
Caroline Halliday
Through DOS 5
Intermediate/Advanced
$24.95 USA
0-88022-729-X, 500 pp., 7 3/8 x 9 1/4

To Order, Call:
(800) 428-5331 OR (317) 573-2500

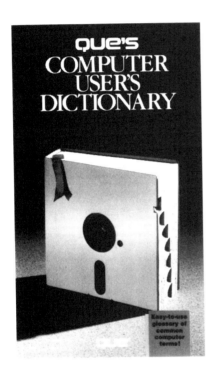

Free Catalog!

Mail us this registration form today, and we'll send you a free catalog featuring Que's complete line of best-selling books.

Name of Book ______________________

Name ______________________

Title ______________________

Phone ( ) ______________________

Company ______________________

Address ______________________

City ______________________

State __________ ZIP __________

Please check the appropriate answers:

1. Where did you buy your Que book?
   - ☐ Bookstore (name: __________)
   - ☐ Computer store (name: __________)
   - ☐ Catalog (name: __________)
   - ☐ Direct from Que
   - ☐ Other: __________

2. How many computer books do you buy a year?
   - ☐ 1 or less
   - ☐ 2-5
   - ☐ 6-10
   - ☐ More than 10

3. How many Que books do you own?
   - ☐ 1
   - ☐ 2-5
   - ☐ 6-10
   - ☐ More than 10

4. How long have you been using this software?
   - ☐ Less than 6 months
   - ☐ 6 months to 1 year
   - ☐ 1-3 years
   - ☐ More than 3 years

5. What influenced your purchase of this Que book?
   - ☐ Personal recommendation
   - ☐ Advertisement
   - ☐ In-store display
   - ☐ Price
   - ☐ Que catalog
   - ☐ Que mailing
   - ☐ Que's reputation
   - ☐ Other: __________

6. How would you rate the overall content of the book?
   - ☐ Very good
   - ☐ Good
   - ☐ Satisfactory
   - ☐ Poor

7. What do you like *best* about this Que book?

   ____

   ____

8. What do you like *least* about this Que book?

   ____

   ____

9. Did you buy this book with your personal funds?
   - ☐ Yes ☐ No

10. Please feel free to list any other comments you may have about this Que book.

    ____

    ____

    ____

QUE

Order Your Que Books Today!

Name ______________________

Title ______________________

Company ______________________

City ______________________

State __________ ZIP __________

Phone No. ( ) ______________________

Method of Payment:

Check ☐ (Please enclose in envelope.)

Charge My: VISA ☐ MasterCard ☐

American Express ☐

Charge # ______________________

Expiration Date ______________________

Order No.	Title	Qty.	Price	Total

You can **FAX** your order to **1-317-573-2583**. Or call **1-800-428-5331, ext. ORDR** to order direct.

Please add $2.50 per title for shipping and handling.

Subtotal	
Shipping & Handling	
Total	

QUE

NO POSTAGE
NECESSARY
IF MAILED
IN THE
UNITED STATES

BUSINESS REPLY MAIL

First Class Permit No. 9918 Indianapolis, IN

Postage will be paid by addressee

que®

11711 N. College
Carmel, IN 46032

NO POSTAGE
NECESSARY
IF MAILED
IN THE
UNITED STATES

BUSINESS REPLY MAIL

First Class Permit No. 9918 Indianapolis, IN

Postage will be paid by addressee

que®

11711 N. College
Carmel, IN 46032